Prophecy and History in Relation to the Messiah
Alfred Edersheim

The Warburton Lectures for 1880-1884

TABLE OF CONTENTS

PREFACE

The volume herewith presented to the reader contains the Lectures delivered during the years 1880-84 in the Chapel of Lincoln's Inn on the foundation of Bishop Warburton. Its object, as expressed in the Will of the founder, is 'to prove the truth of revealed religion in general, and of the Christian in particular, from the completion of those prophecies in the Old and New Testaments which relate to the Christian Church, especially to the apostacy of Papal Rome.'

From the wide range of subjects thus opened, it was necessary to select one—and naturally that, which would most directly meet the present phase of theological discussion, and so best fulfil the purpose for which the Lectureship had been instituted. Not, indeed, that the primary object should be negative, either in the defence of Catholic truth from its assailants, or in the refutation of objections brought against it. For all proper defence of truth must aim after this positive result: more clearly to define, and more accurately to set forth, that which is certainly believed among us. And this, in the good guidance of our God, is the higher meaning and issue of theological controversy. As every schism and separation indicate some truth which had been neglected, or temporarily ignored, by the Church, so each controversy marks some point on which the teaching of the Church had been wanting in clearness, accuracy, or fulness. And so every controversy, however bitter or threatening in its course, ultimately contributes to the establishment of truth—not merely, nor even principally, by the answer to objections which it calls forth, but by the fuller consideration of what had been invalidated, and the consequent wider and more accurate understanding of it. Thus, long after the din of controversy has ceased, with all of human infirmity attending it, and the never ending conflict between truth and error has passed to another battle-field, the peaceful fruits of the contest remain as a permanent gain. In the end it may be so, that much that has proved indefensible—and which all along had only been held because it was traditional, and had never before been properly considered—may have to be given up; and that, the old truth may have to be presented in new forms, as the result of more accurate investigation and more scientific criticism. Yet still every contest, whatever its trials or the seeming loss, ultimately issues in what is better than victory—in real advance. But to each of us, who in loving loyalty has sought to contribute, according to his capacity, to the defence and further elucidation of what we cherish as the Revelation of God to man, comes this comfort of no small inward reassurance. We may have only partially succeeded in our effort; we may have even failed of success. But every defence and attempt at clearer elucidation, unless wholly ungrounded in reason or criticism, at least shows that defence and a clearer and higher position are possible, even though we may not have reached to it; and it points out the direction which others, perhaps more successful than we, may follow. Thus here also 'both he that soweth and he that reapeth may rejoice together.' For, the end is certain—not that full and free criticism may be suppressed, but that it may be utilised, that so on the evening of the battle there may be assured peace, and the golden light shine around the old truth in her new garments of conquest, revealing the full perfection of her beauty.

Some contribution, however humble, towards this end, has been the object of these Lectures. Their form and limits prevented anything like the complete and scientific treatment which I could have wished. Yet the main questions concerning the Old Testament and its Messianic hope have been faced, and, in some respects, viewed under a new aspect. On Prophetism, as essentially distinguished from heathen divination; on Prophecy, as distinct from prophecies; on its wider relation to fulfilment; as well as on other cognate subjects, the views here expressed will, I venture to think, be found different from those hitherto presented. It need scarcely be stated, that at the present time the questions connected with the Old Testament occupy the foreground of theological discussion. Whether, or not, there is in the Old Testament any prophecy in the true and, as we had regarded it, the Scriptural sense; whether there were of old any directly God-sent prophets in Israel, with a message from heaven for the present, as well as for the future; whether there was any Messianic hope from the beginning, and any conception of a spiritual Messiah; nay, whether the state of religious belief in Israel was as we had hitherto imagined, or quite different; whether, indeed, there were any Mosaic institutions at all, or else the greater part of what we call such, if not the whole, dated from much later times—the central and most important portion of them, from after the Exile; whether, in short, our views on all these points have to be completely changed, so that, instead of the Law and the Prophets, we should have to speak of the Prophets and the Law; and, instead of Moses and the Prophets, of the Prophets and the Priests; and the larger part of Old Testament literature should be ascribed to Exilian and post-Exilian times, or bears the impress of their falsifications:—these are some of the questions which now engage theological thinkers, and which on the negative side are advocated by critics of such learning and skill, as to have secured, not only on the Continent, but even among ourselves, a large number of zealous adherents.

In these circumstances it would have seemed nothing short of dereliction of duty on the part of one holding such a lectureship—indeed, inconsistent with its real object—to have simply passed by such discussions. For, in my view at least, they concern not only critical questions, but the very essence of our faith in 'the truth of revealed religion in general, and of the Christian in particular.' To say that Jesus is the Christ, means that He is the Messiah promised and predicted in the Old Testament; while the views above referred to respecting the history, legislation, institutions, and prophecies of the Old Testament, seem incompatible alike with Messianic predictions in the Christian sense, and even with real belief in the Divine authority of the larger portion of our Bible. And, if the Old Testament be thus surrendered, it is difficult to understand how the claims of the New, which is based on it, can be long or seriously sustained. Hence, while attempting to show the prophetic character of the Old Testament and its fulfilment in Jesus Christ, it seemed necessary to secure our position against attack both in front and rear. For the latter purpose I have sought to establish (in Lecture 3) what the primitive belief of the Church really was, by a reference to those portions of the Gospel-narratives which the most extreme negative criticism admits to be an authentic record of the faith of the early Christians, and by making similar examination of the apostolic testimony to the Gospel-facts in such of the apostolic writings of which the genuineness is not called in question. Having thus ascertained what was the earliest tradition of the Church concerning the Christ, say about thirty years after the Crucifixion, I proceeded to inquire what light was thrown upon it by references in Talmudic writings, at the same time describing the earliest recorded intercourse between Jewish Teachers and Christians. By the side of this, there was a second, and, as running parallel to the first, a confirmatory line of evidence from witnesses, not only independent, but hostile. Here it has been sought to ascertain, on the one hand, the full import of the account given by Josephus of John the Baptist, which is generally admitted to be genuine; and, on the other, what light the well-known Epistle of Pliny the Younger about the Christians reflects upon the observances and the underlying belief of the Early Church. While thus the testimony of Josephus was seen to flash light upon the beginning of Christianity, that of Pliny reflected it back to about the year 80 or 90 of our era, the intermediate period—say, from about 60 of our era—being covered by what is admitted to have been the universal tradition of the Primitive Church.

Having thus secured my position in front, I also endeavoured to establish it in the rear, by an examination of the theories of recent criticism in regard to the structure and order of the Old Testament, more especially of the Pentateuch legislation and the historical books, for the purpose of vindicating the Mosaic authorship of that legislation, and its accordance with the notices in the historical books (Lectures 7 and 8). Here an account was first given (in Lecture 7) of the history and progress of recent criticism of the Pentateuch, from its inception to the present time, together with certain general objections to the latest theory of Wellhausen, and an indication of the wide-reaching sequences to which such views would lead. Next (in Lecture 8), the theory of Wellhausen was examined more in detail. The general position on our side of the question having been indicated, it was sought to show, by an analysis of the condition of Israel during the course of its history, that the Mosaic authorship of the Pentateuch legislation is accordant with the notices in the historical books of the Old Testament. Then the theory of our opponents was further combated, first, by certain fundamental objections to it, alike in principle and in detail; secondly, by some arguments intended to show the primitive and Mosaic character of the legislation and institutions of the Pentateuch; and, lastly, by a consideration of what, from an historical point of view, we should have expected to find—or else not to find—in the Pentateuch, if its date and construction had been as modern negative criticism asserts. The arguments in these respects are supported and supplemented by two longer Notes (at the end of Lecture 8), and by two Appendices, embodying chiefly the results of the critical labours of some German scholars. The second Note to Lecture 8 will be found of great interest and importance to the critical student, giving, as it does, a revised list of the passages by which Dr. Hoffmann has proved that Ezekiel had before him, and had quoted from, those portions of the Pentateuch, the publication of which Wellhausen ascribes to the time of Ezra. Similarly, Appendix 2 furnishes an abstract of the summary of Kleinert, giving a general analysis of the Pentateuch; stating its own witness, and that of the other parts of the Old Testament, to its composition; the various phases through which recent Pentateuch criticism has passed, and the reasons by which it is supported; also an enumeration of the passages which are supposed to form what is regarded as the latest portion of the Pentateuch; and, finally, an account of some of the modifications which the Rabbis found it necessary to introduce in that part of the legislation, in order to adapt it to the practical requirements of later times.

After this detailed statement only a brief account appears necessary of the general argument followed in these Lectures. At the outset, it was felt that no good purpose could be served by endeavouring once more to follow the line of reasoning which previous lecturers had so ably and learnedly traced. Besides, the general position taken as to the relation between Prophecy and prophecies, between fulfilment and prediction, and as to the order in which they should be studied, forbade any such attempt on my part. On the other hand, I wished, first, to study anew, and clearly to define, the points just mentioned, and then to trace the history of the great Messianic hope in the Old Testament, through all its stages, from its inception in the Paradise-promise to the last prophetic announcement by John the Baptist. Thus, 'Prophecy and History in relation to the Messiah' was to form the subject of the course. In pursuance of this, the first Lecture is intended to indicate the general ground taken up tracing the origin of Christianity to the teaching of the Old Testament, and showing that the great Messianic hope, of which Jesus presented the realisation, could not have originated in His time, nor close to it, nor yet in the centuries which had elapsed since the return from the Exile. Lecture 2 carries the argument a step further, by showing that 'the Kingdom of God' had been the leading idea throughout the whole Old Testament. At the same time, the form in which prophecy of old was presented to successive generations, and the relation between prophecy and fulfilment, are discussed, while the character of prophetism is defined, and the development of heathenism by the side of Israel, and the ideal destiny of the latter, are traced. In a Note appended to Lecture 2 the ordinary interpretation of Genesis 12:3 is defended against the criticism of Professor Kuenen. Lecture 3 establishes the position, that the New Testament presents Christ as the fulfilment of Old Testament prophecy, by showing that this is borne out by unquestioned Christian, and by most important Jewish and heathen testimony (the Rabbis, Josephus, Pliny). Lecture 4 defines and lays down some fundamental principles in regard to 'prophecy' and 'fulfilment,' and discusses certain special prophecies. It also explains the Biblical terms applied to the prophets, and the functions of 'the sons of the prophets'; and, lastly, refers to some prophecies in the New Testament. Lecture 5 distinguishes between prophetism and heathen divination; exhibits the moral element in prophecy; and discusses the value of the two canons which the Old Testament furnishes for distinguishing the true from the false prophet. Lecture 6 treats both of the progressive character of prophecy, and of the spiritual element in it, and shows how both prophecy and the Old Testament as a whole point beyond themselves to a spiritual fulfilment in the Kingdom of God—marking also the development during the different stages of the history of Israel, to the fulfilment in Christ. Lectures 7 and 8 are devoted to a defence of the views previously set forth concerning the Old Testament, and contain an examination of recent negative criticism, in regard to the Pentateuch and the historical books. Lecture 9 resumes the history of the Messianic idea. It discusses the general character of the post-exilian literature, and gives an analysis of the Apocrypha and of their teaching, of the new Hellenist direction, and of the bearing of all on the Messianic hope. A doctrinal and critical comparison is also made between the Apocrypha and the Old Testament, and the points of difference are marked and explained. In Lecture 10 the various movements of Jewish national life are traced in their bearing on the Messianic idea—especially the 'Nationalist' movement, of which, in a certain sense, the so-called Pseudepigraphic writings may be regarded as the religious literature. Lecture 11 gives an account and analysis of these Pseudepigraphic writings, marking especially their teaching concerning the Messiah and Messianic times. Lastly, Lecture 12 sets forth the last stage in Messianic prophecy—the mission and preaching of John the Baptist, and the fulfilment of all prophecy in Jesus the Messiah.

To this analysis of the general argument, little of a personal character requires to be added. The literature of the subject has been sufficiently indicated in the foot-notes; it is not so large as to have made a special enumeration necessary at the beginning of this Volume. For obvious reasons I have, so far as possible, avoided all reference to living English writers, whether on one or the other side of the questions treated. Lastly— as regards the manner in which the subject has been treated in this book, every writer must be fully conscious, and, where the highest truth is concerned, painfully sensible, of shortcomings in his attempt to realise the ideal which he had set before himself. In the present instance there were special difficulties—first, as already stated, from the form of these Lectures, and the space to which they were necessarily confined, which prevented that more full discussion which, in some parts, I could have desired. Besides this, I must mention at least one other disadvantage under which I laboured. From the circumstance that this course of Lectures not only extended over four years, but that the Lectures in each year had to be delivered at periods widely apart, occasional repetitions of the argument could not be avoided.

That the statement and defence of views so widely differing from what may be described as the current of modern criticism, may call forth strong, perhaps even violent, contradiction, I must be prepared to find. This only will I say, that, within the conditions prescribed by this course, I have earnestly sought to set forth what I believe to be the truth of Revelation concerning Jesus the Messiah, as the fulfilment of Old Testament prophecy, and the hope of Israel in all ages. To Him I would now commend this volume on its way to its unknown readers. As the motto for it I would fain choose the opening sentence with which the first Gospel introduces the history, and on which it grounds the Messianic claims, of Jesus: Βιβλος γενεσεως ʹΙησου Χριστου, υιου Δαβιδ, υιου ʹΑβρααμ. And as my concluding words, I would transcribe these of the Venerable Bede: ʹSi autem Moyses et prophetæ de Christo locuti sunt, et eum per passionem in gloriam intraturum prædixerunt, quomodo gloriatur se esse Christianum, qui neque qualiter Scripturæ ad Christum pertineant, investigat; neque ad gloriam, quam cum Christo habere cupit, per passionem attingere desiderat?ʹ

ALFRED EDERSHEIM
8 Bradmore Road, Oxford:
January 6, 1885

LECTURE 1: ON THE ORIGIN OF CHRISTIANITY IN THE OLD TESTAMENT.

What think ye of the Christ? Whose Son is He? Matthew 22:42.

It requires little consideration to convince us that the question which we propose to discuss in the present course of Lectures, is, from the religious point of view, of supreme interest and importance. In truth, it concerns no less than the very origin of Christianity. Passing beyond the modifications and development which contact with the varied culture of many nations or outward events have effected in the course of these eighteen centuries; passing also through the obscurity around the early age of Christianity, due to insufficient or inexact records, we can happily reach clearer light. We know the period of the rise of Christianity, and, as it seems to me, we can better understand its connection with that which preceded its birth than with that which followed it, and surrounded its infancy. Accordingly, it is in this manner that we here propose to study its origin: inquiring into its connection with that which had gone before, and of which it is the outcome, rather than treading our uncertain steps through the intricate mazes of often dubious tradition and apparently conflicting evidence up to the circumstances of its birth. Thus, the great question before us is this: Christianity, whence is it? The answer will in measure also decide that other: Christianity, what is it, divine or human; a revelation from heaven, or the outcome of determining circumstances? And its issue: is it the Church Universal, or only a new school of thought?

The difference to which we have referred as regards the mode of conducting our inquiry into the origin of Christianity, is the necessary sequence of the standpoint which we occupy in it, and connected with the results which we have in view. From earliest times the historical Church has traced its origin to that which had preceded it. Accordingly it has declared that Christianity was not indeed the counterpart, but the unfolding and the fulfilment of the Old Testament, and it has claimed that the Church was the true Israel of God. It has regarded the whole history of Israel as big with the promise of the world's salvation, and its institutions and promises as pointing to the establishment of a universal kingdom of God upon earth by means of the Messiah. Hence it has set forth, in no hesitating language, that there is unity, continuity, and progress in the teaching of the Old Testament, and that all in it is prophetic of the Christ. As against this view, which admittedly is both grand in its conception and logically consistent in its application, a certain school of modern criticism has followed a different mode of inquiry into the origin of the Church, and reached almost opposite results. Seeking to track the stream upwards, it has been declared that Christianity, as at present we know it, has been shaped by the circumstances, the people, and the culture with which on its introduction it was brought into contact; that its origins were very simple, and due to natural, local and temporary causes; in fact, that it is the result of a gradual accretion of different elements, all historically explicable, around a small and not very important nucleus of facts.

The theory just indicated has, it must be confessed, many attractions. It promises to destroy or supersede the miraculous by tracing to the operation of ordinary causes what otherwise would seem due to direct Divine agency, finding for it what is called 'a rational explanation,' that is, one level with our ordinary perceptions. And the contention is the more important since the Church view of the origin of Christianity implies, if correct, also unquestionable inferences about the Divine character of the Old Testament. Moreover, the new view is in seeming accordance with the general spirit of modern investigation, which everywhere discards preconceived purpose and unity of design, and explains that which is by the gradual operation of inherent forces, adapting themselves under the influence of surrounding circumstances. Lastly, it has the advantage of being set forth by writers not only of acknowledged learning, but of exceeding skill in pleading their case. By the weight of their authority, they too often set forth as undoubted results of critical research what others, even of their own school, have called in question, and which therefore, on any theory, cannot be grounded on indubitable or even clear evidence. Still more frequently, wide-reaching conclusions have been reared on what, after all, is a very narrow basis of facts; most weighty considerations on the other side being either overlooked or ignored. In this manner it has become possible to construct a wholly new theory of the genesis of the Old and New Testament which presents the attraction of unity and consistency, is capable of removing all difficulties, whether real or suggested, and, in fact, is devised to meet them. But strange as it may seem, it is this very facility of explaining and arranging everything which awakens our doubt and suspicion. In real life things do not move in precisely straight or rectangular lines, nor yet with the order and regularity of a tale. Many and varied influences are always at work, and the theory which professes precisely to fit, and exactly to explain, all phenomena though they had to be reconstructed for the purpose, resembles rather the invention of a speculator than the observed course of history.

Happily we shall avoid in our present inquiry all speculation, whether critical or metaphysical, seeking to answer what in the first place is an historical question by means of historical investigation. As a preliminary step, we purpose in the present Lecture to make it clear that the New Testament really points back to the Old. To put it more precisely: we hold that Christianity in its origin appealed to an existing state of expectancy, which was the outcome of a previous development; and further, that those ideas and hopes of which it professed to be the fulfilment had not first sprung up in the immediately preceding period—that is, in the centuries between the return from the Babylonish exile and the Birth of Christ—but stretched back through the whole course of Old Testament teaching.

If we were to view the introduction of Christianity into Palestine, and its spread throughout the heathen world, as an isolated fact, it would seem simply and absolutely inexplicable. For it cannot be conceived that One should have arisen and claimed to be the Messiah; appealed in confirmation to Moses and the prophets; professed to institute a kingdom of God upon earth; and in so doing gained the ear of the multitude and gathered devoted disciples; that, moreover, the temporal and spiritual rulers of Israel should have entered into controversy with Him, not as to the foundation, but merely as to the justice of His claims: and yet that all this should have represented an entirely new movement. We would at least have expected some reference to this circumstance. In thus describing in general outline what Christ professed, did, and experienced, I am not asserting what even the most negative criticism will deny. For even if we were to eliminate from our Synoptic Gospels any part that is called in question by the most extreme criticism, and banish the fourth Gospel to the end of the second century, regarding it as a tissue of ecclesiastical symbolism—sufficient would still remain to establish this position, that Christ professed to be the Old Testament Messiah and to bring the Kingdom of God; that He gathered adherents; and that the justice of His claims was resisted by the Jewish authorities; while at the same time the fact of *a* Messiahship, and the expectation of *a* Kingdom of God, were never called in question. I am warranted in going a step farther and saying, that the unquestioned facts in the Gospel history not only imply the existence of Messianic ideas and expectations, but their depth and intenseness. Only such a state of feeling could explain how One Who taught such evidently unwelcome doctrine was so widely listened to and followed. And the argument as to this Messianic expectancy at the time would only become stronger in measure as we denied the claims of Jesus. For, if even the minimum of such ideas had been a novelty—if no Messianic expectations existed at the time—surely the maximum as formulated by Jesus, and so opposed to Jewish prejudices, could never have been asserted.

All this seems almost self-evident. Yet, to make sure of our position, let me here remind you of what may be termed the most superficial, as certainly they are the least questionable, facts in the Gospel history. Surely, the crowds which from all parts of the country, and from all classes of society, flocked to the preparatory preaching of the Baptist, and submitted to the rite which he introduced, as not only the New Testament but Josephus attests, at least indicate that the proclamation of the Kingdom of God had wakened an echo throughout the land. And again, as we watch the multitudes which everywhere followed the preaching of Jesus; remember how they would fain have proclaimed Him King; and how even at the close of His ministry they greeted Him with *Hosannas* at His entry into Jerusalem, and this in face of the danger threatening them in such a movement from the presence of one so anti-Jewish and so suspicious as Pilate, we cannot but feel convinced not only of the existence, but of the intenseness, of the Messianic hope among the people at large.

It is, indeed, true that all such ideas and hopes are influenced, at least in their intensity and expression, by the circumstances of the time. They gain in depth and earnestness in proportion to the national abasement and suffering. Never did the Messianic hopes of the inspired Prophets rise higher; never was their faith wider in its range, or brighter in its glow; never their utterance of it more passionately assured, than when Israel had sunk to the lowest stage of outward depression. Because the conviction of the prophets and of Israel was so unshakably firm as regarded the glorious future, therefore it was that in such times they most deeply felt and most earnestly expressed the need of fleeing into the strong refuge of a certain future, the realising expectancy of which put a song into their mouth in the night time. So also was it in the long centuries of disappointment, and of apparently increasing unlikelihood that the Hope of Israel should ever become a Reality, that the Apocalyptic visions of the Pseudepigraphic writers gained in vividness and realism of colouring. Similarly, the most pathetically expectant elegies of mediæval Rabbinism date from the times of persecution. In truth it scarcely seems exaggeration to say, that throughout the history of Israel we can trace the times of bitterest sorrows by their brightest Messianic expectations, as if that golden harvest waved richest where the ploughshare had drawn the furrows deepest, and the precious seed been watered by blood and tears. And so the Talmud connects the coming of the Messiah with the time of bitterest woes, when Galilee would be laid waste, and the very mangers turned into coffins, when war and famine had desolated the land, and all righteousness and truth disappeared. Similarly, the mystic Midrash4 sees in the dove in the clefts of the rocks, to whom comes the call, 'Let me hear thy voice,' a picture of Israel as, fleeing before the hawk, it descries, in the rock-cleft, a serpent, and in agony of fear and distress beats its wings and raises piteous cries, which presently bring it the help and deliverance of its Lord. But this intensification of the Messianic hope in times when national glory seemed farthest removed, is only another evidence of the universality and depth of the Messianic hope. And if final proof were required of its existence, it is surely to be found in the circumstance that such hopes were independent of Jesus of Nazareth; that they equally attached themselves to false Messiahs, of whom not less than about sixty are mentioned, and who, despite the absurdity of their pretensions, carried after them such large numbers of the people; and, in the case of so clumsy an impostor as Bar Kokhba, even some of the leading Rabbis, kindling fanaticism to the extent of a conflict which severely tasked the resources of imperial Rome. Nay, is it not so that this hope has survived eighteen centuries, not only of bitter persecution, but of chilling disappointment? Though disowned by the nerveless rationalism of modern Jews, it kindles up in every service of the Synagogue; it flings its many-coloured light over every product of Rabbinic literature; and as year by year each family of the banished gathers around the Paschal table, the memorial of Israel's birth-night and first deliverance, it still rises in the impassioned plaintive cry of mingled sorrow and longing which rings into the desolate silence of these many centuries: 'This year here—next year in Jerusalem!'

A hope so wide-reaching, so intense and enduring cannot, I submit, have been the outcome of one particular phase in the history of the people. Its roots must have struck far deeper than one period of the nation's life; it must be the innermost meaning of their history, the final expression of that long course of teaching in the Law and in the Prophets which, all unconsciously to themselves, has become the very life-blood of Israel's faith.

But on a point of such importance we are not left to general inferences. Even at this preliminary stage of our inquiry, we can appeal to unquestionable evidence that the ideas and hopes which Jesus of Nazareth professed to realise did not arise at His period, nor yet close to it. More than this, we are prepared to show grounds for maintaining that the great Messianic expectation did not originate in the period between the close of the Old Testament Canon and the Birth of Christ. In such case the plain inference would be, that it must be traced up to the Old Testament itself, in the course of whose teaching we must seek its origin, growth, and gradual development.

In regard to the first point just referred to, it may, I think, be fairly argued, that if the idea of the Messiah and His kingdom had originated in the period of Christ, if indeed it had been new, the teaching of Jesus would have either reflected this, at least in its main features, or else indicated and vindicated the fact and the grounds of divergence from the past. In this respect it is most significant, that while Christ so emphatically accentuated the differences between His own and the teaching of the Pharisees, as regarded the most important matters of the Law, He never referred to any such as subsisting between His own and the Messianic ideas of his contemporaries—at least, in their general conception. On the contrary, all implies that, so far from these Messianic expectations first emerging at or near that period, they had been long existing, and indeed had lost their definiteness in a more vague and general expectancy which assumed the colouring of the times. A similar inference comes to us from a consideration of the preparatory Messianic announcement by the Baptist, the questions which it elicited, and the indefinite form of his answers. It represents a very strong but a general expectancy, rather than such definite expectations as one would associate with their recent origination. On the other hand, it is quite evident that Jesus of Nazareth, as He is presented to us in the Gospel history, did not meet the special form which the Messianic thinking of His contemporaries had taken, when called upon to assume a concrete form in accordance with the general direction of the time. For not only did they reject His teaching, denounce Him as an impostor, and crucify Him as a blasphemer, but even His own disciples and followers neither anticipated nor fully understood, in many respects even misunderstood, His doctrine, were utterly unprepared for His death, and had no expectation of His resurrection. In other words, each of the three great elements in His history came as a surprise upon them.

Whatever outward agreement may therefore be traced between the sayings of Christ and contemporary thought, this at least is quite evident, that He did not embody the precise Messianic ideal of His time. And here we must observe an important distinction. In one sense Jesus Christ certainly was a man of His time: He spoke the language of His time, and He addressed Himself by word and deed to the men, the ideas, and the circumstances of His time. Had it been otherwise, He would not have been an historical personage, nor could He have been a true Christ. The more closely therefore we trace the features of His time in His words and actions, in the people introduced on the stage of the Gospel history, and in the general *mise en scène*, the more clearly do we prove the general historical truthfulness of the narrative—that it is true to the time. But in another and higher sense Jesus Christ was not the man of His time, spake not, acted not, aimed not, as they; and hence the great body of the people rejected, denounced, and crucified, while even His own so often misunderstood and were surprised by Him.

What has just been stated naturally leads to the last point in our present inquiry. It has been shown that the Messianic idea could not have originated in the time of Jesus Christ, nor presumably in that immediately preceding. But between the time of Jesus Christ and the close of the Old Testament Canon—or, to avoid controversy, let us say the time of Ezra—roughly speaking, four and a half centuries intervened. Could it be that the great hope of Israel had sprung up during any part of the troubled history of that period? Without at present entering into detailed examination, sufficient reasons can be shown to make this the most unlikely hypothesis. For,—

First. It is impossible to believe that such a hope could have newly sprung up without leaving at least some mark of its origin, and some trace of its growth in the history and literature of the time. Whatever darkness may rest on certain aspects in the development of thought and religion at that period, especially at the beginning of it, or on such questions as the institution of the so-called 'Great Synagogue,' or the influence and development of the new direction of external legalism, or of the national and anti-Grecian party, yet all these tendencies are marked in the history and literature of that period. And it seems unthinkable that the one great, the all-dominant idea in the religion of Israel, the hope of a Jewish Messiah-King, who would bear rule over a world converted to God, should have originated without one trace of its birth and gradual development. But as a matter of fact there is not in the history, nor yet in the literature of that period any appearance of a small commencement, a growth, or a gradual development of the Messianic idea, such as would be requisite on the theory in question. On the other hand, it deserves special notice that such a development is very clearly traceable throughout the Canon of the Old Testament, and that *pari passu* with the progress of Israel's history. It is needless to say that this tells its own most important lesson, both as regards the internal unity of the Old Testament and the origin and development of the Messianic idea. But at present we are only so far concerned with it as to mark that no such progression appears either in Apocryphal, Pseudepigraphic, Alexandrian, or Rabbinic literature. In some respects, indeed, there is retrogression rather than progression in this matter, and this not only in the writings of Philo, where the Messianic idea is, so to speak, sublimated into generalities, but in the Apocrypha, where it is only obscurely referred to. But alike in the one case and in the other, not only is its existence implied, but a previous fuller development of it.

As regards Rabbinic literature, it is universally known that any references to the great Messianic hope of Israel occurring in its pages appear in the most developed form. The only question, therefore, can be in reference to that special kind of literature which bears the name of Pseudepigraphic Writings, and which may in general be described as Apocalyptic in character. Naturally we expect to find the Messianic hope most fully expressed in such works. But although we mark variety and addition of detail in the various books, there is no trace of any development in the underlying conception of the Messiah and His kingdom. As a crucial instance we may here refer to the Book of Daniel, the authorship and date of which are in controversy. According to the testimony of the Church, the Book of Daniel—or at least the greater portion of it—dates from the time of the Exile; according to a large section of modern critics, from about that of Antiochus Epiphanes (175-164 B.C.). In the one case it would belong to the Biblical, in the other to the Pseudepigraphic writings. We have our own decided convictions on this point. But for the present argument it matters not which of the two views is the correct one. Clearly in the Book of

Daniel we have the idea of the Messiah and His kingdom in its full development. If the Book of Daniel belongs to the Canon, then the idea must have existed fully developed in Biblical times; if, on the contrary, it should be regarded as the earliest of the Pseudepigraphic writings, it affords undoubted evidence that the Messianic idea did not gradually develop, but existed in its fullest form in the earliest literary monument of that class. But we can go back farther than this. For,—

Secondly. If the Messianic hope had sprung up during or immediately after the exile, we should scarcely have expected it to cluster round the House of David, nor to centre in the 'Son of David.' For nothing is more marked than the decadence and almost disappearance of the House of David in that period. A national hope of this kind could scarcely have sprung up when the royalty of David was not only matter of the past, but when its restoration was comparatively so little thought of or desired, that the descendants of the Davidic house seem in great measure to have become lost in the mass of the people. And the argument becomes all the stronger as we notice how, with the lapse of time, the Davidic line became increasingly an historical remembrance or a theological idea, rather than a present power or reality. Throughout the Old Testament Davidic descent is always the most prominent element in all Messianic pictures, while in later writings it recedes into the background, as something in the long past which must be brought forth anew. In this respect, also, it is characteristic that the name 'Son of David' was the most distinctive title claimed by, and given to Jesus, while in the case of all spurious Messianic movements this occupied only a subordinate, if any, place.

Thirdly. We may press the argument yet one step farther, and express a strong doubt whether, if this hope had originated in the post exilian period, it would have connected itself with any distinctly monarchic aspirations. The general genius of Judaism is against it, and throughout the whole post-exilian history and literature there is certainly not a trace of any wish for the restoration of the old, or the establishment of any new monarchy. This silence is of itself significant. On the other hand, we have on at least three critical occasions—in the time of Pompey, during the governorship of Gabinius (about 66 B.C.), and after the death of Herod—the distinct expression of objections to monarchical rule and of preference for an oligarchy as conformable to ancient traditions. And if it be supposed that such objections mainly applied to the Herodian house, the attentive student of that period cannot fail to observe that the rapid change of public opinion in regard to the Maccabees from that of unbounded popular enthusiasm to the extreme of general hatred may be dated from their permanent assumption of the royal along with the high-priestly dignity. But, be this as it may, the Davidic house and royalty at any rate may be said to have disappeared from the horizon of practical politics.

It were, indeed, an interesting speculation for which the elements are not wholly wanting, to inquire to what kind of personality the Messianic hope would have attached itself if it had first originated in the post-exilian period. Certainly not to a scion of the Davidic house, probably not to any king. The Messiah would have been a conqueror. This was a political necessity, and in accordance with national thought and ambition, not to speak of the hope of the realisation of a grand contrast between Israel's past and their future. The Messiah would certainly have been a proud and avenging conqueror, whose rule of the conquered would have been anything but that of peace, liberty, and happiness to them. But he would have been a conqueror with whose administration the office of a Chief Rabbi would have strangely blended. He would have been first a Rabbi, then a conqueror, and then again a Rabbi; or his conquests would have been dictated and shaped by the requirements of Rabbinism, and applied and utilised in its service.

We remember that, according to the latest theory which, at least for the present, finds most favour on the Continent, if not among ourselves, the largest and most important part of the Pentateuch, embracing, roughly speaking, the sections from Exodus 25 to Numbers 36, dates from after the Babylonish exile. As containing the great body of the ritual laws and ceremonial observances, it is called the 'Priest-Codex,' and it is supposed to have been introduced by the influence of the priesthood, and to mark in many respects an entirely new departure in, and transformation of, the old Israelitish religion. If the priesthood had such power as to bring in a wholly new document, which initiated a new direction, and if they could gain for it the recognition, ever afterwards unquestioned, of forming the fundamental part of the ancient legislation and religion of Israel—a supposition sufficiently exacting, and which would seem to require the weightiest proofs—we are surely warranted in expecting that some mark of this tendency should have appeared in that Messianic idea which formed the great hope of the people, if it had originated at that time. If they were able to transform the past in the interest of the present, would they not have exercised the same influence as regards the future?

But here, as on so many other points, the theory in question signally fails. The priestly element, which is said to have transformed the Pentateuch legislation, does not appear as in any way connected with the ideal goal of Israel—except from the Christian, theological point of view of the ideal Priesthood of Christ. This, surely, is a very strange phenomenon which demands an explanation, whatever view may be taken of the origin of the Messianic idea. If it originated in strictly Old Testament times, those who could introduce the Priest-Codex into the Mosaic legislation would have had no difficulty in finding a place for the expression of their views in connection with the grand hope of Israel's religion; and if it originated in the exilian or immediately post-exilian period, these views could scarcely have failed to impress themselves upon it.

But, truth to say, this is only one of the historical difficulties of the theory about the late origin of the Priest-Codex. The great objection to it is, that, while it explains certain phenomena in the past religious history of Israel—at least, as these are presented by the advocates of the theory—it not only leaves unaccounted for, but seems inconsistent with, the whole subsequent religious development. And the more carefully the grounds are examined in detail on which the late origin of the 'Priest-Codex' is inferred, the more incompatible with the undoubted facts of the subsequent history will the conclusions be found. Not the origin of the idea of an exclusive central place of worship, but the institution of synagogues everywhere; not drawing together, but expansion, and provision for the 'dispersed,' who not only were, but, it must have been felt, would remain—at any rate, to Messianic times—the majority of the people; not privileges and rights for the priesthood, whom the whole history shows to have been as an order an uninfluential minority, shorn even of some of its ancient prerogatives—in short, not Sacerdotalism but Rabbinism: such was the outcome of the exilian and post-exilian period. And although this transformation was in the first place necessarily carried out by the priests and Levites, there can be no doubt that, even in the case of Ezra, the title 'priest' falls into the background behind that of 'scribe' (Ezra 7; Nehemiah 8), and that his activity and tendency have been rightly indicated when he is designated as 'the father of all the Mishnic doctors.'

But, here we return from our digression: Rabbinism, which is the true outcome of the post-exilian period, is, in its inmost tendency, not only anti-monarchical and anti-sacerdotal, but, strange as it may sound, even anti-Messianic. The Rabbis found Messianism, just as they found the Aaronic priesthood and sacrifices; and they adopted it. They were patriotic and imaginative, and their Haggadists, preachers, and mystics elaborated the idea with every detail which legend, an unrestrained Eastern fancy, or national pride, could suggest. But when we pass beneath the surface, we find that Rabbinism does not well know what to make of this doctrine; that it is a foreign element in it, which may be added to, but will not amalgamate with, the system. The latter is a hard and dry logical development of the Law to its utmost sequences. Beyond the four corners of its reasoning, Rabbinism acknowledges no authority whatever, on earth—be it priestly or royal—or in heaven. And when Rabbi Eliezer appealed, and that successfully, in favour of his doctrines to the Voice from Heaven (the so-called *Bath Qol*), the assembled Rabbis were not silenced by it, but declared that, since the Law had been given on Mount Sinai, it was 'not in heaven' (Deut 30:12); to which, therefore, no appeal could be made. Apart from its somewhat profane witticism, this answer meant that there was finality about the Law as interpreted by the Rabbis by which even the Almighty Himself was bound.

It certainly affords evidence, were such needed, that Rabbinism recognised no authority, not even that of an audible voice from heaven, outside its own hard and dry logic. The only place which the Messianic doctrine could hold in such a system was, that it furnished hope of a temporal deliverance, or even of the national supremacy of Israel, which would make Rabbinism dominant; or else that it opened the prospect of a new law. And this essential antagonism between the Messianic idea as embodied by Christ, and Rabbinism, explains the life and death contest which from His first manifestation ensued between Jesus of Nazareth and the leaders of His people.

Briefly to sum up the conclusions to which the foregoing reasoning points: Christianity in its origin appealed to a great Messianic expectancy, the source and spring of which must be sought not in the post-exilian period, but is found in the Old Testament itself. The whole Old Testament is prophetic. Its special predictions form only a part, although an organic part, of the prophetic Scriptures; and all prophecy points to the Kingdom of God and to the Messiah as its King. The narrow boundaries of Judah and Israel were to be enlarged so as to embrace all men, and one King would reign in righteousness over a ransomed world that would offer to Him its homage of praise and service. All that had marred the moral harmony of earth would be removed; the universal Fatherhood of God would become the birthright of redeemed, pardoned, regenerated humanity; and all this blessing would centre in, and flow from, the Person of the Messiah.

Such at least is the promise of the Old Testament which the New Testament declares to have been fulfilled in Christ Jesus. And if it were not so, then surely can it never more be fulfilled. For not even the most fanatic Jew would venture to assert, that out of the Synagogue could now come to our world a King reigning in righteousness, a Son of David, a Branch of Jesse; and that the present Synagogue would so enlarge itself as to embrace in its bosom all nations of the earth. And thus, unless the old hope of the kingdom has been realised in Christianity, it can never be realised at all. Then also is the Old Testament itself false in its inmost principle, and false the hope of humanity which it bears.

Or otherwise, if it be maintained that ours is not the true meaning of these prophecies, but that they pointed to a great Jewish King and a great Israelitish kingdom, to which all nations were to become subject—then, in such case, the Old Testament—that is, if we take it as seriously meaning what it says—would not be of God. If it had only flattered Jewish national pride; if it had held out only the wretched prospect of a victorious Jewish King, not one in righteousness and peace; if, instead of the universal Fatherhood of God in Christ, it had only spoken of the universal dominion of Israel over men—then would it not have brought good news, and be neither Divine nor yet true. And so it still is, that the New Testament without the Old, and the Old Testament without the New, is not possible. *Novum Testamentum in Vetere latet, Vetus in Novo patet.* And so we all feel it, when in our Christian services we not only sing the Psalter and read the Old Testament, as of present application but speak of Abraham as 'our forefather.' To compare the colourless, declamatory and unspiritual ancient Accadian or Babylonian hymnology with the Psalms seems, even from the literary, much more from the religious point of view, utterly impossible. Conceive our highest spiritual aspirations and our best services expressing themselves in the language of these compositions, or of any possible development of them! No, the Old Testament element could not in this nineteenth century have kept its place in our theology and our worship, otherwise than by an inherent fitness; because the New Testament is the organic development and completion of the Old.

LECTURE 2: ON THE KINGDOM OF GOD AS THE LEADING IDEA OF THE OLD TESTAMENT, AND ON CERTAIN RECENT CRITICISM CONCERNING THE ARRANGEMENT AND DATE OF THE CANON.

Philip findeth Nathanael, and saith unto him,
We have found Him of whom Moses in the law,
and the prophets, did write, Jesus of Nazareth,
the son of Joseph. John 1:45.

Apart from its intrinsic interest and its connection with the narrative of which it forms an episode, this answer of Philip to Nathanael has an important bearing on our present inquiry. It expresses the conclusions at which we have arrived in our former Lecture, and so shows that we have not misrepresented the meaning of the New Testament in saying that it looked back for its origin to the Old Testament. Even in the Fourth Gospel, which a certain school of critics regards as anything but a Judaic document, the early disciples present the claims of Jesus as of Him, 'of whom Moses in the Law, and the Prophets did write.' But although the New Testament writers, and, as we may now say, the Jewish people generally, founded their Messianic expectancy on the Old Testament, it is another question whether, in so doing, they rightly understood its meaning. In other words, does the Old Testament really embody such a hope of a universal spiritual kingdom of God upon earth through the Messiah, as the New Testament writers, rightly or wrongly, saw fulfilled in Jesus of Nazareth; or is this view of the Old Testament only a later gloss put upon it by Christianity? This must be the subject of our next inquiry.

In one respect we might here content ourselves with appealing to the facts established in the preceding Lecture. Evidently the Messianic hope existed at the time of Christ, and that not only among one section, party, or school, but among all classes, thoroughgoing Sadducees perhaps excepted. We might even go farther and assert that the highest springs of the great Nationalist movement, which finally issued in the war with Rome, lay not so much in the aspirations of patriotism and love of independence, as in a misunderstanding and misapplication of the Messianic expectancy. And in proof we might even appeal to the circumstance that some of the disciples of Jesus, notably 'Simon the Zealot,' seem originally to have belonged to the Nationalist party, the *focus* of which was in Galilee. But apart from this, we have also direct evidence, that not only the New Testament writers and later Rabbis, but the people generally, traced the Messianic expectation to the teaching of the Old Testament. Even so unscrupulous a partisan as Josephus can in this instance be cited as a witness on our side, whose testimony is the more important for the manifest reluctance and indirectness with which, in works intended for Roman readers, he refers to the Messianic hope. I am not here thinking of the controverted passage about Christ, but of such (among other) allusions to Messianic prophecies in the Old Testament, as when referring to the predictions of Balaam he infers from their partial fulfilment, even in his own time, 'that the rest will have their completion in the time to come'; or when, commenting on Daniel's interpretation of Nebuchadnezzar's dream (Dan 2), he evades giving an interpretation of the fate of the fourth kingdom, which he evidently identifies with Rome, on the ground that he had undertaken to describe the past and the present but not the future, for the understanding of whose 'uncertainties,' 'whether they will happen or not,' he refers the curious to the Book of Daniel itself, which they would find among the sacred writings. Evidently, then, there was in the view of Josephus, as well as of his contemporaries, a prophetic future for Israel after the destruction of Jerusalem, and the stone cut out without hands predicted to destroy the iron empire of Rome, of which he refused to give the interpretation, must have been the Messianic kingdom. Thus, there was universal Messianic expectancy, and that expectancy was traced to Old Testament prophecy. And, recalling our previous arguments as to the extreme unlikeliness of such a hope springing up in the period between Ezra and Christ, we might content ourselves with challenging those who deny its Old Testament origin to point out the period and the circumstances of its beginning and development.

Still, it is at least conceivable, whatever the presumption to the contrary, that the whole Jewish nation may have been mistaken in their Messianic interpretation of the Old Testament. Yet we have here something beyond an unbroken *consensus* of Messianic interpretation. If the present historical arrangement of the Old Testament Canon may be trusted—not, indeed, in reference to the precise date and authorship of each book (which are here not in question), but as regards the general chronological succession of the

Law and the Prophetic writings—it seems almost impossible to deny that the Old Testament in its different parts is organically connected; and that, as previously stated, alike the connecting, the impelling, and the final idea of it is that of a universal kingdom of God upon earth; and that this idea unfolds together with the development of religious knowledge and life in Israel.

The distinction of terms just made is of such importance in the argument as to warrant a seeming digression. Man's life and understanding develop; God's purpose unfolds. The term 'purpose' is indeed anthropomorphic, and in its strict meaning could not be applied to God, since 'purpose' not only implies a reference to the future, but thinking of the future with the view of acting upon it in a certain definite manner. On the other hand, strictly speaking, we cannot associate (either metaphysically or theologically) the idea of 'future' with the Divine Being, nor yet such planning as implies uncertainty about the future and adaptation to its eventualities. If, therefore, we use the term, it is for convenience' sake, and with the reservations just made. What we know is, that, so far as regards God, all is from the first before Him; and that, in history, it opens up—unfolds to man's understanding, in the course of his development. This may be illustrated from the first intimation of the great Old Testament hope, the so-called Prot-Evangelion, in Genesis 3:14, 15. The substantial accuracy of our translation, 'He shall bruise thy head, and thou shalt bruise his heel,' stands, I think, firm on critical grounds. The rendering advocated by Professor Kuenen, 'This shall lie in wait for thy head, and thou shalt lie in wait for his heel,' would, irrespective of linguistic considerations, yield such feebleness of meaning as almost to transform the pathos of God's final judgment upon sin into *bathos*. It does not seem worthy of record in what professes to be a Revelation, nor yet accordant with the solemnity of a Divine punitive sentence, to decree and declare that in the physical contest between man and the serpent the former is to aim at the head of the serpent, while the latter would, in its stealthy approach, aim at his heel. But if the words mean, as the Church has always understood them, that there must ever be a great conflict between Humanity and the principle of evil, as represented by the Serpent, and that in it Humanity will be ultimately victorious, in and through its Representative: crush the head of the Serpent, although in this not without damage, hurt, and the poison of death—all is changed. In that case the sentence is full of meaning. It sets forth a principle; it ennobles our human nature by representing it as moral; it bears a promise; it contains a prophecy; it introduces the Golden Age. It is the noblest saying that could be given to Humanity, or to individual men, at the birth of their history. In it the Bible sets forth at its very opening these three great ethical principles, on which rests the whole Biblical teaching concerning the Messiah and His Kingdom: that man is capable of salvation; that all evil springs from sin, with which mortal combat must be waged; and that there will be a final victory over sin through the Representative of Humanity. And this first promise does not afterwards develop; it contains initially all that is to be unfolded in the course of the fullest development, so that we might exclaim, with an ancient writer: 'Here begins the book of the wars of the Lord'; or with Luther: 'Here rises the Sun of Consolation.'

This gradual unrolling in the sight of men, as they were able to read it, of what from the first had been written on the prophetic scroll accounts for the peculiar form in which the future is so often presented in prophecy. It explains how so many of the predictions concerning the kingdom of God are presented under a particularistic and national aspect. It was necessary—alike as regarded the people and the prophets; and it belonged to the Old Testament standpoint, quite as much as its sacrifices, rites, institutions, and ceremonial laws. We believe they had a deeper and an eternal meaning which at that time and to that people could only be set forth in such manner. Similarly, the predictive descriptions of the kingdom and the king came to Israel in that nationalistic form in which alone they could have been intelligibly presented. Zion, Israel, Moab, or else the then present enemies of the people of God, and their conquest, had to them a meaning which our later, Christian, ideas could have never possessed, and which, indeed, it would have been impossible to convey otherwise than in such form. And this also must be kept in view, that all these prophecies did historically start from Israel, and that those nations did at that time actually represent the enemies of the kingdom of God. Nor is it meant that all such predictions applied to the kingdom of God. Many of them were what is called *temporal*: that is, they applied only to those times and to the circumstances and nations there mentioned. But, just as the type is always based on the symbol—the application to the future on the meaning in the present—so are the prophecies of the kingdom presented in the forms of, and with application to, the then present. And in evidence that this view is not arbitrary, we point to the circumstance that so often these promises, couched in the particularistic form, alternate with, or merge into others where the horizon is temporarily enlarged and the application is universalistic. This evidences that the world-wide idea of the kingdom was present to the mind of Israel as matter of faith and hope, even though it would ordinarily be clothed in the forms of the time.

From this point of view we perceive the higher need of some facts which recent criticism has established, although a certain school has derived from them inferences adverse to the prophetic character of the Old Testament. *First*, we perceive that generally, though not always, the fulfilment must not be expected to correspond literally with the prophecy. This was the idea of prophecy entertained by the old supra-naturalistic school, and was strictly connected with its mechanical views of inspiration generally. Were it not for our sincere respect for the earnest though ill-directed faith which prompted these notions, we would seriously complain of the misrepresentation of Biblical truth which was their consequence, affording an easy victory to its opponents. But we object, with good reason, that a certain school of critics argues as if the view referred to were the only one possible, and that it directs all its arguments to disprove what we do not, and, in the nature of it, could not hold. It is not controversially—merely in answer to our opponents—but positively, as the outcome of the views previously explained, that we would formulate these principles in regard to the fulfilment of Messianic prophecy: that prophecy can only be properly understood from the standpoint of fulfilment; that prophecy always starts from historical *data* in the then present; and that the fulfilment in each case not only covers but is wider than the mere letter of the prophecy—wider than either the hearers, or perhaps the speaker of it, had perceived. All this in a preliminary way—to be further explained in the sequel.

Secondly. This view of 'fulfilment' leads up to another point, on which we must enter more fully. Here also our opponents have rightly apprehended the facts, while they have laid upon us wrongful inferences from them. For these three things follow from the premises previously stated: that prophecy is not predicted history—which, indeed, would be a quite unworthy view of it; that prophecy had always a present meaning and present lessons to those who heard it; and that, as this meaning unfolded in the course of history, it conveyed to each succeeding generation something new, bringing to each fresh present lessons. Nay, even in its final fulfilment each prophecy has lessons to them who have witnessed its accomplishment. In short, prophecy cannot be compressed within the four comers of a fact: it is not merely tidings about the future. It is not dead, but instinct with undying life, and that life is divine. There is a moral aspect in prophecy to all generations. Under one aspect of it, it prepares for the future, and this is the predictive element of it. Under its other aspect it teaches lessons of the present to each generation; and this is its moral aspect.

It is therefore not discordant with our belief in prophecy, but the reverse, when our attention is called to the fact that, as presented in Scripture, the Prophets were not merely—perhaps not even primarily—foretellers of future events, but that their activity also extended to the then present: that they were reprovers, reformers, instructors. Certainly: for they were God's messengers. But from this it does not follow that the futuristic element had no place in their calling. There is no inconsistency between the two. On the contrary, it was the underlying view of the future which gave meaning and emphasis to their admonitions about the present. I am quite aware that I must be prepared to furnish a formula which will equally cover, and give unity to, these two parts of their activity. My answer is that, when the prophet foretells, he presents the future in the light of the present; and, when he admonishes or reproves, he presents the present in the light of that future which he sees to be surely coming. Thus he is always, and in all aspects of it, the messenger of God to every generation.

It will now be perceived what was meant by the statement that the kingdom of God was the connecting, pervading, and impelling idea of the Old Testament. On the supposition of the trustworthiness of the arrangement of the Old Testament into the Law and the Prophets, Divines of all schools have traced the unfolding—both extensively and intensively—of this idea in the progressive development of the history of Israel through its three stages: the patriarchal, the Mosaic, and the prophetic. And so the history and institutions of Israel would lead up to the doctrinal teaching of the New Testament. It might, indeed, be objected, that in our view of the arrangement of the Old Testament as Law and Prophets there was not progression but retrogression, since the prophetic writings seem to set forth more simple and primitive notions as regards sacrifices and ritual ordinances than those which underlie the directions and arrangements of the 'Priest-Codex.' And it has been argued that this also proves that the right order would be: the Prophets and the Law, not the reverse, and that the Priest-Codex itself must be of late date. But these are ill-grounded inferences. Seeming retrogression may be real progression, because correction, where principles bad been misunderstood, misapplied, or lost from view. If two or three thousand years after this, and in the absence of historical details of the change, it should be argued that, instead of Mediævalism and the Reformation, the historical succession should be the Reformation and Mediævalism, because, as regarded the priesthood, the centralisation of worship, ritual ordinances, and the like, the Reformation marked the more simple and primitive, and must therefore have preceded Mediævalism, the inference would be both fallacious and false. May we not say the same in regard to this argument for the inversion of the order, Law and Prophets?

Let us try to mark the unfolding of the great idea which the Bible places in its forefront, and which, as we have stated, infolds all the religious truth that has come to man in the course of his development. Closely considered, the primeval promise already set before man the outlook on the kingdom of God in its ethical character. And that kingdom was not placed on a particularistic or Judaic, but on a universalistic basis. From this point of view we can observe where the one spring divided, and follow the parting streams of Jewish and heathen development as they issued from the one source. A new meaning here attaches, not only to the fact and the response of conscience to the demands of right, but also to the (however imperfect or even misdirected) striving after the right in the heathen world. We can now understand the appeal to the evidential force of God's works in nature, and much more to that for God in the conscience, as made, not only in the well-known passage of St. Paul's Epistle to the Romans (2:14,15), but also in the Old Testament, as in the sublime appeal to the heathen in Isaiah 40:21-26, in regard to the works of creation, and in that derived from conscience in Psalm 94:9, 10: 'He that planted the ear, shall He not hear? He that formed the eye, shall He not see? He that chastens the nations (viz. inwardly, through their consciences), shall He not punish—He that teacheth man knowledge?' The creator of the human eye and ear must be the living God, Who sees and hears. He Who implanted reason and conscience in man is thereby evidenced as the Rewarder of good and evil, and shall He not eventually so manifest Himself?

It is thus that the Old Testament, starting with a universalistic object, can and does make its appeal to heathendom, both concerning God and for God. And what was the response made both to the first and to the second of these appeals? Only this: In its search after God, the ancient world reached, indeed, beyond the gods many, and came very near, almost touched, the idea of Unity. But this Supreme Unity, to which ultimately men and gods were subject, was not a Personality, not the Living and True God, our reconciled Father—but Fate, blind, impersonal, immovable; and in this struggle between Fate and Virtue lay the mystery, and the misery, and the ultimate self-despair of heathenism. Or again, as regarded the second appeal of the Old Testament to heathendom—that *for* God in the conscience, we recall the despairing expressions of a Tacitus, and the idea of a Cicero, that if ever the ideal of goodness and virtue, for which Humanity had longed, and hitherto with such bitter disappointment, were to appear on earth, all men would fall down before it in universal homage. We recall it to mark the sad contrast of history. Just as the Ideal of Old Testament expectation, for which universal Judaism in its highest aspirations had longed, came to His own, but only to be rejected of them, so did the ideal of all goodness and virtue, the One universally-admitted perfect Man—for whom heathenism in its highest aspirations had yearned—receive, not universal homage, but universal rejection, when Jesus was nailed to the cross.

In truth, the Jewish and Gentile developments are not so far apart as we sometimes imagine. They were at one in their beginning, and they are at one in their ending. And the course of their development also was closely parallel, although in heathenism the issue appeared in the negative; in Judaism, on the other hand, in a positive form. But the unconscious cry of both was after the Life, the Light, the real, the true: after moral deliverance and the Kingdom of God.

Turning from the course of heathen to that of Jewish development, we recall the apt observation, that the Biblical conception of Revelation really looks back upon the account of the Creation, when our world was called into being by the Word, and its life imparted by the Spirit of God. This internal connection between the Word or Revelation and Creation also implies that in Revelation we shall find the same general order which we observe in the physical world—especially the law of historical progress— that is, as we now understand it, progression in history. The one underlying idea of Revelation is, as we have seen, the great ethical prospect in that primeval promise which the Bible places at its forefront—the outlook on a universal Kingdom of God. This primeval promise and principle alike forms the beginning and is the goal; it is the heading and the summary of Revelation. And it was this foundation-truth which unfolded throughout the course of Israel's development—in their history, rites, and institutions, as well as in the more direct communications through the Prophets. We can only indicate this here in briefest outline.

The ideal object of Israel's calling, and hence of their history and institutions, seems expressed in the first promise to their father Abraham: 'In thee and in thy seed shall all the families of the earth be blessed.' This promise is so fundamental as to be thrice repeated to Abraham; it is renewed to Isaac (Gen 26:4); and reiterated to Jacob (Gen 28:14). If this promise had any real Divine meaning, it must have been intended to mark, as it were, the planting-ground for the Kingdom of God, whence in the fulness of time and of preparation it would be transplanted into the heathen world; in other words, the blessings of that kingdom were to be imparted through Israel to the world at large. There is nothing narrow or particularistic, but a grand universalism, even about this earliest presentation of the promise in a concrete form. And that such was the object and mission of Israel, is clearly indicated on the eve of the Sinaitic legislation: 'Ye shall be My property from among all nations, for all the earth is mine; ye shall be unto Me a kingdom of priests and a holy nation' (Exo 19:5,6). As Israel was ideally, so all nations were through their ministry to become really the possession of God: a kingdom of priests, a holy people; for all the earth, as well as Israel, was God's. And the realisation of this would be the kingdom of God on earth.

All the institutions of Israel were in strict accordance with this ideal destiny. Alike the laws, the worship, the institutions, and the mission of Israel were intended to express these two things: acknowledgment of God and dependence upon God. Thus viewed, the whole might be summed up in this one term, which runs through the whole Old Testament: 'The Servant of Jehovah.' The patriarchs were the Servants of the Lord; Israel was the Servant of the Lord; and their threefold representative institutions expressed the same idea. The *Priest* was to be wholly the Servant of the Lord. Hence the smallest transgression of the ordinances of his calling involved his destruction or removal. The *King* was not to bear rule in the manner of heathen princes, but to be the Servant of the Lord, in strictest subordination to Jehovah. Hence Saul, despite his nobler qualities, was really the Antichrist; and David, despite his grievous faults, the typical Christ of Israel's royalty, because of his constant acknowledgment of God's kingship. And the *Prophet* was simply the Servant of the Lord, telling nought but God's Word, in such strict adherence to the letter of his commission, that its slightest breach brought immediate punishment. And the Messiah, as summing up in Himself ideal Israel—its history, institutions, mission, and promises—was to be the Servant of the Lord. Hence the prophecies which most clearly portray Him—those of Isaiah— might be headed by this title: The Book of the Servant of Jehovah; the idea rising, through people, prophet, king, even through a foreign instrumental doer of His behest, up to Him as *the* Servant of the Lord, the ideal Sufferer by and for the unrighteousness of man, the ideal Sacrifice and Priest for his sins, the ideal Teacher in his ignorance, Comforter in his sorrow, Restorer in his decay, and Dispenser of all blessing to the world at large—the Spirit-anointed One, out of Whose fulness all were to receive, and Who would fulfil all that Israel had meant and prepared. Or, going backwards, He was to be *the* Son of Man, the Second Adam, whose victory would restore what sin had lost: the true Son of God, God manifest in the flesh. This, we believe, the Old Testament meant, and Jesus of Nazareth came to fulfil.

In saying this, I am at least not misrepresenting what the Gospels indicate as the meaning of the Old Testament, and as that which stood out before the Christ as the object of His Mission. I cannot express it better than in the language of one who belonged to a school of critics from which I widely differ, but whose deep insight and spiritual appreciativeness contrast markedly with the levity of others of the same direction.

'The call of Jesus,' he writes, 'points back, first to John, and then, much further, into the Old Testament. The conception of the Kingdom of God, which to our modern consciousness seems somewhat obscure...is one of the fundamental ideas of the Old Testament. It was the pride of Israel, not merely because Israel believed in the privileges it would confer on themselves, but because alone of all nations Israel was capable of believing in the possibility of a covenant between heaven and earth, between God and man, in a welding of Divine purposes with the counsels of earth, and in the fact that, even within the modest boundaries of a small nation, the rule of earthly affairs was not unworthy of God. To be sure, this also constituted Israel's sorrow and source of suffering in the course of history; the limitation not only of its free political and purely human, but even of its religious development; the appointed bitter criticism of a Reality which ever fell short and ever contradicted the Ideal. But in this very sorrow and never-ceasing criticism of earthly lamentation and limitation, Israel became the guide and leader in that infinite striving which, by believing in and seeking after the coming Kingdom of God, and by the final real Advent of the Messiah upon earth, would and did join Idea and Reality—the life of

God and that of man, heaven and earth. The one pervading and impelling idea of the Old Testament is the royal reign of God on earth...Almost a thousand years before Christ rises the longing cry after the future Kingdom of God—a kingdom which is to conquer and to win all nations, and to plant in Israel righteousness, knowledge, peace, and blessing—that Kingdom of God in which God, or his Vicegerent, the Messiah, is to be King over the whole earth, and all generations are to come up and worship the Lord of Hosts.' (Keim, *Jesu von Nazara* 2, pp. 35, 36.)

On this only too brief extract I might have been content to rest the case. But I must not forget, even in this preliminary statement, that, since the eloquent words just quoted were written, the study of the Old Testament has entered into an entirely new phase—at any rate so far as its influence on English theological thinking is concerned. The critical conclusions arrived, or at least aimed at, are of the most wide-reaching character. As stated in the previous Lecture, they have this advantage, that they promise to explain every difficulty—though to our mind this is anything but evidence of their truth; that they are propounded by men of great critical learning, and presented by them as the undoubted outcome of the best critical research; and that they are supported by arguments which, to those unacquainted with the details of the controversy, must appear most specious. While reserving for another occasion such answer as may be necessary for the general argument of these Lectures, I must be allowed, even at this stage, to express some general objections. It is not said to create a prejudice, but as a matter of fact, that critics even of the same school are still in hopeless contradiction, not as to minor details, but on such primary questions as the authorship of different parts of the Pentateuch, or their respective dates, on both of which divergent conclusions are advanced—and with equal certitude. From which, I think, we may at least infer that no sure ground has yet been reached in regard to them. Further, some of the arguments are, almost admittedly, unsatisfactory, such as that which would infer the age or composition of certain parts of the Pentateuch from linguistic peculiarities. And the conclusion seems, at least to me, quite clear that the whole question will have to be decided mainly on *internal* grounds. Lastly, the arguments are not unfrequently mixed up with such extraordinary speculations as not only to weaken the force of the general reasoning, but to make us distrustful of the whole direction.

Indeed, *primâ facie*, some of the main conclusions propounded by that school of critics seem to involve the strongest improbabilities. Most of us are in some measure cognisant how books are written. Let us compare with this, for example, the account which Wellhausen—the representative of that school best known among us—gives of the origin of the Pentateuch. Truth to say, it is so complicated that it would be impossible to compress it in one sentence, and so involved as to make it difficult to present it in a quite clearly intelligible manner. Suffice it that the Pentateuch (or rather Hexateuch) is made up of a number of books which themselves have undergone several 'redactions,' and been successively incorporated into yet other books, with still other 'redactions.' Each of these is represented by a special letter, indicative of its authorship or characteristics. Thus we have sources respectively initialed, E, E2, J, J2, D, JE2, PC, and Q, besides the final redaction of them all. Some of these have not only undergone revisions, but P, for example, is 'a conglomerate, the work of a whole school'; while D consists of a centrepiece that had undergone two editions, with additions, respectively, before and after it. As we try to realise the multiplicity of books—not consulted, used, or quoted, but incorporated in the composition of the Pentateuch; remember, that of some of these books only small fragments are preserved, and even those in small pieces cunningly distributed here and there; and finally think of the various additions they have received, and redactions to which they have been subjected—the mind becomes bewildered. No other book has ever been composed in this manner. It may be as Wellhausen says; but in that case the Pentateuch is certainly, from a literary point of view, a unique production. We know that in the composition of a work many sources may be used and various authorities quoted, yet literary history would be searched in vain for another patchwork of the kind in which half-a-dozen or more books are cut up and pieced together in so cunning a manner. Viewed as a purely literary question, the story of the Pentateuch, as told by some of these critics, is not only unparalleled, but transparently improbable.

It need scarcely be said that this post-dating and inversion of the Pentateuch has most important sequences. In the first place, it presents the ancient religion of Israel as something quite different from what we had been formerly led to regard it; indeed, as a form of nature-religion, barbarous, and kindred to those of the nations around. And so the most fundamental questions, such as in regard to human sacrifices, the worship of Baal, and other points of the kind, have to be discussed anew. On the other hand, if the previously received order has to be inverted and we are henceforth to write, the Prophets and the Law—if the Pentateuch, viewed as Mosaic legislation, is, to speak plainly, a deception, we cannot wonder if the so-called Prophets are a delusion. I do not misrepresent Kuenen when I state this as the outcome of the book already referred to, that there is no such thing as Prophetism or Prophets in the sense which the Church attaches to these terms; that what are called fulfilled prophecies are simply a mistake; while unfulfilled prophecies are a delusion. But not only was the future towards which the Prophets looked a delusion, but their activity in the then present did not advance the welfare of the people, and Prophetism was alike ignorant of State policy and dangerous to the State. These self-appointed enthusiasts must, according to the new theory, be placed far below the Roman tribunes of the people. Their only contribution was an ethical monotheism, although, as Professor Kuenen adds, 'Even without their aid Polytheism would, perhaps, have made way for the recognition and the worship of one only God.' And with strange historical boldness, the commencement of such a reformation is discerned in the Roman Empire at the beginning of the Christian era, although Kuenen declares it doubtful whether the monotheism of the people, not of the philosophers, would have been what he calls 'ethical.'

But in cutting away all ground in Old Testament prophecy for an expectation of the kingdom, Professor Kuenen's theory surely condemns itself. For, as a matter of fact, this expectancy did exist, not only in the time of Jesus, but certainly two centuries before. And even Kuenen hesitates to accept the view of Schultz, that many of the Messianic interpretations originated among 'the Jews among whom the Prophet of Nazareth laboured.' But if so, what explanation of them can be offered? Only this: 'In the centuries which preceded the establishment of Christianity a new conception of the words of the Prophets and Psalmists must have been formed, which, in distinction from the actual meaning of these men, could be called the second sense of Scripture.' Probably few persons would call such perversion of the real meaning its second sense. But it is surely a strange use of language when Professor Kuenen calls this the 'allegorical exegesis,' and adds that 'allegorical exegesis is the inseparable companion of the process of the clarification of religious views.' Most students would reverse this epigrammatic generalisation, and characterise such 'allegorical exegesis' as contributing rather to the process of darkening than that of 'clarifying' religious views. But the point to which I wish at present to call special attention is, that, when challenged to show how these Messianic interpretations had originated, Professor Kuenen has no better answer to offer than the assertion, that a new conception *must* have been formed in the centuries which preceded Christianity.

It is perhaps well that all the sequences of so bold and thoroughgoing a theory should clearly appear. And it will afford yet other evidence of the internal and inseparable connection between the Old and New Testament. Nor has Professor Kuenen denied that such did exist, at least, in the mind of Christ and His Apostles. But he declares that in this they had wholly misunderstood and misinterpreted the real and primary meaning of the Old Testament. To quote his own words: 'If they [Jesus Christ and the Apostles] had continued still to occupy altogether the standpoint of the old prophets and poets, Jesus of Nazareth would not have been accepted as the Messiah.' Then must the Synagogue have been right in rejecting the claims of Jesus, and in crucifying Him as a Deceiver of the people!

Surely, this is a startling conclusion. And yet, we repeat, it is well that the issue should be so narrowed, and the real alternative stand out in plain language. With belief in the Christ as presented in the New Testament, the prophetic character of the Old Testament is also established; with the rejection of prophecy in the Old Testament the claims of Christ, as set forth in the New Testament, fall to the ground.

Which of these shall it be? Let history decide.

LECTURE 3: THE FAITH AND RITES OF THE PRIMITIVE CHURCH ARE CONFIRMED BY INDUBITABLE CHRISTIAN, AND BY IMPORTANT NON-CHRISTIAN EVIDENCE.

Whom do men say that I the Son of Man am? And they said:
Some say that Thou art John the Baptist; some Elijah,
and others Jeremiah, or one of the prophets. He saith
unto them, But whom say ye that I am? And Simon Peter
answered and said, Thou art the Christ, the Son
of the living God. Matthew 16:13-16.

IT cannot be regarded as a real digression from the line of our argument if, before proceeding, we guard ourselves against a preliminary objection, since, if it were established, our whole reasoning would be disposed of. Hitherto we have contended that the New Testament in its origin looks back upon the Old; that the one all-pervading idea of the Old Testament is, that of the Kingdom of God through the Messiah; and that the Apostles and primitive disciples saw the realisation of it in the mission, the history, and the teaching of Jesus of Nazareth. But what if this point were called in question, and there be no real ground for believing that the views which we impute to them were held by the primitive Christians? And the inquiry into the primitive belief of the Church gains in importance as we remember that the primitive records in the Gospels have been assailed on many sides: their date and authorship have been disputed; they have been described as partly spurious, partly interpolated; as exaggerated, or else coloured by prevailing superstitions; and as designed to foist later ideas upon primitive teaching, and to bring professedly apostolic authority to bear on existing controversies. Besides, what evidence is there outside the four Gospels (or some allusions in the Epistles)—all of them being in the nature of interested witnesses—that these supposed facts really formed the *data* on which primitive Christian belief rested? It is evident that these questions concern the very existence of the citadel to which we have been seeking to trace the avenues.

Some of the points just mentioned lie, indeed, outside our present inquiry. Our argument only requires us to make sure of the primitive belief of the Church in the facts recorded in the Gospels, and on which the conviction was grounded that Jesus of Nazareth was the Messiah of Old Testament prophecy. It does not require us to establish that this belief was well founded, nor yet that the facts themselves on which it rested were absolutely and literally true. We have at present to deal with the authenticity of the Gospel-records only as expressive of the primitive faith, not with the grounds on which that faith rested. The latter inquiry is, indeed, of the deepest importance, nor would we shrink from making it were this the right place for it. But our present business is only to show that the primitive disciples believed certain facts (whether true or false), on the ground of which they regarded Jesus as the Messiah. Nor is it even necessary for our argument to prove that all that is recorded in the four Gospels represents the primitive tradition and belief of the Church. This also is a most important question, but it forms not the subject of our present inquiry. For our purpose it is enough if sufficient is established on which to ground the conviction that Jesus was the Messiah: sufficient that looked back into the past of Old Testament prophecy, and forward into the future of New Testament history.

But even in this narrowed aspect of the question an affirmative answer will advance us a long way. It will establish the historic continuity of the New with the Old Testament; it will make quite clear what the primitive Christians did certainly believe about the Christ, why they regarded Jesus as the Messiah, and how far their primary belief led them. And more than this, and beyond the scope of our present argument, it will afford presumptive evidence of the reality of the facts on which primitive belief rested. For, if it were proved by the general consensus of primitive tradition that certain facts concerning Jesus were universally held to have occurred, and that certain doctrines were founded on them as inferences from these facts, and certain rites introduced as memorials of them—or, conversely, if certain doctrines or rites can be historically established as primitive which look back upon certain Gospel facts as their necessary basis—then we have such presumptive evidence in their favour that it will be requisite for negative criticism not only historically to prove their incorrectness, but also historically to account for this general consensus of belief regarding them in the primitive Church, and for the origin of the doctrines and rites which were their outcome.

And here, as already stated, we are not limited to the mere historical record of these facts in the Gospels or Epistles. We have other, and quite as strong, evidence that they formed part of the primitive faith of the Church in the doctrines and rites which demonstrably looked back upon them. If we can prove from undoubted and even non-Christian testimony that certain doctrines were held and certain rites practised, which necessarily refer to certain facts recorded in the Gospel-history, we have *pro tanto* confirmation of the reception of these facts—that is, that they formed part of the primitive belief of the Church. We have thus two lines of evidence: that from the unquestioned record of primitive tradition in the Christian writings, and that from the unquestionable evidence of the existence of certain doctrines and practices in the primitive Church. The one will rest on Christian, the other on non-Christian documents; and as regards the latter, it may be found sometimes to stretch beyond the evidence of doctrines and rites to that of some of the facts recorded in the Gospels.

If in the view of some we needlessly narrow the evidence in favour of primitive doctrines and rites by confining it to non-Christian (Jewish and heathen) testimony, there is in the present argument good ground for so doing. It is, indeed, not likely that those possessing at once sufficient information on the subject and calmness of judgment would regard the picture of the primitive Church, or rather of the two fundamentally dissimilar Churches, which M. Renan has painted in his 'Conferences d'Angleterre,' as a portraiture of the original state of matters; still less, that they would accept his views as to the 'posthumous' conciliation of what he calls the Church of St. Peter with that of St. Paul—the Church of Rome with that of Jerusalem—and of their union, which the 'Book of Acts' is supposed, by a pious fraud, to represent as accomplished from the first. The historical assumptions are here too evident, the facts on the other side too numerous, and the explanatory hypothesis is too ingenious, to allow ourselves to be carried away by the brilliant diction and the epigrammatic generalisations of the eloquent Frenchman. It would require far more than this to lead us to attribute to the simple-mindedness of the early Christians such an act of *haute politique* in what to them was matter of deepest spiritual conviction; or to ascribe to them deliberate fraud in that for which they were ready to pour forth their life's blood. And the more you accentuate—as is the wont of that school—the supposed fundamental differences between Petrine and Pauline teaching; the more you insist on the intensity with which each party clung to its principles, the less likely does a 'reconciliation,' such as that described, appear. Not a peaceful fusion that covered the differences, but a life-and-death struggle, would be the likely result with such combatants. But while the line of defence is on all sides good, yet there is such difference of views and such contention about the apostolic, and, on many points, such unclearness about many things in the post-apostolic, Church, that we willingly forego in our present argument all reference to either, so as to avoid what after all would be a needless complication. We shall, therefore, not go beyond the period of the Gospels; and appeal for the rest to non-Christian evidence, in proof that the main facts, on which the conviction rested that Jesus was the Old Testament Messiah, formed part of the primitive belief of the Church.

In other respects, also, it is equally interesting and important to draw the line of distinction between Evangelic and Apostolic times, and between Evangelic and Apostolic literature—the latter including 'the Book of Acts.' The doctrine (διδαχη) which is the outcome of the one we may designate as the faith and rites of the primitive Christians; that of the other, as the dogmas and practices of the Apostolic Church. In regard to the latter, we may say that the one grand principle underlying all is that of *Apostolicity*. I hasten to add that I use the term, not in the sense which in recent theological discussions has been attached to it, but in what is its real meaning—Christsentness. In this sense, apostolicity has a twofold application: as apostolicity of office and apostolicity of teaching. Whatever diversity of gifts or of administration may have existed or been tolerated, above them all was apostolicity of office, which St. Paul, as well as St. Peter, St. John, and St. James, energetically vindicated for themselves against all gainsayers. Whatever was not apostolic or apostolically sanctioned was to be repudiated. And by the side of this supremacy of the apostolic office we have that of apostolic teaching. Whatever differences in views or practices may have been tolerated—and there is evidence of the most wide-hearted liberality in both respects—yet, what of doctrine or practice was apostolic must be absolutely received, while the opposite was absolutely banned. Evidently, we have already passed, or at least are passing, out of the formative into the historic period. The age of historic memorial has already begun, when appeal is made to the teaching and the practice of Apostles, apostolic men, and apostolic Churches. Not so during the first or formative period of the Church. Then the teaching was directly that of Christ, and the rites and practices were simply the outcome of that teaching. And this also is distinctive. Under the Old Testament, doctrine was in great measure the outcome of rites; under the New, rites are the outcome of doctrine. The relation is in accordance with the character of each: in the one case, from without inwards; in the other, from within outwards. The application of these principles is wide-reaching, and, as will appear in the sequel, closely bears on our present argument.

To the Christian heart it must at all times be most painful to follow in detail the criticism of the Gospels as made by the more advanced negative school. Quite irrespective of the valid answer which, we are fully convinced, can, on scientific grounds, be given to their objections, and the good defence which can be made of the positions taken up by the Church, there are preliminary considerations which will, with good reason, weigh with thoughtful persons more heavily than merely logical arguments and ingenious hypotheses. The school in question proceeds in its criticism of the Gospels on the avowed principle, that where they do not preserve the original tradition, they interpolate or intentionally falsify for a definite purpose—that purpose bearing mainly on the supposed two hostile tendencies in the Church of Judaic and Gentile Christianity, the supposed object being to advocate either the one or the other tendency, or else to conciliate them. To adopt the expressive term of German critics: where our present Gospels deviate from the original traditions, they are mainly Tendenz-Schriftenz (tendency writings). But, to my thinking, it seems inconceivable, from the intellectual, and still more from the moral point of view, that the early Christians—and, indeed, it must have been the leading men among them—should have deliberately falsified facts and invented incidents, and that in connection with the Personality of Jesus, Who to them was the all in all. That the writers of our Gospels should have so altered the original traditions and documents (which, according to our opponents, they elaborated into their works), seems, to say the least, intellectually highly improbable, and morally absolutely incredible. That they who so thought of the Christ should, for ecclesiastical purposes, or to bring about a 'conciliation'—which in itself seems psychologically and historically an unlikely undertaking—have falsified and invented, constitutes the very climax of improbabilities. They may have been misinformed; they may have been mistaken; they may have viewed things from the standpoint of their time; they may have exaggerated: all this is conceivable, though historical proof would be required for it—but to associate with them 'Tendency-Literature' seems morally impossible.

But our argument is not merely *à priori*. We have quite a series of witnesses who give incidental confirmation to much in the Gospels. St. Paul, who became a Christian some years after the Crucifixion, must have been acquainted with the traditions and views about Jesus current among those early believers whom he had persecuted. And there is evidence throughout his writings, that after his conversion he had taken pains further to acquaint himself with the historical grounds, that is, with the facts in Christ's history, on which the belief of the Church rested. Indeed this must have been a primary necessity to a nature so logical as his, and to one who had to advocate among Greeks and philosophers a doctrine so inherently unlikely as the Divine Mission, the atoning Death, and the Resurrection of Christ. And his teaching—even limiting ourselves to those epistles which the most severe negative criticism admits as genuine, is in every point grounded upon the data of the Gospels, and hence *pro tanto* a confirmation of them. Besides, the bases of his doctrinal system also rest on the teaching of Jesus, as we gather its spirit from the reports in the Gospels. We remind ourselves here of such teaching as concerning the valuelessness of mere outward observances; concerning the Law as presented by the Leaders of Israel; concerning the opening of the Kingdom of God to the Gentile world; concerning the insufficiency and inefficacy of outward distinctions and advantages; concerning the rule of the Spirit within the heart, and His transformation of our nature; concerning the need of absolute self-surrender to God, like that of Christ; concerning the character and purpose of Christ's Death; His institution of the Last Supper; His Resurrection, and His coming again. All this, and more that could be mentioned, carries with it a train of obvious sequences evidential of the historical character of the Gospels.

But even this is not all. The reference of St. Paul to the Twelve Apostles, (1 Cor 15:5) and to the 'brethren of the Lord,' are not the only direct references to incidents in the Gospel narrative. Even on the admission of negative critics, we have in the undoubted Pauline epistles direct verbal references to passages in the Gospels. Thus, St. Matthew 5:39, &c., is the basis of Romans 12:17, 21; we are reminded of St. Matthew 13:33 in Galatians 5:9; of St. Matthew 22:40 in Galatians 5:14; of St. Mark 11:23 by 1 Corinthians 13:2; of St. Mark 13:26 by 1 Thessalonians 4:17; of St. Luke 6:27, &c., by 1 Corinthians 4:12, &c.; comp.Romans 12:14; and of St. Luke 12:40 in 1 Thessalonians 5:2. These verbal as well as real coincidences are of the most important evidential bearing on the Gospel narratives. And to these might be added similar references in the other epistles of St. Paul, which have not been here adduced, because their authenticity has been questioned by certain critics, our present object being to present only such evidence as is undisputed. Suffice it to state that references to St. Matthew, St. Mark, and St. Luke have been traced in the Epistles to the Ephesians and to the Colossians.

Similar references to the Synoptic Gospels—to which we here confine ourselves—occur in other apostolic writings, notably in the Epistle of St. James and the Book of Revelation. In the former class we mention the following: St. Matthew 5:3 as compared with St. James 1:9; St. Matthew 5:7 with St. James 2:13; St. Matthew 5:9 with St. James 3:18; St. Matthew 5:12 with St. James 1:2, and also 5:10; St. Matthew 5:34-37 with St. James 5:12; St. Matthew 6:19 with St. James 5:2; St. Matthew 7:24-27 with St. James 1:22; St. Matthew 12:7 with St. James 2:13; St. Matthew 21:21, 22 with St. James 1:6; St. Matthew 22:39 with St. James 2:8; and St. Matthew 23:12 with St. James 4:6, 10.

The references in the 'Book of Revelation' are not confined to the Gospel according to St. Matthew, but extend to the other two Synoptists. Thus, we have reference to St. Matthew 10:32 in Revelation 3:5; to St. Matthew 11:15, and to 13:9 and 43 in Revelation 2:7; to St. Mark 13:22 in Revelation 13:13, 14; to St. Mark 13:24, &c., in Revelation 6:12; to St. Luke 12:36-38 in Revelation 3:20; to St. Luke 12:39, 40 in Revelation 3:3, and Revelation 16:15; and to St. Luke 23:30 in Revelation 6:16.

But all this presents only a small part of the evidence at our disposal. We can appeal to the simplicity, vividness, and naturalness of so many of the Gospel narratives; to their psychological truthfulness, their internal connection and reference one to another; to the utter impossibility of accounting for them by notions or expectations prevailing at the time; to the agreement between the narratives in the different Gospels; to the accordance of the persons and surroundings with what we know of the history and the manners of the time, and to many little traits which can scarcely be described, but to which the student of history is sensitive, all bearing their witness to the Gospels. And beyond it all stands out the Figure of the historical Christ, as He was in the days of His Flesh, and as He is to all time and now: Himself the best evidence of the Gospel narratives.

And when from this we descend to the position which even negative criticism concedes to us, we remember that, according to its admissions, the earliest document, or documents, in which primitive tradition found expression dates from less than thirty years after the Crucifixion, and was derived from eyewitnesses of these events and disciples of Jesus. And we feel that this canon of our opponents has a far wider application than they give it: that 'doubt is only warrantable where scientific reasons can be asserted for it.' Further, when we examine what, with frequent forgetfulness of their own canon, the most advanced of that school have selected out of our Gospels as the original narrative, we perceive that, while much more might be inferred from their own admissions, they have left us quite sufficient to establish the grounds on which the primitive Church recognised Jesus as the Messiah promised in the Old Testament.

2. From this we turn to a far different class of evidence: that from the testimony of avowed enemies. We cannot, indeed, expect that either Jews or Romans would furnish us with details about Christian doctrine, unless, in the case of the former, for controversial purposes. But to a certain extent they bear testimony as to facts and practices, and if their witness bears out what we find in the New Testament, this may surely be regarded as giving important support to the fuller account of such persons, practices, or doctrines in the New Testament itself. We can only in the briefest manner follow this line of evidence.

A. *The Talmud*—though containing very early, even pre-Christian notices, is, as a whole, of much later date than the New Testament. Moreover, its statements are utterly unhistorical, and it is charged with bitter enmity to the new faith. Accordingly we cannot look for any positive testimony in its pages. But there are important admissions, ascribed to Rabbis belonging to the Apostolic or Early Post-Apostolic age, which are at least negatively of great evidential value. Thus miracles on the part of Jesus seem to be admitted, and they are not accounted for either by delusion or imposture. However accounted for, we find the belief in the miraculous power of Jesus confirmed. Indeed, miraculous cures are also attributed to the disciples of Christ, and the strict prohibition to avail one's self of them, even if life itself were in danger, only affords additional evidence of the general credence of them. Again, we have undoubted reference to early Christian writings. Whether allowed or forbidden to be saved from the fire—and there were voices on either side—these writings had evidently been intended for the reading of Jews, and must therefore have been written in the Aramæan. Nor can we be mistaken in supposing that they were either documents treating of the history and claims of

Christ, or at any rate connected with the original primitive Christian documents. A distinct quotation, or rather misquotation, of St. Matthew 5:17 occurs in *Shabbath* 116b, as from the 'Evangilyon'—which in the word-play not uncommon in Talmudic writings is styled the *Aven* or else *Avan Gilyon*, 'mischief of blank (empty) paper' (גליון עון, or else און). This testimony reaches up into the first century, and it is comparatively unimportant for our argument whether the quotation was from St. Matthew or from a document earlier or later than our Gospel. Similar remarks apply to what we regard as a reference to the Gospel of St. John on the part of Rabbi Eliezer ben Hyrqanos. In both cases we have—to take the lowest standpoint—confirmation, that what we read in the Gospels as the teaching and mission of Christ formed part of the primitive belief of the Church. And we feel that in so far they also afford confirmation of the Gospels themselves.

The whole subject is so interesting and novel—at any rate to English readers—that we may be allowed to present it, at least in outline, following, so far as may be, the arguments and admissions of Jewish writers, in order to avoid controversy.

It is the contention of certain Jewish writers that at first there was not the same separation between the Synagogue and the primitive disciples as at a later period, and that such would not have ensued had it not been for the Pauline direction and the Anti-Jewish Gentile movement which was its sequence. We mark the concessions which this implies, while we emphatically deny that what is called the 'Pauline direction' is correctly represented in them. And we recall the account in the Book of Acts of the bitter hostility to the infant Church, and the consequent persecutions, which preceded the so-called 'Pauline direction,' and in which, indeed, Saul of Tarsus was himself a principal agent. But we also know that this enmity actually preceded the Death of Christ, and was the cause of it. And as regards the teaching of St. Paul, we are prepared to maintain that, throughout, it had its root and spring in the teaching of the Master concerning traditionalism and Pharisaism. But this in their contention is certainly true, that at first there was much more close religious intercourse between Jews and Christians. Nay, to quote the words of a recent Jewish writer: 'It cannot be denied that the movement which originated within Judaism, and attached itself to the Name of Jesus, drew for a short time also many of the Teachers of the Law into the vortex' (Friedlander).

As a further fact against the Jewish assertion, that Judaism stood in close peaceful relation to the primitive Church, we must here take note of their own admission, that Gentile and Jewish Christian controversialists received far different treatment at the hands of the Synagogue. The former were treated with a kind of benevolent pity; the latter provoked the bitterest hostility, to such extent that the people were warned against all intercourse with those who were regarded as blasphemers. At the same time we mark differences in the statements of the Rabbis concerning such intercourse, and this, not only on the part of different teachers, but even of the same teachers, apparently on different occasions. In general, the principle prevailed that no intercourse of any kind should be held with those heretics; and that even the preservation of life might not be sought by their healing. Sacred as the occurrence of the Divine Name was to the Jew, the Rabbis would have deemed it duty to burn the Gospels and similar heretical books, even though containing the hallowed mention; nay, they would rather have fled into a heathen temple for protection from a murderer or a serpent, than taken refuge among Christians.

In other circumstances, however, opinions would appear changed. At the end of the third and beginning of the fourth century, when Christianity had already become a power, we find that the celebrated Rabbi Abbahu not only called in Christian medical aid, though his colleagues happily averted his purpose, which the Talmud declares would have led to his being killed; but that, when asked whether the writings of the heretics might on the Sabbath be saved from the fire, he replied sometimes affirmatively, at others negatively. But then this Rabbi Abbahu was a sort of ideal personage: handsome, liberal, who favoured Grecian culture, lived at Cæsarea, and was in favour with the Roman authorities. While the Jewish Patriarchate had sunk very low under Gamaliel IV, Abbahu was a sage among sages, and, what was most meritorious, he knew how to inflict the most crushing defeats upon the Nazarenes. No wonder that, according to Talmudic story, the Christians would fain have done away with him—a fate which, as we have seen, was only averted by the timely intervention of his colleagues.

To be sure, they must have been very peculiar controversialists those Christians, if we are to credit the Talmudic accounts of their ratiocination. But, although neither the Christian philosopher nor yet the Jew Tryphon in Justin's 'Dialogue' seems powerful in argument, it is scarcely possible to conceive that statements so utterly puerile as the Talmudists report should have been urged in serious controversy. No wonder the Midrash applied to them the opening words of Ecclesiastes 1:8, declaring these arguments wearisome, wearing; nor yet, that when the colleagues of another noted Rabbinic controversialist, Joshua ben Chananyah, mourned, as he lay dying, that now there would not be any to resist the daring of the Christians, the dying teacher should have comforted them by saying, that if their council had perished, the wisdom of their opponents had become rotten. But the Midrash on Ecclesiastes 1:8 tells us many things which seem to indicate that the words of these heretics must have been more weighty than the arguments reported by the Rabbis. Thus, we find the great Eliezer ben Hyrqanos was so gravely suspected as to be actually arraigned before the civil magistrate on the charge of Christianity, from which accusation he only escaped by a misunderstanding on the part of the magistrate. In truth he made certain important admissions in regard to it. Thus, when his disciples in vain endeavoured to comfort him in his deep sorrow, the Great Rabbi Akiba at last suggested, that Eliezer might on some occasion have listened with pleasure to an exposition by the heretics. The Talmud relates this interpretation, which will scarcely bear repetition. But in view of what we have recorded in another place concerning Eliezer, and what we regard as his references to St. John's Gospel, we may be allowed to doubt whether it represents the whole that had passed. We can scarcely suppose an Eliezer affected by discussions, concerning many of which the Rabbinic students could question their teacher in such terms as these, that he had driven back his opponents with a straw, but what had he to say to them? And in truth the remark of these disciples as to the insufficiency of such replies seems well founded, and, at least on the occasion here referred to, the Christian argument must have turned on the most important points.

Eliezer was the brother-in-law of Gamaliel II, and flourished in the first century. He may have been acquainted with Saul of Tarsus. His citation before the magistrate for suspected Christianity took place during the Trajan persecution. This brings us to the period of Pliny, whom we shall presently adduce as a witness in our favour. It thus connects, in a most interesting manner, the story of the Jewish Rabbi with the evidence of the heathen governor. Meanwhile, I can only express my personal belief that the excommunication which the Rabbis laid upon Eliezer, and their opposition to his teaching, must have been due to far weightier causes than such differences of teaching as are recorded, and which were never otherwise visited with such punishment. But Rabbi Eliezer was not the only great teacher affected by the Christian movement, nor yet Rabbis Abbahu and Joshua ben Chananyah the only Jewish controversialists. Rabbi Saphra, whom Abbahu had praised to the Jewish Christians in most extravagant terms, was apparently worsted by them in an argument based on Amos 3:2, which, I presume, they must have quoted by way of urging that some great national sin must rest on Israel to account for the sufferings that had come upon them.

But we can ascend to an earlier age for evidence of Christian influence on Jewish teachers. As a Jewish writer (Friedlander) argues, Akiba would not have suggested to Eliezer the possibility of such a cause of his misfortunes, if intercourse and discussions with Jewish Christians had been of only exceptional occurrence. Rabbi Ishmael belonged to the illustrious circle of sages who flourished after the destruction of Jerusalem. In his hatred of Jewish Christians and desire to see their sacred writings burned, he yielded nothing to his colleague, Tarphon. Nevertheless, his almost equally learned nephew, Ben Dama, solicited his permission to study 'Grecian wisdom' [יוונית חכמת]—may it not have been Christian writings?—and was in such relationship towards Jewish Christians, that, when bitten by a serpent, he would fain have availed himself of the miraculous healing by one of them, appealing to Scripture for its lawfulness, but was prevented by his uncle, and so perished. A similar story is told of Rabbi Joshua, one of the most celebrated teachers, and who, in his youth, was said to have been among the Levite singers in the Temple. His nephew, Chanina, came under the influence of the Christians of Capernaum; and, to withdraw him from it, his uncle had to send him to Babylonia, where he afterwards exercised the greatest influence. The same Rabbi Joshua is said to have also rescued a disciple of Rabbi Jonathan from the toils of the heretics. The details of the story will scarcely bear repetition.

If true, the Christians, by whom the young Rabbi had been entangled, must have been Nicolaitans. But there is more than this to be told. The ordinance of the patriarch Gamaliel (II), which directed that thenceforth admission to the Academy should only be allowed to such whose 'interior' was like their 'exterior,' has been understood to refer—at least in part—to the fact that many who frequented the Rabbinic schools were under the influence of the new faith, and would have spread the new opinions. This affords striking evidence of the effect which Christianity exercised at its rise upon very many of the best Jewish minds, and gives confirmation to the account of the spread of the faith in the opening chapters of the Book of Acts. Nay, there is evidence that 'heretical,' that is, Christian, prayers were sometimes actually introduced into the worship of the Synagogue by those who led the devotions, against which the sharpest precautions were to be taken. Surely, then, Christianity must have had many and most influential adherents among the Jews at its rise.

But even so the evidence is not complete. We find that the same Gamaliel put to the assembled sages the question, which of them could compose a prayer against the new faith which should be inserted in the most solemn part of the worship—the so-called eighteen benedictions. It has been well argued that while the necessity for, and the introduction of such a prayer in the liturgy are in themselves most significant, the appeal of the patriarch to the sages must have implied the challenge—not which of them could, but which of them would, compose such a prayer. And, indeed, the correct repetition of this formula was henceforth made a test of orthodoxy.

But perhaps the best practical proof of the existence of such intercourse and influence is this, that apparently there were meeting-places for regular religious discussions, and that a special literature seems to have been the outcome of them. The former are mentioned under a twofold name: probably designating assemblies of different character. It is not easy to understand the precise meaning and distinction of these two designations. We read of the *Be Abhidan* ('House of Abhidan'), and of 'the writings of the *Be* Abhidan'; and we also read of the *Be Notsrephi* or *Nitsrephi* ('House of Notsrephi'). Both names seem corruptions of other words, or, rather, as the custom was, word-puns by which a name was converted into an opprobrious epithet. They are universally regarded as having been places for religious discussions between Jews and Christians of different parties. The *Be Abhidan* is supposed to represent a corruption of Ebionites (אבידן = אביוני,) although the Ebionites were also known by their proper name; or it may possibly refer to a Gnostic sect, such as the Ophites. On the other hand, it is easy to recognise in the *Be Notsrephi* a perversion of the term *Be Notsri*, Christian, and to see in it a designation of the Church. The subject is not, however, wholly free from difficulty. The Talmud describes one sage (Samuel) as going to the *Be Abhidan*, but not to the *Be Notsrephi*, while another (Rabh) would not attend the former, much less the latter. Other Rabbis plead age and fear of suffering bodily injury as excuse for their absence from such meetings. And we can readily believe that gatherings for discussion may, among hot-blooded Easterns, have often ended in scenes of violence. Indeed, one Rabbi tells us that he had agreed with his theological opponents that the victor in controversy should be allowed to take bloody vengeance on his adversary, which the successful Rabbi had also done, although this seems to have required considerable effort—whether of the theological or physical kind, does not clearly appear.

To sum up at least some of the results of this long digression. While admitting that Talmudic writings are utterly untrustworthy as regards historical accuracy, this much at least seems established from them, that miraculous power of healing was attributed to Jesus and to the early Christians; that their sacred writings—presumably in Aramæan—existed, were known, and circulated; that there was extensive religious communication between the disciples of Christ and the most eminent Teachers of the Law, and frequent, if not regular, discussions with them; and that many of the leaders of the Jewish world, and naturally many more of the people, were affected by the new movement. In fact, it was supposed that Divine punishment had visited a great Rabbi who confessed to having derived pleasure from their interpretations; while others had to flee or to die, in order to escape the dangerous heresy. Even to hold intercourse with these heretics, who were for ever excluded from eternal life, was regarded as already the first step towards becoming a Christian convert, and was to be carefully avoided.

Thus far all accords with the impressions derived from the Christian records. But we have other and more direct evidence to produce.

B. From the Talmud we pass to the Jewish historian Josephus, whom we may describe as in early life the contemporary of St. Paul. Indeed, there is ground for believing that, as a young man, Josephus was in Rome during St. Paul's first imprisonment there. His systematic ignoring of Christianity will scarcely seem strange when we remember the character of the man, the ulterior object of his writings, and the relations between Christianity and Judaism, on the one hand, and heathenism, on the other. But there are three passages in the works of Josephus, occurring in all existing manuscripts, which bear testimony respectively to John the Baptist, to James the brother of Jesus, and to Christ Himself.

Without entering on detailed criticism, suffice it to say that, while the passage about Christ must have had some genuine substratum, it appears to be so altered and interpolated in its present form as for all practical purposes to be spurious. More credit attaches to the passage about James, the Lord's brother. But even this is in its present form so doubtful that we prefer leaving it unnoticed, as, in any case, not affecting the present argument. On the other hand, sober-minded critics of all schools are now generally agreed that the passage in Josephus concerning John the Baptist is genuine and trustworthy. For evidential purposes it may be described as bearing testimony on these four points: 1st, the exalted character of John and his preaching of repentance; 2ndly, his baptism and its relation to the forgiveness of sins; 3rdly, the crowds which from all parts flocked to him and were deeply moved by his preaching; and, lastly, that John was executed by Herod, because he feared that the preaching of the Baptist might issue in a new movement or rebellion against himself, since the people 'seemed ready to do anything by his counsel.'

This fourfold testimony covers, with one exception, all the main facts recorded in the Gospels about the Baptist, although with such variations as we might expect from the standpoint of the Jewish historian. Thus far, then, it affords important confirmation of the Gospel history. And even the notable omission to which we have referred, that of any allusion to the announcement by the Baptist of the coming Messianic Kingdom, is rather apparent than real. For this rebellion which Herod is said to have dreaded, in consequence of the people's readiness to do anything by John's counsel, must have referred to his proclamation of the near Advent of the Messianic Kingdom and King. Josephus does not give a hint of any political element in the preaching of John; on the contrary, he sums it up as enjoining 'righteousness towards one another, and piety towards God,' 'and so to come to baptism.' If therefore a new political movement was apprehended from such preaching, the inference seems almost irresistible that John had announced the near Kingdom. And here we remember that the claims of Jesus to the Messiahship gave rise to the charge of setting up another King, and that the bare suggestion of the birth of such a Messiah so excited the fears of Herod's father as to lead to the murder of the Innocents at Bethlehem. And, even at the last, when such a claim might seem almost impossible, Pilate discussed it with Jesus; and such deep hold had it taken, that at a later period Domitian summoned the relatives of Jesus to his presence, to see whether their appearance betokened danger to his sovereignty. Hence we can readily believe that this would, under Pharisaic instigation of his fears, be the deeper motive in Herod's conduct towards the Baptist, and that the reproof about Herodias would only represent the climax of offence, and the final occasion of the Baptist's imprisonment. Thus viewed, the silence of Josephus on what would have obliged him to refer to Christianity is itself of evidential value.

But there is even more to be learned from the testimony of Josephus. It not only attests, and that by a witness hostile to Christianity, the exalted character of the Baptist, and implies his announcement of the near Messianic Kingdom, but it affords at least indirect evidence that Jesus brought something new, instituted a new kingdom, such as we know it from the Gospels. We infer this not only from what Josephus records as the subject-matter of John's preaching, but from the rite of baptism which, according to his testimony, John had instituted. We need not here discuss the historically untenable suggestion that the Baptist or his baptism were connected with Essenism. Suffice it to say, that the baptism of the Essenes was not for the people generally, but for the initiated; not once for repentance, but daily for superior sanctity. Indeed, Essenism had nothing to say to men, except to come out and join the Sect; and it fundamentally differed, on almost all important points, from the teaching of John. But if the preaching and baptism of John were not Essene, neither were they Judaic. Rabbinism knows no preaching of repentance such as that to which John called his hearers, or, as Josephus describes it, wherein what the Rabbis would have denounced as sinners—the unlearned, soldiers, and publicans—would have been allowed to continue in their condition, only with changed minds and conduct. Nor was any such baptism either practised or known in Judaism. There were the legal washings connected with Levitical defilements, and the baptism of heathens on becoming Proselytes of Righteousness. But a baptism of Jews as connected with repentance was wholly unprecedented. It inaugurated something different from all the past, something new. Whether viewed in connection with the typical purification preparatory to Israel's reception of the Law at Mount Sinai, or as symbolic of the better washing—in the language of Josephus, 'after that the soul had previously been cleansed by righteousness'—it marked the commencement of a new development, the preparation for a new kingdom, in which righteousness would reign. And in this respect also the silence of Josephus is most significant. Thus, when read in connection with the Gospel narrative, the language of Josephus not only implies the Baptist's proclamation of the coming Messiah, but also that He would found a new kingdom for which baptism was the appropriate preparation.

C. One step still remains. We have had testimony from hostile, and certainly not impartial Jews; we shall now have it from a hostile but impartial heathen. We have been carried to the threshold of the history of Jesus, and have had a look forward into it; we shall now be transported to the period after His death, and from that standpoint have a look backwards on the Gospel narrative. The testimony of Josephus covers the period from the time of St. Paul to that of Trajan—more exactly from A.D. 37 or 38 to after the year 100 of our era. But before that period expires the testimony of another unimpeached and unimpeachable witness begins. I allude here to the well-known Epistle which Pliny the Younger addressed to the Emperor Trajan. The facts are briefly as follows. Under the reign of Trajan (98-117), the younger Pliny, who had already filled the highest offices, became Governor of Bithynia. The precise date of his governorship, and consequently of his Epistle to the Emperor about the Christians, is not quite certain, though the possible difference is only that of a few years— say, between 106 and 111 A.D. But this does not adequately represent the state of the case. For, as some of those by whose examination Pliny ascertained the tenets and practices of the Christians had left the Christian community so long as twenty years previously, the testimony of the younger Pliny concerning Christianity really reaches up to between 86 and 90 of our era—that is, to more than ten years before the death of Josephus. The two witnesses are, therefore, so to speak, historically connected.

The chief points in the information supplied by the Epistle of Pliny may be summarised as follows: The Governor applies to the Emperor for guidance, being in doubt what conduct to pursue towards the Christians. He had not previously been present at any judicial examination of Christians (which at least shows that they were well known), and did not well know with what strictness to bear himself in the matter. Hitherto his practice had been to question the accused, and if they professed themselves Christians, to repeat the question a second and third time, threatening the punishment of death. Those who remained constant were forthwith punished; this, not so much on account of their opinions, of which he seemed still in doubt, as for their obstinacy. But Christianity only spread, and Pliny was beset with anonymous as well as regular information against many, of all ages, of every rank, and of both sexes. Of the persons thus brought before Pliny's tribunal, many denied being Christians, when he applied the crucial test of making them offer heathen worship, and revile the Name of Christ; neither of which, as he had learned, Christians would do under any compulsion. Others admitted having been Christians, but professed to have left the community three or more, and some even more than twenty years before. Although these persons had no hesitation in performing heathen rites, and reviling Christ, they maintained that even while Christians their practices had been wholly harmless, such as Pliny proceeds to describe. And, to be quite sure of it, Pliny next subjected two of the actual Deaconesses to torture, but elicited nothing beyond 'a depraved and excessive superstition' (*superstitionem pravam et immodicam*). In these circumstances, and finding that the number of those who would have to suffer was far greater than he had imagined, and that the new faith had not only taken hold on the towns and villages, but even spread to the country districts, Pliny applies to the Emperor for direction.

Putting aside our natural feeling of indignation at the conduct of Pliny towards those of both sexes, and of all ages and ranks, who were faithful to their convictions unto torture and death, let us see what light this unquestioned historical document—which takes us, say, to about half a century after the death of Christ—casts on the New Testament record.

1. It tells us of a vast number of believers, in all ranks and of all ages, in the province over which Pliny ruled. According to his account, 'the temples had been almost forsaken'; their sacred solemnities intermitted, and it was the most rare thing to find purchasers for the victims (*rarissimus emptor inveniebatur*).

2. As regards the tenets, or rather the observances, of the Christians, we cannot, indeed, expect to derive precise dogmatic statements from criminal informations laid before a heathen judge. The confession of the two Deaconesses under torture may have contained an account of their faith. Pliny describes it as a 'debased and excessive superstition.' But the account given by apostates bore reference to the *practices* of Christians. It deserves special notice that even these persons had nothing evil to say of their former co-religionists. But what they report of their practices is most instructive.

a. The Christians are described as meeting for worship on a stated day. It is impossible to avoid the inference that this was the first day of the week; and as its corollary, that this day was observed as the memorial of Christ's Resurrection. Thus, the Sunday worship and the underlying belief in the Resurrection, are attested within about half a century of the death of Jesus.

b. They are said on these occasions to have offered Divine Worship to Christ, and this, whether we understand the language of Pliny as denoting specifically the singing of hymns or the offering of prayer, to Christ as to a God (*quasi Deo*). Let it be remembered that Pliny here reports the testimony of former Christians, and hence cannot be understood as meaning that the Christians worshipped Jesus as a God in the same sense in which Pliny would offer worship to the Emperor. Moreover, it must be kept in view that, according to Pliny, it was distinctive of these same Christians rather to suffer martyrdom than to offer even the supposed inferior homage to the Roman Emperor, although they fully owned his supreme civil authority. Hence the Christian worship of Jesus must have been consciously and literally offered to Christ as a Divine Person. We have, therefore, testimony that the central point in their worship—that which these former Christians singled out as the distinctive characteristic, was worship of Jesus, with the underlying tenet that He was the Son of God, 'Very God of Very God.'

c. They are said on these occasions to have bound themselves 'by an oath' (*sacramento*), against the commission of all crime or sin, and to all truthfulness and uprightness. We would suggest that this 'oath,' at their solemn meetings, must bear some reference to moral obligations undertaken at the Holy Communion. In any case, we have here testimony of the distinctive holiness of the early Christians, as organically connected with their worship and belief; in short, to the moral theology of the New Testament as the outcome of its dogmatic teaching.

d. Lastly, we have in the account of these former Christians a notice of certain common meals—not in the worship of the Christians, but after it— referring probably to the love-feasts or agapes of 1 Corinthians. We are the more confirmed in this view, since these common meals seem to have been regarded as not of vital importance, for they are said to have been intermitted after the publication of Pliny's edict.

The importance of the historic testimony just analysed can scarcely be overrated. It not only gives historic reality to the picture of the early Church, such as from the New Testament we would trace its outlines; but it fully confirms the power and spread of the new faith, as the Book of Acts and the Apostolic Epistles set them before us. Moreover, it presents, in regard to the Resurrection as the great central truth of Christian faith, the Person of Christ as the grand central Object of Christian worship, and the Holy Eucharist as the main part of Christian ritual, the exact counterpart of the New Testament account. The Christianity of the year 86 or 90 of our era is, so to speak, the coin which bears the device of the mint of the New

Testament. If we were to translate into fact the history which closes with the four Gospels—say in the year 30 of our era—we would have precisely Pliny's account of the Christians in the year 86 or 90. We have here the Sunday worship, with its look back on the Resurrection, and therefore upon the Crucifixion, the Incarnation, and Messianic activity of Jesus; the Divine Worship of Christ, with its upward look to the Saviour at the Right Hand of the Father, having all power; the earnest, conscious striving against all sin and after all holiness, amidst the corrupt, festering mass of heathenism around—a new creation in Christ Jesus by the Holy Ghost, whose living temples Christians are, and this as an integral part of their worship, the outcome of their faith; then, the simple common meetings for prayer and the Holy Sacrament, and, when possible, love-feasts of brotherly fellowship; finally, the enduring perseverance of the Church, even to the loss of all things and to death itself.

Narrow as the line of evidence may seem which we have followed, it has, we trust, fully established the main proposition of this Lecture. What we have learned about the Gospels has not in any part been invalidated, but in many respects confirmed, by such trustworthy notices as we have gathered from Talmudic writings. Then, the testimony of Josephus concerning John and his Baptism has flashed light forward on the beginning of Christ's Ministry, on its object and character; whilst the testimony of Pliny has flashed light backwards to the end of Christ's Ministry, to His Resurrection, and to the faith and practice of the early Church. John the Baptist and Jesus Christ are true historical personages, and the influence of their activity is precisely such as the New Testament describes it. And what we have learned about the power of Christianity and its spread, about the life of Christians, and their readiness to be faithful unto death, sets before us in vivid colouring an historical picture of that primitive Church which saw in Jesus of Nazareth the fulfilment of the Old Testament promises, and the reality of that kingdom which had been the hope of the Fathers.

LECTURE 4: ON SOME FUNDAMENTAL PRINCIPLES REGARDING THE STUDY OF PROPHECY AND ITS FULFILMENT, TOGETHER WITH REMARKS ON CERTAIN SPECIAL PROPHECIES.

He shall grow as a root out of a dry ground. Isaiah 53:2.
I pray thee, of whom speaketh the Prophet this? Acts 8:34.

In the preceding Lecture I have endeavoured to meet an objection which, if established, would have been fatal to our whole reasoning. Having thus, so to speak, cleared the ground before us, we can proceed with our main argument. Nor could we rest it on better foundation than the two Scripture passages just quoted, of which the one points to the grand central Figure in Old Testament prophecy; while the other refers to the question of its counterpart in the Person of Jesus Christ.

It is not difficult to transport ourselves into the scene of the interview between the Ethiopian eunuch and the Evangelist Philip. We have only to follow the most southern of the three—anciently, perhaps, only two—roads, which led from Jerusalem to Gaza. Beyond Eleutheropolis it passed through the 'desert,' that is, through a tract, now—and, as there is reason to believe, in New Testament times—uninhabited. Close by the road, in Wady el-Hasy, is a sheet of water, possibly the place of the eunuch's baptism. It can scarcely surprise us that this stranger, who had just been to Jerusalem to worship, should on this lonely road have busied himself with the Old Testament, nor yet that, in his peculiar circumstances and near the boundary of the Land of Promise, he should in preference have turned to its prophecies, especially to that section in the roll of Isaiah where those boundaries were enlarged till they became wide as the world itself. Nor does it seem strange that, as in thought he climbed the sacred height and stood before the great central Figure of that mysterious Sufferer, he could not recognise His features. To this day has Israel failed to see in that Face marred more than any man's its Messiah-King, the Crown of its glory—only seen in it the impress of its own troubled history. And how could this stranger know it, who had but lately stood wondering in that gorgeous Temple, thronged by thousands of worshippers, and looked, as the crowd of white-robed priests ministered at the great altar of burnt-offering, and beyond it, from out the inner Sanctuary, floated the cloud of incense and shone the light of the ever-burning golden candlestick, while the voice of Levite-psalms filled the house with solemn melody. To lift one's eyes from that scene to the sin-burdened Sufferer, as to the ideal of it all—Who, in His stripes, bore the sin of the world, and so was the crowned Servant of Jehovah—implied a contrast which only Divinely-guided history could resolve, and only God-taught faith comprehend.

We do not wonder then at his question: Of whom does the prophet speak? It is the same which in its ultimate idea, as the mystery of suffering, has engaged all thinking. Very really, it is the same which these eighteen centuries and more has divided us; which the Jew has sought to answer as he stood before the prophetic picture of Isaiah, and the Christian as he gazed on the crucified Christ. How perplexing it has proved to the Synagogue appears not only from the widely-divergent—rather absolutely contradictory—interpretations which the most learned of the Rabbis have given to this prophecy, but even from their own admissions after they had attempted to solve its mystery. The philosophic Ibn Ezra speaks of this Parashah as one 'extremely difficult.' Isaac b. Elijah Cohen says: 'I have never in my life seen or heard of the exposition of a clear or fluent commentator, in which my own judgment and that of others who have pondered on the same subject might completely acquiesce.'

And, to make only one other quotation from Dr. Pusey's Preface to the Catena of Jewish Interpretations on the 53rd of Isaiah, Ibn Amram says: 'There is no little difficulty in giving a sense to those most obscure words of Isaiah in the present; they manifestly need a prophetic spirit.' That, from the Jewish standpoint, such should be the case, every unprejudiced student will readily understand. And we may further remark, that the latest attempt of a certain school of critics to add to the Christian and the Jewish a third interpretation, in some sense more Jewish than that of the Jews, has only resulted in another, and yet more manifest, exegetical impossibility. But amidst these perplexities there seems at least one clear guiding light. The prophecy speaks not only of suffering, but of conquering, and of conquering by suffering. Now suffering is human; conquering is divine: but to conquer by suffering is theanthropic.

But amidst all our diversity there is, we are thankful to know, substantial agreement on one and, as it might seem, the most important point. There is no fundamental divergence between Jew and Christian as regards the translation of this chapter. In this it differs from certain other passages designated as Messianic, such as Genesis 49:10, Psalm 2:12, or the proper meaning of the word *almah* in Isaiah 7:14—which are respectively rendered in the Authorised Version by, '*Until Shiloh* come'; '*Kiss the Son* lest he be angry'; and 'Behold, *a Virgin* shall conceive and bear a Son.' We would go a step further. Even as regards the so-called Messianic prophecies generally, there is, with few exceptions, a similar general agreement as to the translation of the words; or at least generally little that is fundamental is involved in the divergences. In other words, if it were only a question of the meaning of the original, we might hope soon to be at one. More especially is this the case as regards the climax of all Messianic predictions, the 53rd chapter of Isaiah. In the words of Dr. Pusey: 'Next to nothing turns upon renderings of the Hebrew. The objections raised by Jewish controversialists…in only four, or at most five words, turn on the language.' And the matter seems, at first sight, the more perplexing that there is substantial agreement, not only as regards the wording, but also the main contents of this prophecy. All admit that the subject of this prophecy is portrayed as lowly in His beginnings; suffering sorrow, contempt, and death; that He would be accounted a transgressor, yet that His sufferings were vicarious, those of the just for the unjust, and this by God's appointment; that in meek silence and willing submissiveness He would accept His doom; that His soul was an offering for sin which God accepted; that He made many righteous; that He intercedes for trangressors; that He is highly exalted in proportion to His humiliation; and that kings would submit to Him, and His reign abide. To quote once more the language of Dr. Pusey: 'The question is not, "What is the picture?" in this all are agreed; but, "Whose image or likeness does it bear?"' To put it otherwise: the question is not as to the meaning of the passages, but as to their application. 'Of whom speaketh the prophet this?'—of himself?—of his contemporaries, or some part of them?—or of some other One, who sums up in Himself the leading features of all, and yet passes beyond them, just as all fruit in the reality of its fulfilment passes beyond its visible germ-promise, unfolding all its indicated possibilities.

How then are we to account for the differences existing between us? The truth is, we start, indeed, from the same premisses, but into widely different directions. We all start not without preconceived opinions, as some would call them—or guiding principles, as I would designate them. The Jew starts with his preconceived opinions as to what must or must not be in accordance with his general views of the teaching of the Old Testament. The Christian starts with the historical facts concerning Christ and Christianity in his mind. To the one *this*, to the other *that*, is the guiding principle in the application of what both have agreed to be the meaning of the words and the contents of a prophecy. And it cannot well be otherwise. The honest inquirer can only seek to know which of the two directions is the right one. This question, indeed, is of widest application. It covers the entire range of prophecy, and is decisive in the controversy between the Synagogue and the Church, on which, we would here remind ourselves, depend far graver issues than merely intellectual victory. But in answering this question as to the guiding principle in the interpretation of prophecy, it is evident that we must get behind individual prophecies— consider them not merely as isolated, but as a whole, trying to ascertain whether or not the Old Testament, as a whole, is prophetic of the Messiah, and whether or not the historical Christ and Christianity present the real fulfilment of that prophecy.

It is not, I hope, too fine a distinction to make between prophecy as *referring* to Christ, and prophecy as *fulfilled* in Christ. The two mark different standpoints in our view of prophecy, the one being the *prospective* or speculative, the other the *retrospective* or historic view of it. But it seems to me that Christian divines have not only quitted their high vantage-ground of historical fact, but acted contrary, alike to sound reasoning and the example of the New Testament, in disputing whether or not certain individual prophecies referred to Christ, instead of first presenting their actual historical fulfilment in Him. Had they begun with this, they would have exhibited the fundamental principle which underlies all prophecy, and shown the true sense in which these predictions must refer to Christ.

It is altogether a narrow principle which has been applied to the study of prophecy, and which too often results in disputes about words instead of presenting the grand and indubitable facts of fulfilment. There are persons who argue very strangely in regard to this matter. It is sometimes supposed that those who uttered a prophecy, perhaps even those who heard it, must have understood its full meaning, its complete Messianic bearing, or at least have had full conception of the personal Messiah as now in the light of fulfilment we know Him. And when it is shown that this could not have been the case, it is forthwith rashly concluded that the Messianic application for which we contend is erroneous. But it is a kind of Jewish literalism which lies at the basis of this erroneous view of prophecy, a narrow and utterly unspiritual view of it, a mechanical view also, which treats fulfilment in its relation to prophecy as if it were a clock made to strike the precise quarters of the hour. But it is not so. The fulfilment is always both wider and more spiritual than the prediction. It contains it and much more, and it can only be properly understood when viewed in its relation to prophecy as a whole. For it is evident that, if we were to maintain that those who uttered or who heard these predictions had possessed the same knowledge of them as we in the light of their fulfilment, these things would follow: *First*. Prophecy would have superseded historical development, which is the rational order, and God's order. *Secondly*. In place of this order we would introduce a mechanical and external view of God's revelation, similar to that which in theology has led to the fatal notion of a mechanical inspiration, and which in natural science (viewed from the theological standpoint) scouts the idea of development, and regards all as absolutely finished from the beginning—views which have been the bane of much that otherwise would have been sound in Natural Theology and Apologetics, and which have proved destructive to the old supernaturalism, involving in its fall much that was true, and which has now to be digged out of the ruins and built up anew. *Thirdly*. It would eliminate from God's revelation the moral and spiritual element—that of teaching on His part, and of faith and advancement on ours. *Fourthly*. It would make successive prophecies needless, since all has been already from the first clearly and fully understood. *Lastly*. Such a view seems in direct contradiction to the principle expressly laid down in 1 Peter 1:10, 11, as applicable to prophecy.

On the other hand, the principle that prophecy can only be fully understood from the standpoint of fulfilment, seems not only in accordance with all that one would expect—since otherwise prophecy would have been simply foretold history, without present application and teaching—but it must be evident that, if such had been the object in view, it would have been more natural, and, as it would seem, have secured the purpose more fully, to have told it out plainly, without the use of figure or metaphor, in language that could not have been misunderstood or misinterpreted. And so it almost seems as if some persons would fain have it, and that not only in regard to prophecy, but they complain that the New Testament should have told them everything plainly, giving every particular, even to the minutest direction as to the modes of our organisation, the order of our services, and the details of our Church life. But it is not so, and it never can be so, if, as we believe, our religion is of God. What in these demands is true has been granted, though not in the way in which it was expected. The history of the Church has taught us much of that which the New Testament contains, and the enlightened Christian consciousness has learned, as through bilingual inscriptions, to read the characters and the language in which much of the past was written. History has unfolded much that the New Testament had infolded, and under the ever-present guidance of the Holy Spirit we have learned to understand it. Nor does the objection hold good, that in such case they of old must in measure have been ignorant of the truth. In *their* measure they were not ignorant of it, but their measure is not ours. We believe in development and progress, rightly understood. Divine truth and revelation are, indeed, always the same: one, full, and final; and nothing can be added thereto. But with the development of our wants and with our progress its meaning unfolds, and it receives ever new applications. We understand things more fully—if you like, differently—from our fathers, not because *they* are different, but because *we* are different, because questions have arisen to us which had not come to them, because mental and moral wants press upon us which had not presented themselves to them. And what is this but to assert the constant teaching of God? We bring not a new truth, but unfold the old; and from its adaptation, ever fresh and new to all times, to all men, to all wants, we gather fresh and living evidence of its Divine origin.

It is in this manner that prophecy in its application to Christ should be studied: first, the living Person, then His portraiture; first, the fulfilment, then the prophetic reference; first, the historical, then the exegetical argument. These remarks are not intended to deprecate the application of individual prophecies to Christ; only to correct a one-sided and mechanical literalism that exhausts itself in fruitless verbal controversies in which it is not unfrequently worsted, and to give to our views the right and, as we believe, the spiritual direction. For, even an exegetical victory would not decide that inward direction of heart and life which makes the Christian. We fully and gladly add that even in strict exegesis many special predictions can be only Messianically interpreted. But we believe still more that the Old Testament as a whole is Messianic, and full of Christ; and we wish this to be first properly apprehended, that so from this point of view the Messianic prophecies may be studied in detail. Then only shall we understand their real purport and meaning, and perceive, without word-cavilling, that they must refer to the Messiah.

And in this, as in all other things, we take our best guidance from the New Testament. When we ask ourselves whence those quiet God-fearing persons—a Simeon, Anna, Zacharias, Elisabeth, a Joseph, and, with reverence be it added, the Virgin-Mother—took their direction before the manifestation of Christ; and, during its course, His disciples and followers, we unhesitatingly answer, from the Old Testament. But from the Old Testament as a whole; not, in the first place, from individual predictions, since in the nature of things these could only be fulfilled in the gradual development of His history. Nay, even when a prediction was actually fulfilled, as that of Zechariah in Christ's entry into Jerusalem, the reference to it is followed by this significant explanation of St. John (12:16): 'These things understood not His disciples at the first: but when Jesus was glorified, then remembered they that these things were written of Him, and that they had done these things unto Him.' And this also explains how that which to our minds constitutes the central point in all Messianic predictions—the sufferings of the Christ—so far from being prominent in the minds of His disciples, was ever that which they could not understand. It was only after His Resurrection, on that blessed evening-walk to Emmaus, that He could say to those two simple-hearted disciples, who were so sad at the things which had come to pass: 'Oh fools and slow of heart to believe all that the prophets have spoken! Ought not Christ to have suffered these things and to enter into His glory? And beginning at Moses and all the Prophets, He expounded unto them in all the Scriptures the things concerning Himself.' And it was again after that that He more fully taught His Apostles: 'These are the words which I have spoken unto you, while I was yet with you, that all things must be fulfilled which were written in the Law of Moses and in the Prophets, and in the Psalms concerning Me. Then opened He their understanding, that they might understand the Scriptures.' They could not recognise any one single feature, however salient, till the whole Figure stood before them bathed in the heavenly light. Then could each one of them be recognised as it had been portrayed by the prophets. They learned fulfilled prophecies in the light of fulfilled prophecy. And so shall we also best learn it.

Two things here strike the observant reader of the New Testament: first, the sparseness of prophetic quotations in the Gospels; and, secondly, their peculiarity. So far as I remember, only the one prophecy concerning His birth at Bethlehem was ever adduced to guide men to the Christ. And this prediction, itself a *locus classicus* universally accepted, was logically necessary. But even so, it had nothing special to direct to Jesus as the Christ. In all His teaching, except when in the Synagogue of Nazareth, He pointed to His message of the kingdom as fulfilling the prophecy of Isaiah, He did not base His Messianic claims on any special prophecies. He ever based them on what He was, on what He said, on what He did; on the message of love from the Father which stood incarnate before them in His Person, on the opening of the kingdom of heaven to all believers, on the forgiveness, the peace, and the healing to body and soul, which He brought. That was the fulfilment of Old Testament prophecy; this the kingdom for which all had been preparing, and which all had announced. And because He was the fulfilment of all, therefore was He the Messiah promised: the desire of all nations, towards which their conscious and unconscious longings had tended, and the glory of His people Israel, the crowning glory of all their spiritual teaching. Because He was the fulfilment of the Old Testament ideal, the deeper reality of its history and institutions, therefore did all the prophecies refer to Him. And when that stood fully out, then could His Apostles (as in their preaching in the Book of Acts) point to the prophecies as referring to Him. This is the unfolding in the New, of what was infolded in the Old Testament.

Secondly, the observant reader of the New Testament will be struck by the peculiarity of the Old Testament quotations in the Gospels. As regards their form they are mostly neither exactly from the original Hebrew nor from the Septuagint. This in accordance with universal custom. For popular use the Scriptures were no longer quoted in the Hebrew, which was not spoken, nor from the LXX, which was under Rabbinic ban, but *targumed*, rendered into the vernacular; the principle being very strongly expressed that, in so doing, it was not the letter, but the meaning of the passage which was to be given. But as regards the substance of these quotations, we feel as if mostly those passages had been adduced which we would least have expected to be quoted. The reason of this lies in the well-known fundamental principle of the Synagogue, that 'all the prophets only prophesied of the Messiah'—nay, that all events in the history of Israel and all their institutions were prophetic, and pointed forward to a fuller realisation in the Messiah. To whatever extravagance of detail this may have been carried, I have no hesitation in saying that the underlying principle is not only tenable, but both sound and true.

This may be the proper place for some remarks on Prophecy in general, in the Biblical sense of the term, and on the Prophets in the Old Testament application of the designation.

1. Prophecy, in general—perhaps I should have said Prophetism—may, in the Biblical sense of the term, be defined as the reflection upon earth of the Divine ideal in its relation to the course of human affairs. According as the one or the other of these is the primary element, it refers to the future, or else to the present or the past. In the one case it is mainly predictive, in the other mainly parenetic. This from our human standpoint, where we view things as future, present, or past—not from that of Divine reality where all is present.

In this general statement regarding prophecy, nothing has been said as to the medium through which this reflection of the Divine Light is to be made upon earth—whether institutions, events, or persons—and in the latter case, both through those who are in harmony, and those who are out of harmony with the Divine: true or false prophets. In point of fact, prophecy, or the reflection of the Divine upon earth, may be, and really was, through each and all of these *media*. And the more fully we consider it, the more appropriate and even necessary will it appear to us that such should have been the case. For so will history—which is not a fortuitous succession of events, but their orderly evolution from certain well-defined causes towards a Divinely willed end—most properly attain its destined goal.

It may seem a bold statement, and yet, to me at least, it seems logically clear, that our view of prophecy implies only one premise which is indeed a postulate. It is that of the Living and the True God. But this is precisely what the Old Testament teaches us concerning Jehovah. By the Living and the True God, I mean, not an abstraction, but a Person, a Moral Being; the Creator and Owner of all; the Centre of all, with Whom all is in living connection; or, in the words of St. Paul's quotation, He 'in Whom we live and move and have our being.' I am aware that if the view of prophecy here indicated can be historically established, it would, on the other hand, lead by induction to historic evidence of such a God. But I leave this for the present aside, and put my argument, or rather my mode of viewing it, on this wise. The presence of a Living and True God in living connection with His creatures, seems to imply, as a necessary corollary, a Divine ideal in reference to the course of human events. From this again it would seem to follow, that there is at least strong presumption in favour of a Revelation, which is the communication to men of the Divine ideal. And

Revelation and miracles are only different aspects of such Divine communication. But there can at least be no question that, if there be a Divine ideal with reference to the course of human events, that ideal must in the end, and as the goal of history, become the *real*; and, according to Holy Scripture, which in this respect also answers to our former definition of Revelation, this is and will be the Kingdom of God, when the Divine ideal in reference to man shall have become the real. And so it is that all Scripture is prophetic; that all prophecy has its ultimate fulfilment in the Kingdom of God; and that all prophecy points to it, or is Messianic in its character.

Wide-reaching as these statements are in their sequences, they must appear reasonable, at least to every Theist, and they are in accordance with what Holy Scripture sets forth as its object and contents.

2. From these more abstract considerations we turn, somewhat abruptly, to the concrete manner in which Prophetism is presented in the Old Testament. From one point of view, three classes are there designated as Prophets:—Those who were avowedly the prophets of other gods, as of Baal or Ashtaroth; those who, while professedly the prophets of Jehovah (or Jahveh), were not really such—some conscious, some apparently not conscious of imposture; and, lastly, those who were really 'sent' by Jehovah. As all these, however widely differing in character, bear the same name of 'prophets,' it follows—not, as some would have it, that the Old Testament considers them all as equally prophets (which would be the heathen view of it), but that the title 'prophet' must be regarded as simply a generic designation, which implied no judgment either as to the character or the claims of those who bore it. More light comes to us from the root-meaning of the terms by which these 'prophets' are designated in the Hebrew. To a certain extent they show us what ideas originally attached to the functions of a prophet, although we should always keep in view how easily and quickly a word moves away from its original meaning to its common application. Leaving aside such descriptive appellations as 'man of God,' 'messenger of God,' or the like, which afford no help towards the definition of the term 'prophet,' there are three words by which that office is chiefly described in the Hebrew, *Nabhi*, *Roeh*, and *Chozeh*. The etymology and meaning of the word *Nabhi* have been in dispute. According to some, it means primarily a *spokesman*; according to the majority of critics, it is derived from the verb *nabha*, which means to 'well forth' or 'bubble up.' Although the latter seems the more correct, yet there

is practically little difference between the two interpretations. The idea which we necessarily attach to this 'bubbling up,' or 'welling forth,' is, that the prophet was so filled with Divine inspiration that it 'bubbles up' out of his speech, that he 'wells it forth'; in which sense the New Testament also speaks of believers, in virtue of their reception of the Holy Spirit, as those out of whom 'flow rivers of living water' (John 7:38). It will be perceived that this description of the prophet as 'welling forth' the Divine—truly or falsely—is so general as to be universally applicable; and, indeed, the term seems kindred to those used by other nations of antiquity.

Thus viewed, the Prophet is the medium of supposed or real Divine communication—from whatever Deity it be—and the 'weller-forth' is also 'the spokesman.' It is in this sense that, when Moses was sent to bear the Divine communication to Pharaoh, Aaron was promised to him as his *Nabhi*—his weller-forth, spokesman, or medium of communication (Exo 7:1; comp. 4:16). This may also help us to understand the meaning of an institution and of a designation in the Old Testament which is of the deepest interest: that of 'schools of the prophets' and 'the sons of the prophets.' I would suggest that 'the sons of the prophets' stood related to the prophets as the prophets themselves to the Divine. They were the medium of prophetic communication, as the prophets were the medium of Divine communication. And the analogy holds true in every particular. As the prophet must absolutely submit himself to God, and be always ready to act only as the medium of Divine communication, so must the 'son of the prophet' be ready to carry out the behests of the prophet, and be the medium of his communication, whether by word or deed. As a prophet might be divinely employed temporarily, occasionally, or permanently, so the sons of the prophets by the prophets. God might in a moment raise up and qualify suitable men to be His prophets or means of communication, since only inspiration was required for this. But the prophets could not exercise such influence in regard to their 'sons.' Accordingly, special institutions, 'the schools of the prophets,' were required for their training and preparation. Besides this primary object, these establishments would serve important spiritual and religious purposes in the land, alike as regarded their testimony to Prophetism, their cultivation of the Divine, their moral discipline, readiness of absolute God-consecration and implicit submission to Him, and general religious influence on the people.

But the analogy between prophets and sons of the prophets went even farther than we have indicated. For the moral qualifications for the two offices, however fundamentally differing, were in one respect the same. For both offices the one condition needful was absolute obedience; that is, viewed subjectively, passiveness; viewed objectively, faithfulness. Alike the prophet and the son of the prophet must, in the discharge of his commission, have absolutely no will or mind of his own, that so he may be faithful to Him Whose medium of communication he is. Hence—perhaps sometimes purposely, to preach this to an unbelieving generation—the strange symbolisms occasionally connected with the prophetic office, and, on the other hand, the severe and, as it might otherwise seem, excessive punishments with which the smallest deviation from the exact terms of the commission was visited. For, not only each special prophetic mission, but the very meaning and basis of the prophetic office, depended on the exact transmission of the communication.

But we remember that the designation *Nabhi* is not the only one by which the prophetic functions are described in the Old Testament. Of the two other terms employed, *Roeh* describes the prophet as a *seer*, while *Chozeh* presents him rather as one who *gazes*. Although etymological distinctions are apt to run into each other, and in the present instance have actually done so, I would venture to suggest that, originally, the *Roeh* or *seer* may have been the prophet as seeing that which then existed, although unseen by ordinary men; while the *Chozeh* or *gazer* would represent the prophet as, in rapt vision, gazing on the yet future. In any case, the term *Nabhi* would not only be the more general and generic designation, but indicate a higher standpoint, as implying that the prophet acted as the medium of Divine communication.

Very interesting and instructive is the progression from the one to the other designation as marked in 1 Samuel 9:9. From this it appears that he who in the time of the writer was called *Nabhi* had previously been designated as *Roeh* or *seer*. A rash inference has been drawn from the circumstance that nevertheless the term *Nabhi* appears in the Pentateuch as applied, not only to Aaron in regard to Moses (Exo 7:1), but to Abraham in regard to God (Gen 20:7), and that, indeed, it repeatedly occurs in the Books of Numbers and Deuteronomy (Num 11:29;12:6; Deut 13:1,3,5; 18:15,18,20,22; 34:10). But this does not necessarily imply that the Pentateuch was written after the term *Nabhi* had taken the place of *Roeh*, for, in point of fact, it never really did take that place; and the writer of 1 Samuel does not assert that the term Nabhihad previously been unknown, but that before the time of Samuel the designation of the prophet in common use had been that of *Roeh* or *seer*. This seems to us to mark a lower religious standpoint, when the prophet was chiefly regarded as a seer of what was unseen by others. Thus, it would be in character with the period of spiritual decay from the time of Joshua to that of Samuel. But with the ministry of Samuel there was a return to the original idea of the prophet as the medium of Divine communication, when the functions of *Roeh* or *Chozeh* were either subsidiary, or only special aspects of the prophetic office.

2. Leaving aside, for the present, the question of the means indicated in the Old Testament for distinguishing the true prophet of Jehovah from the pretended, or from prophets of Baal, it will be seen that the generic term *Nabhi* might be equally applied to these three classes. They were all *Nebhiim*, or organs of communication, of what professed to be the Divine. Further, this definition of the *Nabhi* will help us to understand the real functions of the prophetic office. We no longer regard the prophet as merely the foreteller of future events, nor yet identify prophecy with prediction. This would introduce a heathen and mantic element, contrary to the whole spirit of the Old Testament, and foreign to it also in this, that it withdraws from its most important institutions the moral and spiritual, which is the primary principle of the Old Testament. Nor do we, on the other hand, so accentuate the recorded facts concerning the work of the prophets as to regard them merely as those who announced to their age the Mind and Will of Jahveh—taught, admonished, warned (the parenetic element). This would lead up to the gradual effacement of the distinctive idea of Prophetism. No, nor yet do we see in it a combination of the two elements, the predictive and the parenetic, but a welding of them into one. The prophet is the medium of Divine communication. When he preaches he does not merely refer to the present; nor yet when he foretells does he refer exclusively to the future. He occupies, with reverence be it said, in a sense, the Divine standpoint, where there is neither past, present, nor future.

And here we must come back upon explanations in a former Lecture. The Prophet, as preacher, views the present in the light of the future; as foreteller, the future in the light of the present. He points out present sin, duty, danger, or need, but all under the strong light of the Divine future. He speaks of the present in the name of God, and by His direct commission; of a present, however, which, in the Divine view, is evolving into a future, as the blossom is opening into the fruit. And when he foretells the future, he sees it in the light of the present; the present lends its colours, scenery, the very historic basis for the picture.

This, as we have seen, will help to explain alike the substance and the form of the prophetic message. To the prophetic vision the present is ever enlarging, widening, extending. These hills are growing, the valley is spreading, the light is gilding the mountain tops. And presently the hills are clothed with green, the valleys peopled with voices; the present is merging into the future, although exhibited in the form of the present. The prophet is speaking of Moab, Ammon, Tyre, Assyria; and these are gradually growing into the shapes of future foes, or future similar relations. And in the midst of such references here and there appears what applies exclusively to that Messianic Kingdom which is the goal and final meaning of all, and of all prophecy. It is an entire misunderstanding to regard such prophecies as not applying to the Messianic future, because they occur in the midst of references to contemporary events. As the rapt prophet gazes upon those hills and valleys around him, they seem to grow into gigantic mountains and wide tracts, watered by many a river and peopled with many and strange forms, while here and there the golden light lies on some special height, whence its rays slope down into valleys and glens; or else, the brightness shines out in contrasted glory against dark forest, or shadowy outline in the background. And the Prophet could not have spoken otherwise than in the forms of the present. For, had he spoken in language, and introduced scenery entirely of the future, not only would his own individuality have been entirely effaced, but he would have been wholly unintelligible to his contemporaries, or, to use the language of St. Paul, he would have been like those who spoke always in an unknown tongue.

To make ourselves more clear on these points, let us try to transport ourselves into the times and circumstances of the prophets. Assume that the problem were to announce and describe the Messianic Kingdom to the men of that generation, in a manner applicable and intelligible to them, and also progressively applicable to all succeeding generations, up to the fulfilment in the time of Christ, and beyond it, to all ages and to the furthest development of civilisation. The prophet must speak prophetically yet intelligibly to his own contemporaries. But, on the other hand, he must also speak intelligibly, yet prophetically to the men of every future generation—even to us. We can readily understand how in such case many traits and details cannot have been fully understood by the prophets themselves. But we are prepared to affirm that all these conditions are best fulfilled in the prophecies of the Old Testament, and that, if the problem be to announce the Messianic Kingdom in a manner consistent with the dogmatic standpoint then reached, the then cycle of ideas and historical actualities and possibilities, and yet suitable also to all generations, it could not have been better or equally well done in any other manner than that actually before us in the Old Testament. As a matter of fact, the present generation, and, as a matter of history, all past generations—admittedly the whole Jewish Church and the whole Christian Church—have read in these prophecies the Messianic future, and yet every successive generation has understood them, more or less clearly, and in a sense newly. If I might venture on an illustration: the reading of prophecy seems like gazing through a telescope, which is successively drawn out in such manner as to adapt the focus to the varying vision.

And yet the telescope is the same to all generations. We do not propose the clumsy device of a twofold application of prophecy, to the present and to the future, but, taking the prophetic standpoint, we regard the present as containing in germ the future, and the future as the child of the present, so that it can be presented in the forms of the present; or, to revert to a statement in a previous Lecture, it is not a progression, nor even a development, but an unfolding of the present. Viewed in relation to the Messianic Kingdom, it is one and the same thing, which to the eye of the prophet now is, and ever shall be. We might almost apply to prophetism this in the Epistle to the Hebrews: 'Jesus Christ, the same yesterday, and to-day, and for ever.' Canaan is a prophetic land, and Israel a prophetic people, of whom God says to the world: 'Touch not Mine anointed, and do My prophets no harm.' And their whole history is prophetic. It is not merely one or another special prediction that is Messianic: everything— every event and institution—is prophetic and Messianico- prophetic, and what we one-sidedly call special predictions are only special points on which the golden light rests, and from which it is reflected. And it is in this sense that we understand and adopt the fundamental principle of the Synagogue, repeated in every variety of form, that every event in Israel's history, and every prophecy pointed forward to the Messiah, and that every trait and fact of the past, whether of history or miracle, would be re-enacted more fully, nay, in complete fulness, in the times of the Messiah.

We repeat, that this fundamental view of the Old Testament prophecy, or rather of the prophetic character of the Old Testament in contradistinction to the theory of merely isolated predictions in single verses or clauses, or even in isolated chapters, must not be misunderstood as if it implied that there are not absolute and definite predictions in the Old Testament. Unquestionably there are such, that had no basis in the then present—as when a sign was to be given, or an immediate judgment or deliverance enounced. But the principles which we have laid down are most wide-reaching in their bearing. They find their application also to what are called the types of the Old Testament, which are predictions by deed, as prophecies are predictions by word, and in the study of which the reference to the future must be learned from their teaching in the then present: their typical from their symbolical meaning. And the same principles also apply to what of prophecy we have in the New Testament. This bears chiefly on these three points: the Second Coming of Christ, the Antichrist, and the visions of the Apocalypse. The subject is so interesting, that without applying in detail the principles laid down in this Lecture, we may be allowed at least to indicate their bearing on each of these three groups of prophecy.

As regards the Second Coming of Christ, it will scarcely be questioned that it was somehow connected with statements, which we now see to have primarily referred to the destruction of Jerusalem and the Temple. Equally there can be no doubt, that the men of Christ's time expected His Advent, and also that every age since has done the same; and, indeed, was intended to do so. The application of our principles seems to introduce harmony into all this. It was the all-engrossing and all-influencing fact, to be viewed through the telescope of prophecy. And the destruction of Jerusalem and of the Temple was not only a symbol, but in an initial sense the very coming of Christ into His Kingdom. That coming of Christ into His Kingdom, which had been denied in explicit words, and negatived by public deed, when by wicked hands they slew Him, was vindicated, and, so to speak, publicly enacted when the Roman soldier threw the torch into the Temple, and when afterwards Jerusalem was laid level with the dust. As regards the men of that land and generation, it was the public proclamation, the evidence, that the Christ Whom they had rejected had come into His Kingdom. By the lurid light of those flames no other words could be read than those on the Cross: 'This is the King of the Jews.' I say, then, the burning of Jerusalem was to that generation—and whatever kindred events successively came within the focus of the telescopic vision of following generations, were to them, the fulfilment of that prophecy, of which the final completion will be the Personal reappearance of Christ at the end of the Æon.

Similar inferences come to us when we turn to the prophecies concerning the Antichrist. In that generation the mystery of iniquity was already working. Antichrist had already come, in those Gnostic heresies, defacements and displacements of Divine truth, and in the political antagonism, which almost threatened the extinction of the Church. And in every generation does 'the mystery of iniquity' work; and it worketh now—nay, as the holy Apostle explains, it shall work—in the children of disobedience, and so long and wherever there are such, till that which now letteth is taken away, and the dammed-up waters rush into those ready channels, from which they had so long been held, and so Antichrist be fully revealed. Or, lastly, as regards the prophetic visions of the Apocalypse, it is not difficult to perceive that the forms and imagery—so to speak, the groundwork—are taken from the then present: either from the Temple and its services, or from current Apocalyptic imagery, or else from the political history of the time, from Nero, and the events then occurring. But because critics recognise, for example, Nero and that period, it would surely be a very rash conclusion that these visions are so jejune as to present merely an Apocalyptic description of that time.

To sum up in practical conclusions what has been stated in this Lecture. It is in the light of the wider view of fulfilled prophecy which, as a whole and in all its parts, refers to the Kingdom of God upon earth, that we must study individual predictions. They pass far beyond anything actual at the time of their utterance to the underlying ideal. They are not exaggerated Orientalisms for simple facts, but there was one grand moving idea set forth with ever unfolding clearness: the hope of a great Fatherhood of God, of a great brotherhood of man, in which the grand connecting link, alike with God and man, should be the One Who embodied all that was ideally possible in man, and Who manifested all that could be manifested of God; Who united the highest point in the human with the utmost condescension of the Divine—God and man; Who brought God's reconciliation to man, and by it reconciled man to God, combining in Himself these two: the suffering of man and the conquering of God, and organically united them in conquering by suffering; One Who, by so doing, made possible, and introduced the Messianic Kingdom of God, through the willing submission of man. Thus the God-Man fully realised the theanthropic idea of the whole Old Testament.

As each event in His history kindled into light, it shone upon the individual prophecies, and made them bright. And here let us mark the inward connection of these Messianic prophecies. If, putting aside controversial criticism, we range them side by side, and in their order, we perceive that which modern philosophic science seeks, in all its departments: a grand unity. This unity cannot be accounted for on the modern negative theory, which treats the prophecies as *disjecta membra*, having each sole application to some one historical event of the past. Even as regards the older view of prophetism, which I have disclaimed, Kuenen himself has admitted at least its attractiveness and grandeur. But further, there is not only unity, but manifest progression. The fundamental idea does not change, but it unfolds, and applies itself under ever-changing and enlarging circumstances, developing from particularism into universalism; from the more realistic preparatory presentation to the spiritual which underlay it, and to which it pointed; from Hebrewism to the world-Kingdom of God. And, lastly, this Messianic idea is the moving spring of the Old Testament. It is also its sole *raison d'etre*, viewed as a revelation. Otherwise the Jewish people and their history could only have an archæological or a political interest for us. Hebrewism, if it had any Divine meaning, was the religion of the future, and Israel embodied for the world the religious idea which, in its universal application, is the Kingdom of God.

Or, else, if we discard this view of prophecy altogether, then must we also surrender the Old Testament itself as of any Divine authority, or as other than a form of ancient religion. For we can never believe that a narrow, national, and exclusive creed and institutions could have been Divine in the strict sense, or intended to be permanent—'for it is not possible that the blood of bulls or of goats should take away sins' (Heb 10:4). But if you remove the Old Testament, then the New Testament which is built on it must also fall. For not only do Christ and His Apostles avowedly stand upon Old Testament ground, but the Church itself is built 'upon the foundation of the Apostles and Prophets' (Eph 2:20). This issue we can safely leave to the arbitrament of time, or rather, as Christian believers, in the hands of our God. Modifications of form and of presentation may, and will come—other perhaps than we either expect or fear. But we have received a kingdom that cannot be shaken (Heb 12:28)—the revelation of which, whether as prophecy under the Old, or fulfilment under the New Testament, is, with reverence be it said, worthy of God to have given, worthy of Christ to have manifested, worthy of humanity to be received and submitted to; worthy also, let us add, to be accepted by us in the reverence of a humble, earnest, and personal faith.

LECTURE 5: ON PROPHETISM AND HEATHEN DIVINATION, THE MORAL ELEMENT IN OLD TESTAMENT PROPHECY, AND THE BIBLICAL CANONS FOR DISTINGUISHING THE TRUE FROM THE FALSE PROPHET.

And He said unto them, These are the words which I spake unto you, while I was with you, that all things must be fulfilled which were written in the Law of Moses, and in the prophets, and in the Psalms, concerning Me. Then opened He their understanding, that they might understand the Scriptures. Luke 24:44, 45.

We may almost be pardoned the wish that St. Luke had, at least in this instance, not so closely adhered to his plan of narration, and told us in detail to what special lines of prophetic thought Christ had pointed the minds which He opened, and what special prophecies, dimly apprehended of old, He had now illumined with the radiance of His risen glory. Yet it is perhaps best for the Church that to all time only these gigantic measurements should have been laid to the Scriptures of the Old Testament: that they form one organic whole, being bound together by the prophetic element which is common to them all; that their prophecy is of the Christ, that He should suffer and rise again, and that repentance and remission of sins should be preached in His name to all nations—in other words, that they tell of His humiliation, exaltation and reign; of the story of sin, righteousness, and judgment; of man, Christ, and God; or, in more scientific language, that they contain the anthropology, soteriology, and eschatology—in short, the history of the Kingdom of God.

But whatever prophetic Scriptures Christ may have opened at that time, their Messianic interpretation would, to judge by the Old Testament quotations in the Gospels, not have been according to the *straitness of the letter*, which regarded a prophecy as exhausted by one special event, but in the *expansiveness of the spirit*, which, starting from a definite event as the *terminus a quo* of fulfilment, followed the prophetic element in it through its unfolding to its finality in the Kingdom of God, which is the goal of all prophecy. As the words of our Lord imply, the whole Old Testament is prophetic, not only in its special predictions, but even in its history, from the 'Out of Egypt I have called My Son,' to 'A prophet like unto me shall the Lord your God raise up unto you.' Thus the Old Testament pointed beyond itself to the perfectness which it announced and for which it prepared. That perfectness consists in the removal of all the evil which sin has wrought, in the restoration of man to God, and in the fulness of blessings which flows from fellowship between God and man. This is the Kingdom of God. To announce it and to prepare for it, was the object of the Old Testament. More especially was Prophetism the moral and spiritual element in the Old Testament, which was intended to meet the people in their successive stages of development, to point out to them the lessons of the past, to explain the meaning of the present, and so to prepare them for that future which it announced. God's dealings with Israel in the past were ever on the lips of the prophets. In their hands the Law lost its deadness of the letter and became instinct with a new life. Circumcision, sacrifices, the priesthood, and all the other religious institutions in Israel—and what institution in Israel was not religious?—were shown to have a spiritual background, to point to spiritual realities, and to have a spiritual counterpart in that blessed future which the prophets were specially commissioned to announce, that so through the lessons of the past and the discipline of the present they might prepare men for that future which was the end and goal of all.

To this moral element in prophetism as its inmost characteristic the present Lecture will be devoted, leaving another aspect of it for future consideration.

1. All prophecy has the moral and spiritual element, I shall not say for its aim, but as its basis and essential quality. The distinction seems important in this, as in the case of miracles, especially those of our Lord. An endeavour has sometimes been made to vindicate for them what is called a moral object. But this would be to transfer our human modalities to what is Divine. The Divine has no object outside its own manifestation. The moral is its quality, not its aim. And it is the moral and spiritual in man, the remnant of the Divine in him, and that which renders him capable of restoration, which, consciously or unconsciously, stretches forth its hands towards God, rises towards its spring, tends heavenwards. Consciously or unconsciously, it underlies not only the idea of, but all the great institutions that are common to all religions. It forms the fundamental idea of sacrifices, priesthood, prayers, prophetism, and of that grand thought of a

reign of universal peace and happiness which, in one form or another, exists in all religions. In part these may be regarded as the result and survival of a primeval tradition; and, in part, they are the outcome of the deepest aspirations, and (why should I not say it?) of the true Divine instincts of the human spirit.

Even that which in some respects is farthest from, and yet is also nearest to, prophecy—heathen divination—was not destitute of this moral element. It were a narrow and mistaken view, judging it by its later development, to regard heathen divination as merely imposture or delusion. In its fundamental idea it represented deep consciousness of distance from God; a longing to know His will, to be guided by it, and to have fellowship with Him; and, finally, a feeling that God was indeed near to man, that He cared for him, and guided the events of his life. These are also among the premisses on which the Old Testament proceeded. Only, starting from the same premisses, the Old Testament pointed in a totally different direction, and accordingly reached the opposite results from heathenism. Heathenism endeavoured to attain its desire by divination (*mantic*), which sought all either in nature or from man; while the Old Testament pointed for all to the living God. Heathen divination was either by means *external*, such as signs, auguries, the stars, conjuring the dead; or else by means *internal*, such as dreams, visions, and the ecstatic state. But neither in the one nor the other case did it seek its satisfaction in spiritual fellowship with God. That element was wholly wanting. The direct opposite of this is characteristic of the Old Testament and its prophecy. Here everything is spiritual, comes from, and points to God. Divine revelation meets the moral wants of man, and directs him to God. This one thing appears most clearly throughout the whole Old Testament: that there is absolutely no power in any outward things to produce prophecy, nor yet has the prophet himself any power to produce it within himself by any means of his own, but that in all cases it comes straight from God, to whom, when, how, and where He pleases; that a man becomes a prophet as God gives him the message, and is such only and so long as God continues to send it. On the other hand, God did meet this deep want and longing of His children by sending His prophets and putting His Word into their mouths. Hence to receive or else to resist them could not be matter of indifference, since they were the direct ambassadors of God; but it involved either obedience to Him, or else guilt. And in the New Testament we have in this also progressed to the finality of widest fulfilment. Of old there were intermittent springs, now we have a perennial fountain; then the Holy Spirit fell on individuals at special times, now He dwells permanently in all His people; then there were prophets, now we have One ever-living Prophet, an everlasting link that binds us to God, One Who not only brings the promises, but in Whom they are Yea and Amen.

Otherwise, also, the points of contact between heathenism and revealed religion are most important. They seem to start from the same point (as *terminus a quo*), for the outgoings of the human spirit are ever the same. But the road they take, and hence their end (the *terminus ad quem*), are widely different, for they are under very different guidance. These common underlying ideas: a sense of guilt, longing after the Divine, and belief in His connection with our earth, equally express themselves in heathen and in Jewish sacrifices, in the belief in the Golden Age, and in the expectation of the Kingdom of God. As regards the latter, there is indeed this characteristic difference, that, except as directed by the Jewish Sibyl, the Golden Age is past, while in Revelation it is the goal towards which all God's manifestations and all man's developments tend. But these institutions and ideas were the outcome of the common consciousness, wants, aspirations, and expectations of all mankind, and, as we believe, the result of a common original tradition. But how differently they were developed, and to what different goal they led in heathenism and under the Old Testament, appears best when we compare the final outcome of the two: in the one case Jesus Christ, in the other the heathen world. And, as regards this period of comparison, Hoffmann has well expressed it, that what Cæsar Augustus is for the understanding of Roman history, that Jesus Christ is for that of the history of Israel. And the absolute contrast of final results between the two developments starting from the same point is due to this, that, as St. Paul indicates, heathenism sought not the realisation of its wishes and wants by seeking it from God—they retained not God in their knowledge nor glorified Him—whereas revelation in the Old Testament pointed to the living and true God, to simple faith or receptiveness, and to submission to His Word and Will, and then met that faith by a reality which bound heaven to earth, made sacrifices a type of Christ, prophecy a direct message from God, and the great hope of the future a Kingdom of God on a ransomed earth. And to go one step further: Even as regards the knowledge of God, heathenism closely approximated to, yet remained at infinite distance from the Old Testament. In its highest outcomings heathenism reached to a unity, but it was the unity of a principle, or an abstraction—an It, not He; Fate, not Jehovah. And even under the Old Testament the standpoint of present knowledge was only that of Jehovah as the God of all the earth and the Father of His people Israel. It was prophecy which pointed beyond this to the finality of all in the Christ, and to God as in Him the God and Father of all His people. In a world of which politically and religiously the one great characteristic was the most rigid nationalism, it stood alone in the moral grandeur of setting forth the brotherhood of humanity, the sonship of adoption, and the universal Fatherhood of God.

It is this moral element as leading up to God, whereas heathenism led away from God, which is characteristic of Revelation and of the Old Testament in every one of its institutions, and which also clearly marks the difference between mantic and prophecy. And this leads back to a question left unanswered in the former Lecture. It will be remembered that, so far from seeing anything incompatible—a dilemma in which we must make our choice—between the prophet as preacher to his times, or as the predicter of future events, we perceived in these two aspects a deeper unity. We are now prepared to go further, and to recognise the necessity of this union of the preacher and the predicter in the prophet. It is due to the moral element in prophecy. Moreover, we have here the means of understanding and applying that test by which the Old Testament would have us distinguish the true from the false prophet. Commonly two passages are quoted for this purpose. But, as generally interpreted, it must be admitted that the tests which they are supposed to supply would be vague and unsatisfactory. For in Deuteronomy 13:1-5, we have only this characteristic of the false prophet, that he leads the people away from Jehovah and after other gods; while in Deuteronomy 18:9-22, the canon is laid down, that if the thing predicted did not come to pass, the prophet had not spoken from God, but presumptuously and from himself. At first sight it might seem as if both these tests were practically worthless. For, this test that the false prophet led away from God, might, from the standpoint of Anti-Jehovahism, seem to involve a *petitio principii*; while, as regards the test of a prediction by its fulfilment, many years might have to elapse before it could be applied, so that it would scarcely afford the means for present discernment whether a prophet spoke from the Lord or from himself.

But further consideration will correct this superficial view. For, first, we mark in these two canons a distinction between prophet and prophecy. The latter might be either prediction in the narrowest sense, or else prophecy in the wider sense. If prediction in the narrower sense, it would, with rare exceptions, which mark special high-points in prophetism, be a sign or an announcement of immediate judgment or deliverance. In that case, the second canon—that of fulfilment or non-fulfilment (Deut 18:9-22)—would naturally apply. On the other hand, prophecy in the wider sense would grow out of exhortation, warning, or consolation, and, in the nature of it, form part of, or be connected with, a whole group of teaching. To it the first Canon—about leading away from God—would, as we shall presently show, be applicable as a moral test. And that the second Canon in Deuteronomy 18:22, chiefly referred to predictions of signs or judgments in the immediate future, appears from this, that the words, 'if the thing follow not, that is the thing which the Lord hath not spoken, but the prophet hath spoken it presumptuously,' are immediately succeeded by these, 'Thou shalt not be afraid of him (or, of it).' Manifestly this addition would only have meaning if the prediction referred to the immediate future.

But what of predictions in the more distant future? The test of these is, as already hinted, furnished by the first canon (Deut 13:1-5), which, be it carefully marked, applies not to prophecy, but to the prophet. Israel is emphatically warned, that even if signs or wonders were wrought, the guidance of a prophet was not to be followed if he led away from the Living and True God. This canon embodies most important and wide reaching principles, distinctive of the Old Testament as compared not only with heathenism, but we had almost said with every other school of thought. It sets forth the dominance of the moral and spiritual over every other consideration. Power, even that of working miracles, is but of inferior consideration: truth, right, God—the Divine, the spiritual—are everything. This is a height not only far beyond the ideas which we commonly attach to the Old Testament, but, I venture to add, beyond the horizon of modern society, which worships power as such, whatever its origin or character may be. It is the spirit of that Pan-Jehovahism which found utterance in the sublime proclamation, unique in its meaning and bearing; equally marvellous as coming from little Judæa and down-trodden Israel, and as spoken at that age into all the world; marvellous as a dogma, a prayer, a call, and a prophecy; marvellous also as a summary of the Law and the Gospel, of Providence and Grace; of the past, the present, and the future: 'Jehovah reigneth, let the earth be glad; let the multitude of isles be glad thereof' (Psa 97:1). The words of the original, in their rugged grandeur, seem like steps hewn in the eternal ice, leading up to some Alpine height. We need not quote this Psalm further, nor compare it with the others in the Psalm-range, among which it rears its crest. But I venture to assert that none but a Jehovahist, an Old Testament prophet, could have so written, because none but he had the living burning conviction that Jehovah He is God. Such a history as that of the Old Testament produced such belief; and such belief produced such expectancy and utterance. It produced a Moses, an Elijah, a Daniel, and, even when crumbling into decay, had its unnumbered martyrs. Such utterances could not have been those of uncircumcised heathen lips, nor can we conceive them as the conviction or outcome of heathen minds, whose highest speculations have nothing of the true Divine life pulsating in them.

First God, then everything else: be it man, kingdoms, demons, power, even Word as from God, or signs and miracles! This is the truth which Israel's history had evolved, which Israel's institutions embodied, which Israel's prophecies set forth, and by which, in turn, according to Deuteronomy, Israel's prophecy was to be tested. This then is the meaning of the canon in Deuteronomy 13: Try the prophet by his confession of God. And similarly, we read it in the New Testament: 'Try the spirits, whether they are of God…Every spirit which confesseth that Jesus Christ is come in the flesh is of God, and every spirit which confesseth not Jesus is not of God; and this is the spirit of the Antichrist' (1 John 4:1-3).

Nor was the application of this canon so difficult as at first sight it may appear. In the case of a prophet or a prophecy which, avowedly, led away from God, there could be neither doubt nor question. But even in the case of a prophet, professedly of God, who brought a message as from Him, the mode of decision is indicated. The Old Testament offers a leading case, hitherto too much overlooked, which furnishes, so to speak, a supplement and an explanation of its canon. In the 28th chapter of Jeremiah, a prophet is introduced, who prophesied differently alike from his predecessors and from Jeremiah. It is after the deportation to Babylon, and Hananiah is within the sacred precincts of the Temple, in the presence of priests and people, and in that of Jeremiah himself, predicting the speedy restoration of the holy vessels, of the king and the people, that had been carried to Babylon. Apparently Jeremiah does not charge him with being only and always a false prophet. But the question arose, whether in this special instance Hananiah, differing from all others, acted as a true or was a false prophet? To apply the canon in Deuteronomy: would it lead to, or away from, following Jehovah, the Living and True God? The answer could not be difficult. It was the Will of God, frequently expressed, that in the then state of the people, their captivity, and the cessation of the Temple-service, should *not* be of short duration; and that Judah should willingly submit to God in this judgment, and to the instruments which He had appointed to execute it. But the prediction of Hananiah was in precisely the opposite direction from this leading of God, and to have given credence to it would have led away from God. It is this to which Jeremiah referred when, after expressing as a patriot Israelite his intense desire that the prophecy of Hananiah might prove to have been God-sent, he added: 'Nevertheless hear this…The prophets that have been before me and before thee of old, prophesied both against many countries, and against many kingdoms, of war, and of evil, and of pestilence.' This, in the then state of Israel and the world, was evidently in accordance with the mind of God; there was moral evidence that it was of God. 'But,' continued the prophet: 'the prophet which prophesieth of peace, when the word of that prophet shall come to pass, then shall the prophet be known, that Jehovah hath truly sent him' (vv 6-9). In other words, such prophesying, as leading away from Jehovah, wanted the moral evidence. Let it be tried by the test of fact.

Looking back upon it, I shall not call this the vindication, but the manifestation and assertion of the moral element in prophecy. This self-limitation of prophetism, this submission of itself to the criterion of God-obedience, not only contrasts with all divination, but is absolutely grand in its moral elevation, and affords yet another evidence of its Divine character. Once more we come, as we might have expected, on New Testament lines. For it was this moral element which our Lord presented to His enemies as evidence of His own Prophetic Mission, when He said: 'If any man will do His will, he shall know of the teaching, whether it be of God, or whether I speak of Myself. He that speaketh of himself seeketh his own glory; but he that seeketh His glory that sent him, the same is true' (John 7:17,18).

Closely connected with this moral test, there is another aspect of the moral element in prophetism, another self-limitation and submission to God. In heathenism, prediction was absolute; in the Old Testament, prophecy was never absolute, but always subject to moral conditions. Commenting on the 33rd chapter of Ezekiel, which declared that the prediction of death to the wicked and life to the righteous were not absolute, but would be reversed on their moral change, St. Jerome aptly observes: 'Nor does it follow that because a prophet foretold, that which he foretold should come to pass; for he does not foretell in order that it might take place, but lest it should take place (*'nec statim sequitur ut quia propheta pædixit, veniat quod pædixit. Non enim pædicit ut veniat, sed ne veniat'*). It, is in this sense that Holy Scripture, taking the human point of view, so often speaks of God's repenting. All the prophets who announced judgment also called to repentance, and all such calls—as so many in the prophecies of Isaiah; in Jeremiah 4:3-5; Ezekiel 18:30-32; Joel 2:12-14, and in other passages—were accompanied by the promise that in case of obedience the predicted judgments would be averted. More especially do we here recall the words of Jeremiah (18:7-10): 'At what instant I shall speak concerning a nation, and concerning a kingdom, to pluck up, to pull down, and to destroy it—if that nation against whom I have pronounced turn from their evil, I will repent of the evil that I thought to do unto them. And at what instant I shall speak concerning a nation, and concerning a kingdom, to build, and to plant it: if it do evil in My sight that it obey not My voice, then I will repent of the good wherewith I said I would benefit them.'

It is not fate that presides over prophecy, nor does fatality follow it. But there is a Living and True God Who reigneth, and the moral is the rule and characteristic of all prophecy. The Old Testament has settled, or rather anticipated, this great theological problem of so many ages: the combination and compatibility of God's sovereignty and decree with man's liberty and responsibility—not by either of our two clumsy devices or modes of cutting the knot,—that from above in what is called Predestinarianism, or that from below in what is known as Arminianism—but by putting the two in juxtaposition. And this lesson of what may be called the moral conditionalness of prophecy is specially indicated in that marvellous allegorical history, the Book of Jonah, which more than any other reaches beyond the Old Testament standpoint, and anticipates the lessons and facts of the New Testament. Nor, I trust, will it be considered presumptuous to suggest that this moral conditionalness—with all the possibilities resulting in this case—would, in part, be the answer to such a question as this: What, if the Jews, instead of rejecting and crucifying, had received Jesus as the Messiah? And it is in this sense that I would understand the words in which our Lord explained the true position of the

Baptist: 'And if ye are willing to receive (it, or him), this is Elias, which, was for to come' (Matt 11:14).

But even thus I have not yet given a full view of the moral element in prophecy. For this purpose I must refer to at least two other points. For, first, prophetism, while confirming the historical reality of all the institutions of the Law, presented their spiritual bearing, without which it declared the observance of the letter to be not only meaningless, but an absolute perversion of their Divine purpose. Beyond the *opus operatum* and the letter were the Spirit and the spiritual reality to which they pointed. Circumcision of the flesh pointed to that of the lips and the heart; by the side of Israel after the flesh was Israel after the Spirit; by the side of the Levitical, another Priesthood, to which 'Holiness to the Lord' was the consecration. Sacrifices were meaningless without brokenness of heart and spirit, and they pointed to one great sacrifice of suffering. Festivals, fasts, and all other rites were a perversion and an abomination, unless pervaded by the moral and spiritual element.

Secondly. Prophetism emphatically presented itself, not as a finality, but rather as a preparation for a higher, better, and more spiritual state of things. Even as in the New Testament we are told that those miraculous *Charismata* of the Spirit: prophecies, tongues, and knowledge, belonged to a still imperfect or preparatory state of the Church, so did prophecy, while with one hand pointing back to the Law of Moses, and with the other to prophetism, tell of a time when God would make a new Covenant with His people, and give them a new Law, not graven on stone, but written on the heart, of which the seal would be circumcision of the heart: a Covenant of which the fundamental fact would be a new deliverance, not from the bondage of Egypt, but from that of sin, when He would forgive their iniquities and remember their sins no more—or, to quote the imagery of another prophet, when He would sprinkle clean water upon them and they would be clean (Eze 36:25). Then would prophecy indeed cease; no man would any more teach his neighbour, for they would all know Him, from the least to the greatest of them. Nor would the spirit of prophecy rest then only upon a few chosen individuals, but the wish of Moses of old would be fulfilled concerning all Israel, and the Holy Spirit be outpoured on all their sons and daughters, nay, even on the slaves and handmaidens, so that all would prophesy (Joel 2:28,29)—for in those days would He cause the Branch of Righteousness to grow up unto David, Who would execute judgment and righteousness in the land.

Thus prophecy pointed beyond itself, and to a spiritual fulfilment connected with the Advent of the promised Messiah. And not only so, but it also pointed to that period as that of the Kingdom of God, not now of narrow Judaic dimensions, but wide as the world; not of national glory, but of spiritual righteousness. This is the highest moral element, the moral climax in prophecy, and in that sense is Jesus the Messiah also most fully *the* Prophet. But this line of argument stretches too far to be followed to its end in the present course of Lectures.

In conclusion we may gather together the threads of this argument in a few plain and easily-answered questions. Is it not so that the goal which the Old Testament indicated when pointing beyond itself, beyond its rites, institutions, and prophetism, to a spiritual fulfilment, has, as a matter of fact, been attained in the New Testament and in Christ? In His own language: is it not so, that the salvation which is of the Jews has come to all men, since, not in Jerusalem only, but everywhere, the true worshippers worship the Father in Spirit and in truth? And is not all this because of, in, and through Jesus of Nazareth? Then 'Is not this the Christ,' the Messiah? and did not Philip truthfully say it, 'We have found Him of whom Moses in the Law, and the Prophets did write'? And, lastly, have not all things been fulfilled which were written in the Law of Moses, and in the Prophets, and in the Psalms concerning Him?

Here we might, under ordinary circumstances, have paused for the present. But the terrible circumstances in which we find ourselves at this time, not only require language the most explicit and emphatic, but excuse that which is most impassioned. A great crime is being enacted over the world, which cries to Heaven for vengeance, and to the Church for testimony and self-vindication. While we speak of that salvation which is of the Jews, and of the joyous fulfilment of all promises in Christ, other thoughts obtrude themselves, and, like heavy clouds, crowd our horizon, and darken out the light of our gladness. For once more has the wild howl of unchained passion against Israel risen above the sweet music of the dying Saviour's last prayer: 'Father, forgive them, for they know not what they do.' Once more has the blood-stained hand of rapine, lust, and murder sought to shake from out the jewelled memorial cup, in which the Church had gathered and held up in a constant Prayer of Intercession, the tears which Jesus had shed over the Jerusalem that would not receive Him—tears, that can never be dried up. And once more has the white raiment of the Church been fouled with blood; her fair name been made a byword, and her hymn of charity drowned by wild orgies. The hand raised to point to the Cross drops in anguish. How can we strike Judah's lyre when her captives lie murdered, mangled in our streets? How can we respond with the Antiphony of Fulfilment to the Hymn of Promise made to the virgin daughter of Zion when her maidens are outraged, her old men murdered, and her dwellings plundered by those who bear the Name of Him in Whom all these promises are Yea and Amen? The Church veils her face in mourning; a thrill of horror, a pang of anguish, a cry of indignation pass through universal humanity. Whether and what in the wonder working Providence of Him who brings good out of evil may be the outcome of this to Israel, we cannot say. But in the name of God, let us clear ourselves of all complicity in this sin and shame. We who do believe in Christ, and because we believe in Him, as the true Messiah—we protest with one heart and mind against this and all like movements! In the name of Christianity, in the name of our Church, in the name of this land of liberty and light, in the name of universal humanity, we abhor it, we denounce it, we protest against it. And yet more, as we believe, so we pray: Come, Lord Jesus, come quickly, and by Thy glorious reign put an end to bloodshed, rapine, and sin!

LECTURE 6: ON THE SPIRITUAL ELEMENT IN PROPHECY: THE OLD TESTAMENT POINTED TO A SPIRITUAL FULFILMENT IN THE KINGDOM OF GOD.

Of which salvation the prophets have inquired and
searched diligently, who prophesied of the grace that
should come unto you: searching what, or what
manner of time the Spirit of Christ which was in
them did signify, when it testified beforehand the
sufferings of Christ, and the glory that should follow. 1 Peter 1:10, 11.

It needs not a detailed analysis of these verses to show how closely their teaching agrees with the record of St. Peter's preaching. For, in his first sermon on the day of Pentecost, and especially in his second on the occasion of his healing the lame man in the Temple, his argument addressed to the Jews was, as might have been expected, to this effect: There is nothing new or unexpected in what you see and hear; it is simply the fulfilment of prophecy, for 'all the prophets from Samuel, and those that follow after, as many as have spoken, have foretold of these days.'

But the Apostolic statement which we have chosen as text for this Lecture goes farther than this. It implies: Firstly, That all prophecy was the outcome of the Spirit of Christ in the prophets; secondly, that it pointed to the sufferings of the Messiah, and the glory that should follow; and, lastly, that while the prophets understood the general Messianic bearing of their prophecy, the details of the manner and time of its fulfilment were not understood by them, but remained reserved to the historical unfolding of the latter days.

This takes us another step in our argument. It sets before us the historical character of prophecy, as progressing *pari passu* with the history of Israel, till at last its meaning fully appears in its fulfilment. Accurately considered, this forms indeed part of that moral element which in the last Lecture was shown to be the great characteristic of Prophecy. For it was not something mechanical and dead, thrust upon the world, as it were, but an active power for good, which grew with the moral growth of the people, and unfolded with their capacity for receiving and understanding it. From the first all was present—as St. James puts it: 'Known to God from the first beginning' (Acts 15:18), or, in St. Paul's language, 'part of the mystery hid from all ages in God' (Eph 3:9,10), and finally made known in Christ. And each advance in history was preceded by Prophecy, of which the object was not only the announcement of events, but preparation for them. And because the prophets, although they knew that their prophecies pointed to the end, understood not the time nor the manner of their fulfilment, therefore do we find so often the beginning and the end, the immediate and the final fulfilment, laid quite closely together, without apparent connection or transition—the Assur or Edom of the then present by the side of the final foes of the Kingdom; the Israel of the present along with that of the future; the restored services of the Temple beside the renewed worship of a Temple made without hands, and the heavenly beside the earthly Jerusalem. All this awaited the 'Let there be light' of the last days. Meantime that which was known to God from the beginning was successively revealed by Him through His prophets, for the spiritual training of His people. In the language of Amos (3:7), 'Surely Jehovah God will do nothing, but He revealeth His secrets to His servants the prophets'; and in that of Isaiah (42:9), 'Behold, the former things are come to pass, and new things do I declare; before they spring forth I tell you of them.' And so Prophecy and History proceeded, the one as the forerunner of the other, the Spirit of Christ in the prophets ever pointing forward to the period of fulfilment. Then would all the great lines of prophecy meet, and in their meeting would their meaning become manifest.

If this historical view of prophecy characterised the preaching of St. Peter as the Apostle of the Jews, it is not less apparent in what may be termed the Biblical representatives of the opposite, or Alexandrian, direction: St. Stephen and the Epistle to the Hebrews; and in St. Paul, who in a marvellous degree combined the Palestinian and the Grecian direction. This explains how the largest part of St. Stephen's address to the Council was occupied by an historical sketch of God's Revelation, and of Israel's progressive disobedience thereto. Similarly, in the Epistle to the Hebrews, after a general introduction, chapters 3, 4, and 11, trace the prophetic view of Israel's history, while the intermediate chapters give that of Israel's institutions—and so the main proposition in chapter 2 is carried to its practical application in the concluding part of the Epistle. Lastly, we mark the same line of argument in the preaching of St. Paul to the Jews. Thus, in his first sermon in the Synagogue of Antioch, in Pisidia, the prophetic history of Israel from the Exodus to David is passed in review; then the predictions are referred to, which accompanied and explained this history, and pointed from David, nay from Moses and the Law, to Christ, the conclusion being an application of the prophetic warnings of Isaiah and Habakkuk to their contemporaries, as that of which the fulfilment threatened St. Paul's hearers (Acts 13:17-41). There is, indeed, another line of thought regarding prophecy, followed by St. Paul, and, so far as I know, by him alone, in which the absolute or dogmatic view of it is taken, the Law with its demands being presented as the schoolmaster unto Christ, while the provisions regarding sin and satisfaction—sacrifices and atonement—are shown to point to Christ as their fulfilment. To this aspect we shall refer in the sequel.

We may safely assume that the historic and prophetic character of the Old Testament, as preparing for, and pointing to, the Messiah, would not be seriously questioned by the Synagogue—at least, by the orthodox part of it—however strenuously the fulfilment of the prophetic Scriptures in Christ might be denied. But if the Divine authority of the Old Testament is accepted, it appears to me only possible to challenge the New Testament conclusion on one of three grounds:—*First*, it might be contended that the Old Testament must be taken in an exclusively literal sense. We have already shown that this could not have been the case in reference to the prophecies of the coming Kingdom of God. But it might be argued against our general view of the prophetic character of the Old Testament, that at least the ordinances and institutions of the Old Testament had no further meaning beyond themselves, no absolutely spiritual bearing—were merely external, and not intended to be superseded by a new and spiritual dispensation to which they pointed. Or else, *secondly*, it might be maintained that what may be called the Christian view of the Messianic idea in the Old Testament is entirely imaginary and erroneous. Or, *thirdly*, it might be said that even if that view were correct, the Old Testament picture of the Messiah was essentially different from that presented by Jesus of Nazareth.

As concerns these three objections, I think I may say that the last may be dismissed without discussion. For, if it were proved that the Old Testament pointed beyond itself to a larger and a spiritual Law, rites, and institutions, and if, besides, it were shown that the Christian view of the messianic idea in the Old Testament is correct, few would, I suppose, be disposed to question the inference that Jesus Christ did embody the Old Testament ideal as conceived by the Church. In such case we would have only to appeal to history, and it would almost seem logically impossible to resist the argument from the historical Church. And if it were further objected that a great majority of Christ's contemporaries did not recognise in Him the Old Testament picture of the Messiah, this answer would be sufficient, that these men had no longer the proper Messianic ideal before their minds; that their conception of Him was no longer true to the Old Testament, nor yet spiritual, but that traditionalism had overgrown and crushed out the Old Testament teaching in its higher bearing: in one sentence,—that the religion of the Old Testament had already become transformed into Judaism. Our Lord indeed bade them search the Old Testament Scriptures as bearing testimony to Him, but their eyes were holden by the hand of their Pharisaic leaders, and their heart was hardened not to perceive their meaning. And this: that the contemporaries of Christ, or at least a majority of them, under the teaching of traditionalism, did not any longer occupy the Old Testament standpoint in its spiritual presentation of the Messiah, we are prepared to affirm as a substantive proposition. Accordingly, we have here to deal really with only these two questions: Did the Old Testament in its ordinances and rites point to something spiritual, and indicate that its observances were only temporary, intended to merge into a new and spiritual dispensation? And, again, as quite kindred, and, indeed, connected with it: Is what may be called the Christian view of the Messianic idea and ideal in the Old Testament the correct one? The first of these questions has in part been touched upon in the previous Lecture, but it must now receive more systematic and detailed consideration.

I. The Old Testament embodies not only a code of outward observances, but points beyond their letter to a deeper spiritual meaning in the present, and to a higher spiritual fulfilment in the future. This does not involve, even in part, the old principle of allegorical interpretation which characterised Alexandrian Judaism or Jewish Hellenism, although I am ready to admit that this embodied a certain aspect of truth, as is even witnessed by the manner in which it prospered and bore good fruit. But Alexandrian allegorism was not only exegetically ungrounded; it had no historical basis, and was purely imaginative in its origin and character, with all of attractiveness, but also of logical defect, which this implies. It invented—or at least discovered—the interpretation for the sake of the truth which it wished to teach. Not so the mode of interpretation which we propose to adopt. Method is not fanciful, but historical, inasmuch as it proceeds on that which actually was, and seeks to explain institutions, not by what they may be supposed to mean, but by the meaning which in other parts of the Old Testament, notably in the prophetic writings and the Psalms, is expressly attached to them. This will appear as we pass in review the principal institutions of the Old Testament.

We have already seen that the initiatory rite of the Covenant, circumcision, was, even in the Pentateuch, presented in its symbolic aspect, and shown to point to another circumcision, that of the lips and the heart, which in the future would become a great spiritual reality to all men. It is in this view of circumcision that Moses speaks of himself as of 'uncircumcised lips,' that is, as unprepared for great spiritual work (Exo 6:12), while in Leviticus 26:41 we read of 'uncircumcised hearts,' and in Deuteronomy the command to circumcise the heart is explained as equivalent to being 'no more stiff-necked' (10:16). Quite in accordance with this view, Jeremiah expresses his call to repentance in the words: 'Circumcise yourselves to Jehovah, and take away the foreskins of your heart, ye men of Judah and inhabitants of Jerusalem' (4:4). And that this was intended to point to something very real, appears from the circumstance that it forms the great Divine promise of the latter days: 'Jehovah thy God will circumcise thine heart...to love Jehovah thy God with all thine heart and with all thy soul' (Deut 30:6). Circumcision then was not a merely outward rite, but symbolic of a spiritual reality; and it pointed beyond itself to the time of its spiritual accomplishment. Accordingly we find that in the prophetic writings it is associated with the glory of the latter days. Thus Isaiah calls on the Holy City to awake and put on her beautiful garments, for that henceforth the uncircumcised and the unclean would no more enter her gates (52:1). And that the outward rite could not have been referred to, appears from this, that Jeremiah foretells that the days would come when Jehovah would equally punish the circumcised with the uncircumcised, for that while the Gentiles were uncircumcised, 'all the house of Israel were uncircumcised in the heart' (9:26). But what is this other than the New Testament argument of St. Paul: 'He is not a Jew which is one outwardly; neither is that circumcision, which is outward in the flesh. But he is a Jew, which is one inwardly; and circumcision is that of the heart, in the spirit, and not in the letter; whose praise is not of men, but of God' (Rom 2:28,29).

And as in regard to circumcision, so, and perhaps even more emphatically, as to sacrifices. The spiritual, as distinguished from the merely external, view of sacrifices is always prominently brought forward. Even the well-known (and too often misapplied) words of Samuel to Saul: 'To obey is better than sacrifices, and to hearken than the fat of rams' (1 Sam 15:22), not only imply that sacrifices had a deeper meaning and bearing than the mere outward act, but that this was generally known and admitted. But when we pass beyond this to the prophetic writings and the Psalms, which, as Professor Delitzsch well reminds us, must be taken into account in all such discussions, the teaching of the Old Testament unmistakably is, that sacrifices pointed to a higher reality. Psalm 50 reads like a withering irony on the mere *opus operatum* of sacrifices, as if God would eat the flesh of bulls or drink the blood of goats (v 13). In Psalm 51 the penitent pleads: 'Thou desirest not sacrifice, else would I give it: Thou delightest not in burnt-offering. The sacrifices of God are a broken spirit' (vv 16.17). It is in the same spirit and manner that Isaiah (1:11-14), Jeremiah (6:20), Amos (5:21,22), Hosea (6:6), and Micah (6:6-8) speak of sacrifices as in themselves of no value. And we are carried beyond this chiefly negative view in this most important retrospect of the Prophet Jeremiah, 'I spake not unto your fathers, nor commanded them in the day that I brought them out of the land of Egypt, concerning burnt-offerings or sacrifices. But this thing commanded I them, saying, Obey my voice, and I will be your God, and ye shall be my people (7:22,23). It almost seems as if it were intended to teach the absolute worthlessness of sacrifices, viewed by themselves, and to point to the substitution of a spiritual worship in their room. We seem to be catching a faint whisper of these words in the Epistle to the Hebrews: 'It is not possible that the blood of bulls and of goats should take away sins' (10:4). And beyond this did the prophets speak of another sacrifice which would be of intrinsic value. Thus we read it in Psalm 40: 'Sacrifice and offering Thou didst not desire...Then said I, Lo, I come: in the volume of the book it is written of me, I delight to do Thy will, oh my God' (vv 6-8). However the exegesis of this passage may be disputed, we believe that it presents this threefold view of sacrifices: their symbolical and transitional character; the moral element in them; and the great Sacrifice of inherent value by the self-surrender of the Righteous One—and that it points forward to, and finds its fullest explanation in, the great prediction of the 53rd chapter of Isaiah.

The argument, which we have sought to set forth, gains greatly in cogency as we remember that these utterances were not caused by any depreciation, on the part of the prophets, either of sacrifices or of the other ritual observances of the Old Testament. On the contrary, if we read in Psalm 51 that the sacrifices of God are a broken spirit, we find it immediately followed by this: 'Then shalt thou be pleased with the sacrifices of righteousness, with burnt-offerings and whole burnt-offerings; then shall they offer bullocks upon thine altar' (v 19). And, again, it is the same Psalmist who so earnestly pants after spiritual fellowship with the Living God, who also longs to go up to the hill of God, to His tabernacle and altar (Psalm 42, 43).

Most important in this respect are the references in the prophecies of Daniel and Malachi, but especially those in the book of Ezekiel, to ritual and Levitical ordinances. They prove beyond question that the prophetic standpoint did not imply any depreciation of the ordinances and institutions of the Law. And yet by the side of all this we find what some have, in perhaps exaggerated language, termed an anti-ritual direction. The solution of this seeming difficulty must not be sought in the supposed priority of the Prophets to the Law, but in another consideration which forms one of the main points in prophecy. Ultimately all prophecy points to 'the last [latter] days,' or the end of days (the *Acharith hayyamim*). This was to be the goal of the religious development and of the history of Israel. Thus we read it in the prophecy of Hosea (3:5), that after many days in which Israel would be without king or sacrifices—true or false—they would return and seek Jehovah their God and David their king, and fear Jehovah and His goodness in the latter days (the *Acharith hayyamim*). It was not for a gradual development into a more spiritual worship that the Prophets looked; their gaze was bent on the *Acharith hayyamim*. They expected not a religious reformation but a renovation, not the cessation of sacrifices but the fulfilment of their prophetic idea in the latter days, which were those of the expected Messiah and of His Kingdom. But, for the reason previously indicated, that they knew not the manner nor the time of fulfilment, these two—the present and the future—lay as yet in close, and to them, though not to us, undistinguished, contiguity. Thus Jeremiah introduces the sacrificial services into a restored Jerusalem, the starting point of his prophecy being the return from the Babylonish captivity, and its goal-point that from the final dispersion of Israel, or the latter days (Jer 17:26; 31:14; 33:10-16). The same undistinguished conjunction appears in the prophetic Book of Isaiah. In the 56th chapter of it we have a burning description of 'the latter days.' Then would the sons of the strangers join themselves to Jehovah and be brought to the Holy Mountain, and their burnt-offerings and sacrifices be accepted on His altar, because His house would be called a house of prayer for all nations. It is not an enlargement but a transformation of the Jewish dispensation which is here anticipated; not a conversion to Israel, but to Israel's God; not a merging of all nations into Israel, but a breaking down of separating walls; not a universal Synagogue, but a universal Church, in which all that had been national, preparatory, symbolic, typical, would merge into the spiritual reality of fulfilment. But what is this prophecy from the Book of Isaiah other than a prediction of the words of Christ concerning those other sheep of His not of the Jewish fold, whom He must bring, and who should hear His voice, that so there might be one flock and one Shepherd—words (John 10:16) which He consecrated by His latest prayer (John 17:20,21). Assuredly, it seems as difficult to understand how the fourth Gospel which records this can be regarded as un-Jewish, as how these prophecies of Isaiah can be represented as merely Jewish and anti-Gentile.

To pass over other and kindred prophetic utterances, those in the 60th chapter of the Book of Isaiah must claim our attention, as specially illustrative in our present argument. Here we find in strange juxtaposition two apparently contradictory series of facts. The prophecy opens with what almost seems a denunciation of Temple and sacrificial worship. Heaven was God's throne, and earth His footstool: where then was the house which man would build for Him, unless it were in the heart of the humble and contrite? Similarly, as regarded sacrifices, he that offered a lamb or an oblation was in the view of the prophet as if he had killed some unclean animal. And yet, by the side of these apparent denunciations, we have a glowing description of the restoration of that very Temple and of its sacrifices, yet of such kind that the Gentiles would, not as proselytes of righteousness, but as proselytes to God, have their part in all, by the side of spiritually converted Israel. Surely, clearer evidence than this could not be given, that the present was ever regarded as prophetic of the future; that the future was presented in the language and forms of the present; and that the sacrifices, which symbolised spiritual realities, were also typical of that future in 'the latter days,' when around the Great Sacrifice, and in the great World-Temple of the Church, all nations would be gathered.

To the same effect is what the Old Testament says concerning the Levitical priesthood. It is not the Epistle to the Hebrews only, but the Old Testament itself, which teaches that, beyond the letter, there was a deeper significance attaching to the Old Testament idea of the priesthood; and that, beyond the present institutions and ministry in the outward Temple, it pointed to higher spiritual realities, of which it was both symbolic and prophetic. Even the circumstance that the Levites were appointed in place of the first-born in Israel, (Num 8:16,17) is most significant. Like the claim to the first-fruits, it indicated the claim of Jehovah upon His people. This fundamental principle includes all detailed instruction that was afterwards given. Accordingly, we find that in Exodus 19:5, 6, all Israel are designated Jehovah's peculiar possession, although only on condition of being faithful to the covenant. It is in this sense also that we understand it, that all Israel 'shall be to me a kingdom of priests.' The same view of the meaning of the priesthood, as typical of God-consecration, is expressed in the Book of Deuteronomy (7:6; 14:2; 32:9), in the Psalms (135:4), and in the prophetic books (Isa 41:9; 43:1). But the final fulfilment of this fundamental idea was reserved for the future—and is presented in that mysterious priesthood after the order of Melchisedec (Psa 110:4), and in that prophecy concerning 'the latter days,' when, with reference to a far other than the Aaronic priesthood, one probably including the Gentiles also, this promise was to become true: 'And I will also take of them for priests and for Levites, saith Jehovah' (Isa 66:21). And as we recall the circumstances of Israel in relation to Babylon, and the stage of revelation when these words were uttered, and compare, or rather contrast them with the narrow Judaism of the time of Christ, we can in some measure realise the spiritual altitude of these prophecies, and feel that we must look in the pages of the New Testament for their fulfilment.

But it is not only one or another institution, but the whole Old Testament, which points beyond itself and to a higher fulfilment in the future. Here we specially mark how frequently and emphatically the Law is referred to, not as a code of outward commandments, but in its deeper and spiritual bearing on the inward man. This especially in the Book of Psalms, which may be described as being equally of the Law and the Prophets, converting the teaching of both into spiritual life-blood. Here we would refer, as a most characteristic instance, to the teaching of the Psalms in regard to holiness and forgiveness, which, as in the New Testament, are conjoined. A prominent influence in reference to these two is ascribed to the Law—necessarily, not as a code of outward commandments, but in its spiritual aspect. Thus in Psalm 19 the Law of the Lord is spoken of as 'converting the heart,' the prayer being immediately added for forgiveness of secret sins. Similarly, in Psalm 51 the prayer for forgiveness is joined to one for the creation of a new heart by the Spirit. This conjunction of the prayer for forgiveness with that for regeneration is exceedingly characteristic of the spirituality of religious aspiration. Psalm 119 may be described as a grand eulogy of the Law in this aspect of it. And when, with the time of Israel's completed inward departure from God, came that of their greatest outward need, the Prophet was not commissioned to give them any new commandment, still less to admonish to strict observance of the old, but to bring the promise, which characteristically was to this effect, that God would give them a new heart to know Him that He was Jehovah (Jer 24:7). And that it was not in any wise connected with ignoration of the Law, nor, on the other hand, expected in conjunction with a return to its merely outward ordinances, appears from this, that the great promise of 'the latter days'—of the Messianic time of completion—was, that Jehovah would then make a new covenant with Israel, not according to that when He brought them out of Egypt, but one in which He would put His Law in their inward parts, and write it on their hearts. And most important as adding yet another element: then would one man no longer teach his neighbour, but all be taught directly of God (Jer 31:31-34). This indicates the existence of the old elements, while at the same time it points to an entire change in the future. Then would not only the old Covenant and the old Law, but even prophetism be superseded, or rather fulfilled. All this in the 'latter days,' or Messianic time, when, as Zechariah predicts, all ritual ordinances would merge in that universal consecration to God, in which 'Holiness unto Jehovah,' the inscription on the High-Priest's mitre, would, so to speak, be that on all vessels in common use in Jerusalem (Zech 14:20,21). But what does all this mean, when translated into the prose language of history, but the fulfilment of the Law in its spiritual aspect, such as we find it described in the Epistles of St. Paul and, indeed, throughout the whole New Testament?

But even this is not all. If Psalm 51 had combined these two, the spiritual renewal of the heart and the forgiveness of sins, we are told that in the days of the promised New Covenant this would be the gift of God to all His people. Thus Jeremiah connects with the prediction of the new Law, which was to be written on the heart when man's teaching would give place to universal knowledge of God, this promise deeply significant, even if in its then form it applied to Israel: 'For I will forgive their iniquity, and I will remember their sin no more' (Jer 31:34). Similarly Ezekiel, the priest-prophet, speaks of the time when God would sprinkle clean water upon them, and cleanse them from their filthiness, give them a new heart, put His Spirit within them, take away their stony heart, and make them to walk in His statutes (Eze 36:25-27). And that these promises would find their fulfilment in the time of the Messiah, the Son of David, is thus expressly stated by the same prophet in the following chapter of his predictions: 'And David my servant shall be king over them: and they all shall have one shepherd: they shall also walk in My judgments, and observe My statutes, and do them' (Eze 37:24). And this is what Ezekiel emphatically designates as the covenant of peace, the everlasting covenant which God would make (Eze 37:26-28). Lastly, with this also agrees both the saying of Zechariah (13:1): 'In that day there shall be a fountain opened to the house of David, and to the inhabitants of Jerusalem, for sin and for uncleanness,' and this of Micah (7:19,20), that God would cast all their sins into the depths of the sea, and thus 'perform the truth to Jacob, and the mercy to Abraham' which He had 'sworn unto our fathers from the days of old.'

Detailed as these references have been, they have only brought us, as it were, to the threshold. For beyond all these individual predictions we have the glowing descriptions by all the prophets, but especially in the Book of Isaiah, of the time of the new covenant, with its blessings to Israel and to mankind. That these bear reference to a spiritual world-wide dispensation in the Messianic days needs scarcely argument, any more than that all the conditions of it have been fulfilled in that dispensation which was introduced under the New Testament. It could scarcely be imagined that at any future period Judaism, whether of the Rabbinic or the Rationalistic kind, would unfold into such a universal religion and Kingdom of God, as the Prophets describe. In such case the alternative must be, either to renounce the Old Testament hope, or to translate it into the platitudes of a vapid Deism. Or else if we cling to the spiritual hope set before us by the Prophets, then must we look for the wider fulfilment of all in that dispensation which is set before us in the New Testament, even though it may not yet appear as a concrete reality, but as that towards which we are tending, and which forms the promise and the goal of the present development.

From Judaism, which is either an anachronism, or a revolt against the inmost idea of the Old Testament, we turn again to the Old Testament, and in regard to it claim to have established these positions: that the Old Testament itself pointed to spiritual realities of which the external and the then present were confessedly and consciously the symbols. And, secondly, that in this it pointed for the fulfilment of all to the 'latter' or Messianic days.

Another, and a kindred argument, comes to us from what we have previously referred to as the absolute or dogmatic view of the prophetic character of the Old Testament, as taken by St. Paul. In this aspect he regards the whole Old Testament as prophetic of the New, 'the righteousness of God without the Law is manifested, being witnessed by the Law and the Prophets' (Rom 3:21). From what might be called the purely rational standpoint, it might be argued, and, indeed, was argued in the Epistle to the Hebrews, that the ceremonial and ritual Law could not have been intended as permanent, nor its provisions have been regarded as sufficient for the atonement of sin. But St. Paul takes even higher ground than this. As he explains it, the Law could not reach within, and, therefore, did not remove, rather did it call out, that sin on which it pronounced the sentence of death. Accordingly, the object of the Law could only have been to call forth longing after salvation. It follows, that the Law could only have been intended as a temporary institution and to be a schoolmaster unto Christ. But the grace to which it pointed was from the first, and long before the Law, conveyed unto the fathers in the promise which could not have been annulled by that which came after, and which was only intended for temporary purposes and to serve as preparation for the future. Such is the argument of the Epistle to the Romans, of a portion of the 2nd to the Corinthians, and especially of that to the Galatians, the main position being summed up in these words: 'Is the Law then against the promises of God? God forbid; for if there had been a law given which could have given life, verily righteousness should have been by the law. But the Scripture hath concluded all under sin, that the promise by faith of Jesus Christ might be given to them that believe. But before faith came, we were kept under the law, shut up unto the faith which should afterwards be revealed. Wherefore the law was our schoolmaster to bring us unto Christ, that we might be justified by faith. But after that faith is come, we are no longer under a schoolmaster. For ye are all the children of God by faith in Christ Jesus' (Gal 3:21-26).

II. The detailed answer which we have sought to give to the first question we had proposed to ourselves, in measure also implies that to the second great inquiry: whether or not what may be called the Christian view of the Messianic idea and ideal is true to the Old Testament. What we have still to say, may perhaps be best presented in the form of a rapid review of the historical development through which the fundamental religious ideas passed in Israel.

The ante-patriarchal age may be described as the stage of infancy. During its course the general foundations were laid, and that condition of things was established to which the provisions of the Divine Covenant would in the future apply. The grand facts which then emerged to view were these: Man's original God-relation, as God- created, and still God-like; law, sin, death, and the promise of final recovery. But sin was not only an outward transgression of an outward command. Springing from evil thoughts within, sin would progress to its furthest limits, and that which had begun in disobedience to the Divine Father would end in murder of the human brother. Yet by the side of sin appeared also from the first, and on the ground of the Divine promise, the *origines* of worship; Divine warning also, and Divine acknowledgment, as well as Divine judgment. Next emerged the grand outlines of the distinction between those who called upon God, and who followed the merely material, and with the increase of the latter, the corruption of the former, and thereupon a universal judgment, yet with preservation of the believing righteous. From this sprung a new order of society, still bearing, however, the Cain seal of judgment, which resulted in the confusion of tongues, and the severance of mankind into separate nations. By the side of these originesmight range, as their counterpart, the historic fulfilment in the New Testament, beginning with the Incarnation of the Christ, and ending with the outpouring of the Holy Ghost.

What here distinguishes and gives such unique grandeur to the Old Testament narrative, is that it professes to give not the physical, philosophical, literary, nor political, but the purely moral and spiritual history of our *origines*, at the same time laying the foundations of the most distant future. Even the hope of such a future is significant, since heathenism as such had no *Acherith hayyamim*. To the Old Testament the future is everything: the condition of its existence, the *rationale* of its aim, the impelling power of its development. It comes into our world, young, fresh, and tending towards a Divine manhood. And, dim as the primeval promise may be, it is the Gospel. For it tells us that man is not to be for ever oppressed by sin, but that sin is in the end to be utterly crushed, and that out of the moral contest between the Representative of humanity and that of sin, of which the condition is suffering to the former, victory and universal deliverance would come.

The next period was the patriarchal stage, or the age of childhood. It is characterised by a child's simplicity of faith, and absoluteness of obedience. The great future now appeared mainly through its contrast to the present. The lonely wanderer was to become the father of all nations; the homeless pilgrim, the heir of all the land, nay, of all the earth. This sets forth another feature in the development of the Kingdom of God: that of the contrast between the seen and the unseen, the present and the future, appearance and reality. And this also is most fully exhibited in the history of Christ and His Church. Moreover, on further consideration, it will be perceived that this must be the necessary outcome of the prevalence of evil, and of that contest of suffering which is the characteristic of the Kingdom of God, when introduced into the world. But at the same time the original promise began also to assume more definite form. These two things were now clearly marked in the further unfolding of the promise: that its starting-point was to be in the individual, 'in Thee'; and that its goal- point was 'all nations,' which were to be blessed in Him. But to mark this starting-point was to enter into covenant, as God did with Abraham, as father of the faithful. The sign of it was circumcision, which indicated that, while this covenant was to be transmitted from father to son, its transmission was not to be merely by hereditary descent, but that it also implied personal submission to God's ordinance, and voluntary taking up of the covenant obligations. From this point onwards alike the starting and the goal-point are marked with ever increasing clearness.

The period which we next reach, and which may be designated as that of Israel's youth, was the constituent period of the Covenant history. The promise which had found its location in an individual, and then in the patriarchal family, was now to enter the field of the world, being, so to speak, embodied in a nation, whose life, history, and predictions were to be identified with the Kingdom of God. The idea, which was symbolically and typically presented in the history and institutions of Israel was—as we have seen—that of the Servant of the Lord, in opposition to that service of sin which was unto death. This, with all of struggle and suffering, but also with the ultimate victory, attaching to it. The whole subsequent history of Israel was the outcome and development of that in the patriarchal and ante-patriarchal period. Alike the ceremonial, the ritual, and the moral Law, as well as the promises, have their explanation and starting-point in the idea of the Servant of the Lord. The same contrast between the seen and the unseen, the present and the future, which had emerged in patriarchal history, characterised that of Israel in their relation to the other nations of the world. And the varying events which befell Israel were determined by their faithful adherence, or the opposite, to the Divine idea which they were intended to embody.

Another stage, and we reach the period of the monarchy, which was that of Israel's manhood and maturity. To the idea of priesthood and of prophetism, which had during the previous period been expressed in outward form, that of royalty was now added, but still with the underlying principle of the King as 'the servant of the Lord.' The great promise connected first with the patriarchs as God's anointed, and then with Israel as a royal nation, now attached itself to Israel's king, and became, so to speak, individualised in David and his seed. The picture presented in the history of David is still that of the suffering servant of Jehovah. But, by the side of it, that of the reigning servant of God is also placed. And as we follow the outward history of Israel, its great spiritual lessons appear with increasing clearness. The fate of the people is more distinctly shown to be dependent upon faithfulness to the covenant; the prophets point out with growing clearness the spiritual character of the Law and its institutions; above all, the great hope of Israel in regard to the spiritual kingdom and the king over all nations, is presented with ever-increasing particularity and definiteness as being the goal of fulfilment.

The prophetic line which indicated the starting point was now well-nigh completely traced; that in regard to the goal-point yet remained to be more fully marked. This was done in the last stage of Israel's history before the great pause of expectancy—that of the exile. It was the period of Israel's decay; but, as always, the casting off of Israel was to become the bringing in of the Gentiles. Israel was now placed in closest contact with the great world-monarchies, and those new relations gave rise to another stage, in which the grand hope entered, so to speak, on its world-mission and history. Israel was to become a John the Baptist to the heathen world; a voice in the wilderness crying to them of the coming Christ. Once more did Providence and grace work together. The greatest miracle was accomplished without sign of outward miracle. The Jewish dispersion, the spread of Grecian culture, and the establishment of the rule of Imperial Rome, were the three great factors, acting independently yet harmoniously towards one great object. Then, after the pause of expectancy, when, as regarded literary preparation, Grecianism, and, as regarded political preparation, the rule of ancient Rome, had united all mankind, the Old Testament in its Greek rendering, and the New Testament in its old and new world-meaning, could go forth into the arena of the world. And so the days of César Augustus became those of the coming of Christ, and of the final fulfilment of prophecy.

Clearly as, from the standpoint of fulfilment, we perceive all this, we can readily understand how till after the coming of Christ it would appear only dimly even to those who believed. But there is one book in the Old Testament which, more than any other, must have kept alive these thoughts and hopes in Israel. It is the Book of Psalms. Let it be borne in mind that this was at the same time the liturgy, the hymnody, and in great measure the dogmatics of the Old Testament Church. Then realise that its first beginnings date from the primitive and, in some respects, barbaric times of Saul. And yet, in a sense, it has been, and still is to the Church and to individuals, what it had been to Israel during the changeful periods of their troubled history. Its grandeur of God-conception, its intense pathos of suffering, its sweet tenderness of feeling, its child-like simplicity of faith, and the absoluteness of its trustfulness, still best express our deepest religious experience. And, beyond these subjective characteristics, are the objective earnestness of its God-proclamation into the wide world, its view of the City of God as the ideal State, its expectancy of the fulfilment of all the promises, and of the beatification of the world. Above all does it set forth in clear lineaments the portraiture of the Messiah-King. Thither all the lines of thought run up. The wail of the righteous Sufferer leads up to the agonies of the Cross; the shout of the king to the gladness of the Resurrection-morning. Over and above the noise of many waves and the rebellion of heathen nations rises loud, clear, and for ever, the God-assertion of His kingdom upon earth, and the God-proclamation of the Christ into all the world. The answering voices of the Church and of ransomed nations, that stretch forth their hands towards Him, respond: 'He hath made us, and for Himself; we are His flock and the sheep of His pasture'; all nations shall worship Him—ride forth prosperously, and reign forever, 'David's greater Son!'

LECTURE 7: ON THE HISTORY OF THE RECENT CRITICISM OF THE PENTATEUCH, AND ON SOME DIFFICULTIES CONNECTED WITH ITS RESULTS.

But we hoped that it was He which should have redeemed Israel. Luke 24:1.

We have reached that stage in the inquiry proposed in these Lectures, when we might have been expected to gather together the individual predictions in the Old Testament, with the view of presenting in them a prophetic picture of the Messiah. But the exigencies of the time, and indeed of the present argument, impose on me another duty than once more to attempt what, in one or another part of it, has been so often and so well done by my predecessors. In truth, it must have been felt in the course of this argument, that those great questions regarding the date and component parts of the Pentateuch, or rather of the Mosaic legislation, and its relation to the Prophets, which are at present so largely engaging the attention alike of scholars and of general readers of the Old Testament, are of vital importance in our present inquiry.

Notwithstanding the interest awakened in the subject, it may be doubted whether the history and progress of this question are sufficiently known, intelligently to follow its discussion. Accordingly, I propose to give a brief sketch of its history, before considering the results arrived at—avoiding, so far as possible, merely technical details.

What may be called the traditional or Church-view of the Mosaic date and authorship of the Pentateuch (entertained not only by the Roman Catholic, the Greek, and by all the Protestant Churches, but also by the Synagogue) prevailed with but little and not influential exception or dissent till the second half of the last century. The first systematic attempt to trace different documents, in the first place, in the book of Genesis (inclusive of Exodus 1, and 2) was made by Jean Astruc (1684-1766), a French physician, the son of a Protestant pastor, and afterwards a convert to Roman Catholicism. His work, 'Conjectures sur les mêmoires originaux dont il paroit que Moyse s'est servi pour composer le livre de la Genèse,' appeared anonymously at Brussels in 1753, when the author was nearly seventy years old. Starting from the exclusive use in different parts of Genesis of the terms Elohim and Jehovah, he ascribed the portions in which either the one or the other designation occurred to separate documents, which he respectively marked by the letters A and B. Those parts in which there were repetitions of the same narrative, and the name of God did not occur, he ascribed to another document (comprising Genesis 7, 20, 23, 24) which he called C. Finally, those narratives which seemed to him foreign to the history of the Jewish people he ranged in yet a fourth column, D, which, however, really comprised various documents (eight in number), and which he marked by the letters E to M. Thus the book of Genesis was composed of eleven documents (A, B, C, and E to M).

The investigations of Astruc soon found a more congenial soil, and received fuller development, in Germany. Here (after a few not influential predecessors) we have specially to name J. G. Eichhorn, whose 'Introduction to the Old Testament' (in 5 vols.) appeared at Leipsic in 1780-1783, and rapidly passed through several editions. The work of Eichhorn lays down the main principles and lines which have since been followed in German criticism of the Pentateuch. After stating the various reasons for his distinction of the two documents which he traces in Genesis, Eichhorn endeavours to prove that each of them is again based upon a previous document, arriving at the final conclusion that the Jehovah-document had finished with the death of Joseph, the Elohim-document with the public appearance of Moses, and that these two documents may have been put together by someone before Moses (p. 94)—although not in their completeness, but often in fragmentary form, in accordance with the plan of the compiler, and with not unfrequent glosses and interpolations. These three elements (the Elohistic, the Jehovistic, and glosses) Eichhorn traces in detail through the Book of Genesis (pp. 107-110). The author next proceeds to vindicate the genuineness of Genesis and to defend its high antiquity (pp. 135-172) by arguments well worthy of consideration. Exodus, Leviticus, Numbers, and Deuteronomy, Eichhorn regards as older than all the other books in the Old Testament, proving this both from their language and contents (pp. 187-193), and from later history. These books cannot be post-Mosaic, notably they have neither been written nor compiled by Ezra, although these Mosaic documents have passed through many hands and received glosses and additions. But all this before the time of Ezra, since otherwise the Samaritans would not have accepted the Pentateuch (pp. 204-205). Other reasons confirmatory of this view are given. It is further shown that these books could not have been composed at the time of Josiah (2 Kings 22), nor yet between that of Joshua and David, but must have originated from documents by Moses and some of his contemporaries, although (as already remarked) not without later interpolations, alterations, and additions. The notices of these by Eichhorn mark the points of departure for later and more destructive criticism. The arguments by which all these views are supported in detail are very interesting and deserve the attention of modern critics. Emphatic is the testimony of Eichhorn in favour of what is now known as the 'Priest-Code,' and very detailed the examination of Numbers, which is followed (p. 322) by a refutation of objections and a demonstration of the authenticity of the Pentateuch which, it is declared 'not even the most boundless scepticism could regard as fictitious'—the analysis closing with the literary history of the subject.

I have been thus detailed in the analysis of Eichhorn's argument, as not only the beginning of modern criticism, but because it deserves more serious attention than it has of late received. To complete this part of our account, we add that K. D. Ilgen sought to show the existence of a second 'Elohist,' against which Eichhorn protested, and that the contention of Ilgen was further followed out by Hupfeld, and by Ewald in his 'History of Israel.' To mark yet another step—De Wette claimed a separate authorship for Deuteronomy; Bleek showed, that the Book of Joshua really formed part of what originally was a Hexateuch; while Ewald and others extended the proposed criticism to all parts of this work. The denial of the Mosaic authorship of the Pentateuch was, as might be expected, further developed by successive critics, whose special views it were out of place to describe in detail—the final result being briefly this, that the existence in Mosaic times of almost any part of the Pentateuch was denied.

2. From this review of the history, we pass to a sketch of the present state of the controversy. Generally speaking, the various views advocated may be grouped under three headings:—

A. The first of these bears the name of the 'Fragments-hypothesis.' According to its advocates, we can discover so many interpolations, glosses, and repetitions in the Pentateuch, that the work must be regarded as a collection of separate documents, thrown together without order or care by one or more redactors, with the view of preserving all the literary remains of the past. With this theory, which is now generally abandoned, the names of Vater, of our own countryman Dr. A. Geddes, and of A. Th. Hartmann, are connected.

B. According to the second theory, which is designated the 'Supplement-hypothesis,' the work of the Elohist was the oldest in the collection, and then supplemented by that of the Jehovist, Deuteronomy having been added at a later period. With this view the names of Tuch, Bleek, Lengerke, and formerly also of Delitzsch, are identified. This hypothesis also has been virtually abandoned by modern critics.

C. The third theory, known as the 'Document-hypothesis,' is that which at present is most generally received. According to its advocates the whole or most of the Pentateuch consists of various documents, which have been redacted by two or more persons—the original documents themselves being classed as the 'First Elohist,' the 'Second Elohist,' the 'Jehovist,' and the 'Deuteronomist.'

It will be noticed that, in its outline, this hypothesis is both general and vague. It leaves room for the widest differences in regard to the documents, all, or some, of which may, in our Pentateuch, appear in their original or in an altered form—'redacted' and 're-redacted'; or may have been incorporated in a previous work, and then re-incorporated in another. Moreover, the theory itself does not settle the question as to the date of the composition, emendation, redaction, or incorporation of the various documents—leaving all these points undetermined, or rather in dispute, between the various critics. And yet, manifestly the most important question is that about the date of the contents of the Pentateuch: whether, broadly speaking, it truly represents, as a whole, the Mosaic legislation, or else must be pronounced, in regard to any such pretension, as in the main a later forgery. On this point it seems, to me at least, difficult to understand how the alternative and question at issue can be misapprehended, although it is only fair to say that there are scholars, both on the Continent and among ourselves, who hold the late date and non-Mosaic composition of so large a part of the Pentateuch, and yet utterly refuse the sequences which seem to me the logical inference from these views. Lastly, it should be added that there are still scholars in Germany and, no doubt, in our own country, who defend the unity and Mosaic authorship, or at least redaction, of the whole Pentateuch. It must, however, be admitted that their opponents have justice on their side in charging them with want of consistency in their views.

We have said that there was room within the document-hypothesis for the most divergent views on many important questions. Till lately it might, indeed, have been boasted that, although many, and, as we should have thought, serious differences prevailed on matters of detail, there was substantial agreement on all leading points, such as the relative age of the chief documents composing the Pentateuch; the existence of certain sections which are older than any of the documents of which the Pentateuch is composed; and the combination of the other principal documents into one work which was completed before the time of the Deuteronomist. But this agreement no longer exists, so far as the most important, points are concerned, unless it were in this, that only small fragments in the Pentateuch are dated from Mosaic times, and that even these have been arranged and rearranged in strangest manner. But, by the side of this, there are on many questions absolute and irreconcilable differences between various critics. These concern: the number of documents in the Pentateuch, and the number of 'redactors,' who, in a certain sense, may be regarded as additional writers; the relation, order, and succession of these documents and of their redactions; and, lastly, the respective date or age of some of these documents and redactions. In evidence of the differences prevailing, the various views on the supposed age of the documents composing the Pentateuch have been arranged in *seven*, or, more strictly speaking, *ten* separate classes, to each of which the name, or names, of distinguished critics are attached. In other words, on the important question of the arrangement and relative age of some of the documents composing the Pentateuch, seven, or, more properly, ten, diverging views prevail; while in regard to some of them it may be said that opposite conclusions have been derived by equally competent scholars from the same *data*. From all this the impartial observer will derive at least this inference, that, where these conclusions so differ, they cannot rest on irrefragable grounds, but must to a large extent have been influenced by subjective considerations.

But all other differences pale into insignificance by the side of the fundamental divergence introduced by what is popularly known as the theory of Wellhausen. We call it by his name, not because it originated with him, but because of his lucid and popular advocacy, and his thorough application of it to all questions connected with Hebrew history and literature; and because its recent presentation, both in Germany and in this country, has identified the theory with his name. On the other hand, it is only fair to state, even at this stage, that many scholars whose names are identified with Hebrew learning have, on critical grounds, refused to accept his conclusions. The *genesis* of the theory is not without interest. Vatke and George contended, chiefly on philosophical grounds, that the Book of Deuteronomy, which was supposed to date from the time of Josiah, was older than the legislation of the other books in the Pentateuch. This position was next advocated on critical grounds by other writers. Thus E. Reuss (since 1833) laboured to establish that the notices in the historical books implied what was contradictory to the provisions of the so-called Mosaic law, and hence that the latter could not have existed at the time; that the prophets of the eighth and ninth centuries B.C. knew nothing of a Mosaic code; that Jeremiah was the first prophet who spoke of a written Law; and that his references were exclusively to Deuteronomy; and, lastly, that Deuteronomy (4:45 to ch. 28) was the oldest portion of the Pentateuch-legislation, being the very book which the priests in the time of Josiah pretended (*prétendaient*) to have found in the Temple; while Ezekiel (40-48) was anterior to the redaction of the ritual code and of the laws (the 'Priest-Code') which the Jewish priesthood afterwards introduced into the Pentateuch.

The most important argument on which this theory rests is the supposed ignoring of the Mosaic Law in the historical books, and the inconsistency of its provision with the state of matters then existing. Full reference will be made to this in the sequel. At present we only add, that this argument was capable of wide application, notably to all the religious institutions referred to in the Pentateuch: sacrifices, the priesthood, the central place of worship, and the great festivals. The theory just described broke with all the past. For, whereas Deuteronomy had formerly been regarded as being, on any supposition, the latest book in the Pentateuch, it was now declared to be the earliest, while the Levitical legislation in the Pentateuch was relegated to the times of the Exile. It follows that there must have been an immense difference between the times before, and those after, Josiah, when Deuteronomy first emerged. It would further follow that the earlier period of Jewish history was one of religious barbarism, confusion, and mostly worship of nature, when the voice of the prophets brooded over the moral chaos, and sought to introduce order in it. To other sequences of a theory so destructive, and which, even at this stage, I venture to designate as utterly incompatible with the facts of the case, reference will be made in the sequel.

The theory of Reuss was at first coldly received, and only gained adherents when developed by his pupils. One of them, K. H. Graf (1869), maintained that the 'original document' [the old historical work of the Elohist] had been successively recast by the Jehovist and the Deuteronomist, while the code of the middle books in the Pentateuch was certainly post-exilian. This view he afterwards modified, retracting what he had said about the 'original document' (the *Grundschrift*), which, in direct contradiction to his former contention, he now declared to have been post-exilian, and, indeed, to form the latest part of the Pentateuch. Graf was followed in much the same direction by Kayser.

We have now, lastly, to sketch the system of Wellhausen, which may most conveniently be studied in his 'History of Israel,' of which only the first volume has as yet appeared; and in the article 'Israel' in the 'Encyclopædia Britannica,' where it is presented with much greater moderation of language and form than in the 'History.' To avoid the possibility of personal bias in our account of Wellhausen's views, we propose, so far as possible, to follow the sketch of Professor Strack, verifying it by constant reference to Wellhausen's writings.

At the outset we are warned not to look in the Pentateuch for anything really Mosaic. Even the Decalogue is not Mosaic; in truth, the song of Deborah, in Judges 5, may be the oldest historical monument in the Old Testament. It is indeed true that the foundation-document which Wellhausen calls the 'Priest-Code,' assumes the guise of the Mosaic age, seeking, so far as possible, to mask itself (p. 9), and that it seriously pretends to be the legislation of the wilderness, assuming an archaic appearance so as to hide the real date of its composition (p. 10). But the true critic has no difficulty in seeing through this disguise. The 'book of the Covenant' (Exo 20; 21:1-23:19) is 'Jahvistic.' The Jehovist (JE)—who must not be confounded with the Jahvist (J)—dates from the golden age of kings and prophets, before the Assyrian conquest of Israel or Judah. The substance of the two works, J and E, of which that of the Jehovist is composed, dates from before the prophets, but each of them has been repeatedly re-edited before the work appeared in the form of JE, or the Jehovist. We are bidden to remark that J presents more of the real original state of things, and shows less trace of prophetic influence than E (p. 371). The document J breaks off suddenly at the blessing of Balaam, although there may be traces of the work in Numbers 25:1-5, and Deuteronomy 34. But when we speak of JE (the Jehovist work), we must remember that, as already stated, the documents do not appear in their original form, but have been edited and re-edited with additions; in fact, they are J3E3. Deuteronomy, or rather the original D, appeared shortly before the eighteenth year of Josiah, when it only contained chapters 12-26i. Then, 'not before the exile,' D underwent a twofold redaction, of which the first prefaced D by Deuteronomy 1-4, and tacked to it chapter 27, while the next redaction added at the beginning chapters 5-11, and at the end chapters 28-30. The combination of these two editions and the insertion of the work into JE was probably made at the same time and by the same Deuteronomist as the combination of J and E into JE (p. 370).

But this is not nearly all. The section Leviticus 17-26, is said to represent what originally was a separate and distinct code of laws, the writer of which made manifold use of previous documents. It dates from the close of, or after the Exile, and is more cognate to Ezekiel than to the 'Priest-Code,' into which, after due redaction, it was inserted. In fact, the redaction was made by the same hand as the Priest-Code (pp. 388, 391, 396). Putting aside JE and D, we have still to consider the 'Priest-Code' itself, which embraces the legislation of the middle books of the Pentateuch. It is posterior to Ezekiel (his supposed legislation: Ezekiel 40-48), and must be viewed, not as the product of one person, but 'as a conglomerate, as it were, the outcome of a whole school.' In its language and contents, as well as by direct references, it is interwoven with an historical document Q (the book of the four—*quatour*—covenants), to which originally the following had belonged: Exodus chapters 25-29; Leviticus chapter 9; 10:1-5,12-15; chapter 16; Numbers 1:1-16; 1:48-3:9; 3:15-10:28; chapter 16 in part; chapters 17; 18; 25:6-19; chapters 26; 27; 32 in part; 33:50-chapter 36: The whole Pentateuch—unknown as such till then—was finally published by Ezra in or about the year 444 (Neh 8:1-10:40), although many minor amendments and considerable additions may have been made at a later date. It should, however, be added, that other critics of that school, such as Reuss, Graf, Kayser, hold that only the work P, or even its main part, was published by Ezra, the rest at a later period. But, as Strack rightly objects: in that case it seems impossible to explain how D, which is supposed, in many points, to contradict P, could have remained 'latent' for a considerable period after the Exile; and still more, to understand how the Samaritans had accepted the Pentateuch at a period not later than Nehemiah. These objections might evidently be applied and extended to many other points in the system.

3. Probably the first impressions derived from the analysis of the system of Wellhausen will be that of its extreme elaborateness and intricacy. Indeed, we fear that with all our care we have failed to make it quite intelligible in its details—the main fact only standing out, that the great body of Mosaic legislation, such as we have been wont to regard it, is declared to be post-exilian. The theory reflects great credit on the industry, and especially the ingenuity of its author; but common sense instinctively rejects it as incredible. A work so elaborately tesselated, into which so many different documents, redacted and re-redacted, have been so cunningly inserted, that one piece breaks off in the middle of a chapter, or even of a verse, to which a piece from a different document is joined, and so on, till the mind becomes bewildered amidst documents and redactions: such a piece of literary mosaic has never been done, so far as we know, and we refuse to believe that it could have been done. Whatever objections may be raised against what is called the 'traditional' view, whatever difficulties may attach to the conciliation of the supposed differences between notices in the historical books and the enactments of the Mosaic code, the theory of Wellhausen is not the thread to lead us out of, rather that to lead us into, the labyrinth. Viewed quite from the outside, it only adds to our difficulties. Indeed, although the distinction between the two great documents known as those of the Elohist and the Jahvist does not depend merely on the distinctive use of the designations Elohim and Jehovah—being supported by other and weighty considerations—it makes us almost doubt what weight should be attached to this fundamental distinction. We put aside this, that the different use of the two Names has been explained as expressing a difference of meaning, each presenting a special relation of God to man—because, to our thinking, this explanation does not fully meet the case. But, supposing the workmanship of the composition and redaction of the Pentateuch to have been so manifold and so cunning as Wellhausen's theory implies—indeed, in almost any case of multiple composition, unless of the most clumsy kind—it seems almost impossible to believe that one of the later writers or redactors, into whose hands E and J had come, might not sometimes have interchanged, for reasons of his own, the two designations; or else himself have used them promiscuously, as he leaned towards one or the other document, or the exigencies of the narrative pointed to the use of either one or the other. Hence it seems extremely difficult entirely to rely on the great test, with which the absolute separation of documents originally started.

And more than this requires to be taken into account. Ewald had long ago remarked, that the last writer or redactor of the Pentateuch could not have thought that it contained any mere repetitions or contradictory accounts of the same facts. This most reasonable canon gains immensely in application as we recall, on Wellhausen's theory, the elaborateness of workmanship, the immense skill displayed in it, and the multiplicity of composition and redaction in the Pentateuch. Only a very clumsy *litterateur* would have left so many contradictions and inconsistencies unnoticed, if indeed they existed. And it seems utterly inconceivable—nothing short of impossible—that, in a work which had passed through so many hands, all of them admittedly able, and which, on Wellhausen's supposition, was, at least in great part, designed—shall we not say, falsified—for a definite purpose, so much should have been left, which was transparently inconsistent with, and opposed to, the purpose in view. And when we go a step further, and recall that the historical books which contain the notices that are said to be in direct contradiction to the Pentateuch legislation, were at least manipulated by those to whom we owe the Pentateuch, it seems still more impossible to believe that these notices could have been considered, or, indeed, could have been, quite inconsistent with the arrangements introduced by the Pentateuch. These writers must have seen some mode of conciliating the seeming discrepancies, or else—and this seems not too bold a statement, on Wellhausen's theory—they would have unhesitatingly removed them.

These considerations cannot, we feel assured, be overlooked when thinking of such a theory as that under review. There are others which must weigh with every serious mind and every critical student. I have previously expressed, with all gravity, my personal feeling that, if the theory in question, with all that it implies, were true, it would seem logically impossible to maintain the claims of Christ as the Old Testament Messiah of Moses and the Prophets, and the Son of David. This is not said with the view of foreclosing inquiry, or influencing its results. On the contrary, I would insist, as strongly as our opponents, that every question should be examined on its own merits, irrespective of preconceived opinions or possible consequences. In fact, I claim for our side equal, if not greater, independence, since those acquainted with the controversy will scarcely deny that much of the reasoning on the other side has been prompted by, and grounded, on *à priori* conclusions about the possibility of the miraculous, prophetism, the supposed relation between God and Israel, and similar matters. But, while not wishing to prejudice inquiry by the consideration of the consequences involved, these are sufficiently grave to render extreme care and caution imperative. When we read, as the outcome of the theory we are combating, that 'what has gained for the history of Israel pre-eminently the designation of sacred is mostly due to what a later period has painted over the original picture,' we feel that the whole basis of our religion is being seriously shaken. For, if the largest portions of the Old Testament are myths, legends, and forgeries, it would be difficult to retain any belief in the trustworthiness of the rest. And, in truth, this school of criticism has spoken with sufficient plainness on the subject. We are assured that we do not owe to Moses any of the laws or historical notices in the Pentateuch; nor yet, in all probability, to David any of the Psalms, nor to Solomon any of the Proverbs. The historical books are often recast and retouched in the spirit of the later Law, and indeed unreliable. And here I must add that the manipulations of passages in the historical (and in the prophetical) books which appear inconsistent with the new theory of the date and authorship of the Pentateuch, are sometimes, to say the least, peculiar. It is easy to get rid of such passages by declaring them interpolations or corrupted texts, but solid reasons of an absolute character must be adduced for the assertion, and not merely such *à priori* assertions as that they are inconsistent with the proposed Pentateuch theory. It were easy in this manner to cut off, so to speak, the head of every opponent so soon as he emerges; but the justice of the procedure has in each case to be vindicated before the tribunal of criticism. And, although the impression made by the accentuation of difficulties and seeming inconsistencies, which are all removed by the new theory, may be that of a brilliant discovery, we distrust it from its inception, not only for the reasons already adduced, and for those which will be stated in the sequel, but for its very brilliancy, and the ease with which everything may be fitted into its Procrustes-bed.

Similar violence is done to much in the prophetic writings and the Psalms by the new school of criticism. More especially is this the case in regard to Ezekiel. A careful investigation, the results of which have not yet been met by the school of Wellhausen, has established that Ezekiel reflects back upon the Pentateuch, and not the reverse. Nor can we even at this stage for a moment hesitate not only to dissent from the theory of Wellhausen with regard to the post-exilian date of the legislation in the Priest-Code, but also to express our conviction that Deuteronomy could not have been composed so late as about the time of its recovery in the reign of

King Josiah. To begin with, the statement that the account of its finding (2 Kings 22:8) means that it had not previously existed, but been just written, is merely an a priori gloss upon the text—a *suggestio mali*, for which the text itself affords no warrant. It might seem almost as reasonable to deny the truth of the whole narrative as that of the part which speaks of the finding of the Law. Moreover, this view of 2 Kings 22:8 is not only inconsistent with what is expressly characterised in verse13 as the sins of their fathers in not formerly obeying 'the words of this book,' but the whole account about the finding of the Book of the Law presupposes a general knowledge and belief in the existence of such a code, which it would be most unreasonable to assume could have been palmed off by Hezekiah as Mosaic, or received by the people as such, if no one had ever heard of the existence of a written Mosaic legislation. Lastly, there are many provisions in the so-called Priest-Code inconsistent with the idea of its post-exilian origin, just as there are notices in Deuteronomy incompatible with the theory of its composition in the time of Josiah. But to these points we shall have to refer at greater length in the sequel.

Let it not be said that the line of argument which we have hitherto followed proceeds, in great measure, upon *à priori* considerations, which we have contended our opponents must not bring to that criticism of the facts on which their theory rests. For there is great difference between establishing an hypothesis on *à priori* considerations which determine our criticism of facts, and proving by *à priori* considerations that such an hypothesis is not only highly improbable but morally impossible. The latter method is lawful; not so the former. If a document, such as a will, were propounded in a court of law, it would not do to argue that its provisions were spurious—introduced by a later falsifier—because they seemed to the advocate incredible, such as that such a person could not have made certain charitable bequests; or, to apply it in the present argument, that miracles, prophetism, direct revelation, and the like, are contrary to our ideas. In both cases direct evidence would be required. And if such direct evidence were offered from the incompatibility of these provisions with certain supposed indications in the document, it would not do to brand as spurious and falsified other indications in the same document which are in accordance with the provisions invalidated, on the ground that they accord with provisions which, on the hypothesis of the advocate, are spurious. This were vicious reasoning in a circle, and evidence on which a jury would not pronounce against a document. On the other hand, it would be quite lawful for the advocate who defended the document to show, that the opposition to it proceeded on a theory and on grounds intrinsically so improbable and so inconsistent as to involve moral impossibility.

But the issues of this controversy are so important that I must emphasise what, from fear of seeming to prejudge the question, may have been too lightly touched. There are, no doubt, many, scholars and general readers, who would earnestly refuse to attach to the theory in question the absolutely destructive sequences which seem to me logically involved in it. But quite irrespective of this, that Christ and the Apostles, in appealing as so often they did to Moses and the Prophets, must, on the theory in question, have been in such grave and fundamental error as cannot be explained on the ground of popular modes of speaking, and seems incompatible with the manner in which the New Testament would have us think of them—there are other and most weighty considerations. If there really is no Mosaic legislation; if the largest, the central, and most important part of what professes to be such, was the invention of the priesthood about the time of Ezra, foisted upon Moses for a specific purpose; if there was not a 'Tabernacle,' in our sense of it, with its specific institutions, nor a central place of worship, nor the great festivals, nor a real Aaronic priesthood; and if the so-called historic books have been coloured and elaborated deuteronomistically, or in that spirit; if they are full of spurious passages and falsifications—as, for example, in the history of Solomon; and if every now and then 'a prophet is put in' (*einqelegt wird*) who expresses himself in the spirit of Deuteronomy and in the language of Jeremiah and Ezekiel; if the 'anonymous prophets of 1 Kings 20 have all been afterwards inserted for the purpose of a detailed *vaticinium ex eventu* [prophesy after the event], because Israelitish history is never complete without this kind of garnish'; if, in short, what has gained for the history of Israel pre-eminently the designation of sacred is mostly due to what a later period 'has painted over the original picture': then, there is in plain language only one word to designate all this. That word is *fraud*. Then, also, on the supposition that, what we had regarded as the sacred source of the most sacred events, was in reality the outcome of fraud, must the Gospel narratives and the preaching of Christ lose their historical basis, and rest in large measure on deception and delusion. For Holy Scripture, as the communication of God to man by man, does indeed contain a distinctively human element, but that element cannot have been one of human imposture.

In thus arguing we are not setting up any extravagant theory of Inspiration, nor are we ignoring either the repeated redactions which the Old Testament has undergone, nor yet the fact that scarcely any religious documents of that period can be expected to have come down to us without bearing the marks of redaction. We are simply proceeding on a broad line of demarcation, visible to all men: that between falsehood and truth. Nor is it to the point to argue that pseudonymic literature was so common in antiquity. Even were this the case in regard to what we call the 'canonical' writings, there is clearly a great difference between the assumption of a spurious name and the assertion of spurious facts, such as that to have been given or ordered of God by Moses, which was the invention of the priesthood in the time of Ezra. 'Every literary untruth,' writes one of the distinguished modern historians, 'brought forward for the purpose of deception, was treated in the first centuries of the Church, by all those Fathers whose writings have come down to us, as an abominable sin.' The Apocrypha and the so-called Pseudepigraphic Writings form no part of the Canon, and therefore cannot be quoted as instances in point. Such books in the Old Testament as we sometimes, though erroneously, associate with certain names, will, on examination, be found not strictly to claim such precise authorship. Besides, as already stated, the Old Testament Canon has undergone repeated investigation and discussion. And we know sufficient of the discussions in those early Jewish assemblies which fixed the Old Testament Canon, to assure us, that a book would not have been inserted which was known to be false in its title—still less, one that was fraudulent in its object. And these assemblies—at least the earlier of them—sat close on, if not in the very time, that the fraud is supposed to have been published! Or, to go back a step, and to Old Testament times, how can we reconcile the introduction of such a fraud as the 'invention' of the Book of Deuteronomy in the time of Josiah with the denunciations of his contemporary Jeremiah, who inveighs in such stern language against the Prophets that prophesied lies in God's Name, when He had not sent them, neither had commanded them, nor spoken unto them, but they prophesied a false vision, a thing of nought, the deceit of their own hearts, and so caused the people to err? (Jer 14:14; 23:16, 31, 32)

We have yet another consideration to urge before closing this preliminary part of our inquiry. If we were to accept the views of the school of criticism to which we have referred, much more than what has already been stated would seem logically to follow. When we have relegated the so-called Levitical legislation to the time of Ezra, and resolved all that is really distinctive in the Biblical history of Israel into legends and myths, a blank remains which must be filled up. What was the history of Israel, and what their religious institutions? Take away all the sacred element, and Israel appears as only a horde of barbarians and of slaves, lately emancipated, and not distinguishable from the Canaanites around. In such case their religion was really the old indigenous nature-worship (as they call it 'naturwüchsig'), in which Jahveh is really Moloch and Baal; sacrifices, often those of human beings; and where all the abominations of the races in Palestine have their place. In drawing such sequences we are not making inferences of our own. We do not, indeed, impute them to Wellhausen, although he designates the Ark as 'an idol'; but the sequences mentioned have been made; they are stated in the most pronounced manner; and they have, in consequence of the new theory, become present and pressing questions, which are being discussed as 'the chief problems of ancient Israelitic religious history.' Moreover, they really are the logical sequences of the new treatment of Jewish history, although they had been propounded before that theory was broached. Such statements as those of Kuenen, that the religion of Israel was only one of the old religions—neither more nor less; and that Judaism and Christianity belong, indeed, to the principal religions, but that between them and all others there is not any specific difference—point out the direction which has been followed. And such titles of books as 'The Fire and Blood Service of the Ancient Hebrews, the Ancestral, Legal, and Orthodox Worship of the Nation' (Daumer, 1842), 'The Human Sacrifices of the Ancient Hebrews' (Ghillany, 1842), 'Mythology and Revelation' (Noack, 1853), 'Mythology Among the Hebrews' (Goldziher, 1876)—or the attempt to show that the original sanctuary of Mecca was founded by emigrants from the tribe of Simeon in the time of David, and that the religion there enacted was that of Abraham (Docy, 1864)—point out the manner in which this direction has been followed.

I have mentioned the titles of these books, of which many are not recent, because they most readily present to the general reader the character of the views which, as before stated, are undoubtedly at present among the burning questions in connection with the new theory of the history and religion of ancient Israel. It is distinctly asserted, that 'the worship of Moloch was that of Abraham, Moses, Samuel, and David,' and that 'the idolatry inveighed against was the primeval national religion of Israel.'

One of the latest writers of the Wellhausen school, Stade, seems even to doubt (although in this against Wellhausen), whether there had ever been any Hebrew clan in Egypt, while Jahveh is represented as a national deity by the side of other gods, and much in the worship and religious life of the ancient Hebrews as kindred to that in the cognate nations. I have stated the case briefly, because, without affectation, it is painful to state it at all. The curious reader must be referred to the works of Kuenen, Stade, and others, to learn how such views are carried out, by different writers to different lengths, and by what strange Scriptural references they are supported.

But to what extremes a perverted ingenuity may lead a critic, will appear from the following instance. There is not a name among modern scholars which deservedly stands higher, as regards Semitic learning and literature, than that of Paul de Lagarde. Yet this is one of the conclusions propounded, and these are the grounds on which it has been arrived at, by perhaps the greatest living Semitic scholar. Deriving the term *Levite* from the verb *lavah*, to cleave to another, to accompany him, Lagarde refers to Isaiah 14:1, and 56:3, in both of which this verb (rendered in the A. V. 'joined to') is connected with 'strangers.' From this he infers that the Levites were those who, according to Exodus 12:38 (Num 11:4?), had 'joined' themselves to Israel on their exodus from Egypt—the 'mixed multitude,' which Lagarde regards as Egyptians. The latter notice he accepts as historical, on the ground that otherwise the Jews, the most vainglorious of men and conceited of nations, would not have admitted that theirs was not pure 'blue blood.' On the other hand, he pronounces the account in Exodus 2:1-10, which gives the Israelitish genealogy of Moses, as not worthy of more serious notice than the fable of the Persians that Alexander the Great was the son of Darius. And Lagarde further argues that, regarding Moses not as an Israelite, but as an Egyptian, we can understand how he sought and found support from the Levites, his Egyptian compatriots [why not, if they were his Israelitish tribesmen?]; how the Levites, as the better educated Egyptians, could undertake the intellectual training of the Israelites [where is this stated?]; why the Levites did not appear in the promised land as a real tribe [as if no other reasons had been given for their scattering]; while, lastly, it also explained the manner in which the exodus was referred to in Egyptian documents. And as in ancient times the Ark of the Covenant had marched before the Israelites, those who 'accompanied' it were the Levites.

I have reproduced in detail an hypothesis so manifestly untenable, and supported by such flimsy reasoning, because the great name of Lagarde attaches to it, and because it affords a convenient example, how sweeping, and yet how unsatisfactory, in many instances, is that criticism which is destructive of the history and sacred legislation of the Old Testament. As an almost parallel instance of critical violence we might refer to Wellhausen's treatment of the history of Solomon in 1 Kings 11:1-13. But in view of the issue before us in this great controversy, supported by such arguments, a certain degree of warmth of language may be excused on the part of those who hold and cherish the truth of the Old Testament. Much more will have to be done, before they shall have shaken from their hinges those 'everlasting doors' by which Christ the King of Glory has entered in. As we think of the blessings of life with which His coming has enriched the barrenness of our earth, or of the spring of hope with which it has gladdened the winter of our hearts, we tremble as we realise what the hand of science, falsely so called, might have taken from us. For if, indeed, they were words, not of Divine truth, but of delusion or of deceit, when, on that Sabbath evening walk to Emmaus, 'beginning at Moses and all the prophets, He expounded unto them in all the Scriptures the things concerning Himself,' then may we fold up within our hearts that pang of bitterest disappointment: 'But we trusted that it had been He which should have redeemed Israel.' But, thank God, it is not so. As with a thousand chimes from heaven, the voices of the Law and Prophets ring it out into all the world on this Advent Sunday: Ring out the old, Ring in the new—as on a thousand altars we worship the mystery of the Incarnation, and ten thousand hearts are filled with the joyous assurance that their sins are forgiven. For Christ has come: the reality of all types, the fulfilment of all promises, the Son of David, the Saviour of the world. 'For unto us a Child is born, unto us a Son is given, and the government shall be upon His shoulder; and His name shall be called Wonderful, Counsellor, the Mighty God, the Everlasting Father, the Prince of Peace!'

LECTURE 8: SOME FURTHER CONSIDERATIONS REGARDING THE COMPOSITION AND DATE OF THE PENTATEUCH.

But neither so did their witness agree together. Mark 14:59.

It will, I trust, not be deemed an entirely unwarrantable application of these words, when we recall them in connection with the great controversy about the date and authorship of the Mosaic legislation. For if the witness of critics on the other side could be established, no reasonable appeal for the Messiahship of Jesus could be made to Divine prophecy, in a book where even human history was so mendacious, and where the pretensions as to the origin of so-called Divine institutions and laws were so fraudulent. At most—and we hesitate as we express it—we would have to apologise for Jesus and His Apostles as occupying a lower critical standpoint. But it would seem a strange postulate to regard Him as the Christ, the Son of God, or His Apostles as divinely inspired.

And yet this inference would be carried too far, if it were supposed necessarily to imply what may be called the old traditional standpoint, either as regards inspiration or the authorship and composition of the Pentateuch, with which alone we are here concerned. The traditional view errs by excess perhaps as much, though not with such fatal consequences, as the new by deficiency. As regards the mode of Divine communication in the Holy Scriptures, or, to narrow it: objectively, revelation; subjectively, inspiration—the human element must be taken as fully into account as the Divine. And specifically, in reference to the Pentateuch—or rather, the Hexateuch—it is not requisite, nor in any way implied, that it represents one homogeneous work. As the history of our Lord is derived from four different Gospel-sources, which, in turn, look back upon the universally accredited tradition of the Church and on special sources of information, and as the Gospels view the same Divine Life from different standpoints, and mutually supplement each other—so may the Pentateuch consist of several original documents or sources, welded together by one or more redactors. And there may even be emendations and additions—glosses, if you like to call them so —by redactors, revisers, or final editors. This is simply the historical aspect of the Book as it presently exists, and with which criticism has to busy itself. It concerns the human element in it, but is in no wise inconsistent with, nor yet invalidates, the higher and Divine element in revelation and inspiration. But what we have to insist upon is the general truthfulness and reliableness of the Book, alike as regards its history and legislation: that it is, what it professes, an authentic record of the history of Israel, and a trustworthy account of what was really the Mosaic legislation. This is to draw a sufficiently broad line of demarcation, and to take up a sufficiently intelligible position, with which, I believe, all the facts of the case will be found to accord.

In order better to understand this, it is necessary to transport ourselves, more fully than is generally done, not only into Mosaic times, but into those which followed the occupation of Canaan by the Israelites. Let us first state the general position taken up by us in this argument. It is held, that the legislation of the Pentateuch is of Mosaic authorship and of Divine authority; that the settlement of Israel in the land was followed by a period of religious decay and decadence, which called for the interposition of the Prophets, who pointed back to the Law, and explained and applied its deeper spiritual meaning; that this decadence continued, with brief interruptions, throughout the period of the Kings, thus further calling for the continued activity of the Prophets, and making it intelligible how, in the utter breakdown of the Law with its provisions, they should have pointed forward to another Law to be written in the heart; and that, in the decadence of Israel and its conformity to heathenism, instead of the transformation of heathenism into a kingdom of God, through the chosen race, the Prophets, should have set before them the coming of the Messiah and the establishment of God's kingdom upon earth as the great hope of Israel and of the world.

But probably this is to state the case in too general terms. We are apt, unconsciously to ourselves, to transport our modern and Western ideas into the premises from which our conclusions as to the earlier history of Israel are drawn. Let us remember that the Israelites, at the time of their entrance into Canaan, were the wilderness- generation, a purely nomadic race, with all of intellectual disadvantage—indeed, infancy—which this implies. During their years of wandering they had not been brought into fructifying contact with any of the cultured nations of antiquity. What they had inherited from their fathers was, morally, mostly of the evil gotten in Egypt. The intellectual culture derived from them may, indeed, have become more generally spread in that second generation, to which the results of that culture, and the general ideas awakened by it, would come as an heirloom. But, from the nomadic habits of the people and the general circumstances of the sojourn in the wilderness, this inherited culture would decrease in intensity, even if it increased in extent. And this decline, once begun, would be furthered, rather than hindered, by the close contiguity of the mass of the people at their halting-places, by the briefness of their sojourn at each of them, and by all the circumstances attending an Eastern progress from one station to another. Morally viewed, we have to deal with a people semi-barbarous, and, therefore, prone to all superstition and excess, whose newly re-awakened religion had been tainted by Egyptian idolatry, and deteriorated by the educational influence of the evil example of their fathers and mothers. We have before us an Eastern nation, sensuous and sensual by nature, lately emancipated, with declining culture, and which, as we have abundant evidence, is ready at the first temptation to lapse into gross idolatry, and to pass into the most unbridled licentiousness, which, in turn, formed part of that idolatry which was essentially a nature-worship. Licentious nature-worship was—alike physically, mentally, and morally—the natural religion of the races inhabiting those lands.

When we realise these various elements, we feel what absolutely Divine truth and power must have been about the religion of the Pentateuch—the direct Divine element of Revelation in it—to make of such a people and in such circumstances what, after all, Israel was; still more, what Israel might have become, and what, even in its miserable failure, it has become to mankind at large. The evidential force here is analogous to that from the influence of the Gospel on the Jewish and heathen world,—perhaps even stronger. And the production of such moral effects seems necessarily to imply direct Divine guidance, such as appears in what are called the miraculous portions of Israel's earlier history. Here also the Divine wisdom—if, consistently with reverence, the expression may be employed—appears in the special religious institutions of Israel. Let it be remembered that the special legislative, religious (and even political) institutions of the Pentateuch bear reference to what was then future, rather than to what was then present—to the settled, rather than the migratory, state of the people. Many—I had almost said, most—of these institutions had no place in the wilderness. This holds specially true in regard to what constitutes the central and really all-determining institution of the Mosaic religious legislation: sacrificial worship. On its existence depend in great measure the appointment of one exclusive central place of worship, the institutions connected with the priesthood, as well as those about the great annual festivals. Take away sacrifices, and most of the distinctive peculiarities attaching to these three institutions cease; suspend them even partially, and the other three great institutions will also be partially suspended, or require extraneous supplementation, such as we find it in the historical books. Indeed, the religious institutions of the Pentateuch might be likened to the wood laid in order on the altar, and the actual observance of the Pentateuch sacrifices as the fire—significantly sent from heaven at the consecration of the Temple—which is to set the whole in flame.

But there is not any point which, to my mind, is better established, than that sacrifices were not offered in connection with the Tabernacle during the pilgrimage in the wilderness. The only sacrifices mentioned in connection with the Tabernacle are those brought at its consecration and at that of the priesthood, and the offering of incense. It requires little consideration to understand that it could not have been otherwise. Hence the name, which the Tabernacle bears, is not 'Tabernacle of sacrifices,' although these were really to form the central part of its worship; but its common designation is 'Tabernacle of Meeting' (*Ohel Moed*) —that is, between God and Israel, the place where God would meet with His people, as expressly stated in Exodus 25:22; 29:42, 43; 30:6, 36; Numbers 7:89; 17:4. To this designation the other 'Tabernacle of Witness,' or 'Testimony' (as in Num 9:15; 17:8; 18:2) is subsidiary, although parallel. It follows that, during the wilderness period, the sacrificial worship—although existing initially (in the consecration services), and institutionally (in the altar of the Tabernacle and throughout the legislation), and also symbolically and by anticipation present (in the burnt incense)—would not stand out before the people as a real, *de facto*, service; and that, in the absence of it, this bond, which held together all the other fundamental institutions, would likewise be loosened. For without such sacrifices the idea of one exclusive sanctuary could scarcely have been truly carried out (indeed, it would have no present real meaning), nor yet that of one priesthood, nor yet that of great central festivals. Thus we have, even at this stage of our inquiry, to accentuate, in most emphatic language, that, when the Israelites took possession of the land, they were unaccustomed to a sacrificial worship in the great central sanctuary. They did not bring this great idea with them into the land, as an actual reality—and this, as we remember, must have involved the loosening of all the ideas connected with the other great institutions, organically connected with sacrifices. Even the manner in which this central sanctuary was spoken of, might further contribute to loosen the hold which the idea itself might have had upon the people from its Divine institution, and from the actual existence among them of the Tabernacle, constructed, consecrated, and divinely honoured as it was. Such general references as: 'in all places where I record My Name, I will come unto Thee'; and, 'the place which the Lord your God shall choose,' so frequent in Deuteronomy, might, especially in the circumstances after the conquest of Canaan, rather tend to decentralise the idea of the Sanctuary. For, while directing that sacrifice should be offered only in the place which God had selected, it was not stated that this would to all time be one and the same place.

As we recall that this non-observance of sacrifices in the regular services of the Tabernacle during the wilderness period was, unquestionably, a necessity imposed by the circumstances, we feel the more deeply the wisdom by which, notwithstanding the present impossibility of realisation, the idea of sacrificial worship in the sanctuary was fixed in the popular mind as the central fact in their religious institutions. And this, together with what has already been stated about the condition of the new generation in Israel which entered into Canaan, will show the need of a repetition of the Law in Deuteronomy—but now, with modifications and special adaptation to the new circumstances of territorial settlement. And realising the whole condition of things on the entrance into Canaan, we see the absolute value of the two great sacraments of the Old Testament: circumcision and the Sabbath (with their kindred domestic institutions of tithing, as God-consecration of property, the sabbatic year, &c.). These fixed the permanent landmarks of Israel in the period of unsettledness and confusion which followed—to some extent, necessarily—after the death of Moses.

What has been stated in regard to the intellectual and moral condition of the people, and the nonexistence of regular sacrificial worship in the Tabernacle, must now be applied to the actual state of things in the period following. In general we must repeat, that the religious institutions of Israel were adapted not to what Israel then was, but rather to what Israel was intended to become. If Israel had developed in the right direction, if it had come up to its institutions, then—but only then—would these institutions have been possible, and have become a practical reality. But it will not be denied that, so far from rising to them, the next period witnessed a great and growing religious decline among the people.

It is not difficult to transport ourselves into the circumstances of the time. The first necessity of Israel was to fight, so to speak, for existence. They had to obtain possession of the land; and they could only achieve this by continual warfare. For they were not confronted by merely one, nor even by a few hostile nations. The land was divided among a large number of independent clans, each under its own king. They might, at least in part, combine against Israel, but for all practical purposes they were separate nations. A victory might be decisive in one locality; but an advance of only a few miles would bring Israel into new territory where the whole contest had once more to be gone through. Accordingly, this period must have been one of constant preoccupation, constant movement, and constant contact with new elements. And the absolute removal of the heathen elements from the land would have been most difficult—well nigh impossible, since they would spring up behind the Israelites on leaving a district, and before them as they advanced into another territory. It was certainly not a period when new institutions, which had never before been actually carried into practice, could be established. And to this must be added the gradual spiritual decline of the people, and the influence upon them of the surroundings of that heathenism, towards which, as we have seen, they were so predisposed—intellectually, sensuously, and sensually. And here we can in some measure realise the religious importance and the necessity of such a religious ceremony in the centre of the land as the renewal of the covenant on Ebal and Gerizim (Josh 8:30-35).

We have seen that the circumstance that the great religious institutions of Israel were not immediately introduced in practice, must have tended to weaken their hold upon the people, to whom they were as yet rather a theory than a reality. Indeed, it would render their future establishment, at least, in their integrity and purity, increasingly improbable. This, even irrespective of the ever growing religious decay already referred to. Every month that passed, and every additional contact with the heathen world, would render the absolute prevalence of the Mosaic institutions practically more difficult, or rather render it increasingly likely that these institutions would appear tinged and modified by the circumstances around. And when the tribes were finally settled, they presented the appearance of so many separate republics, not even joined together into a Confederation, but consisting of as many independent States. There was not any central authority nor bond. Everywhere we mark tribal jealousies and hostilities. Foreign invasions and wars specially affected individual tribes, and only on rare occasions did a sense of common danger unite even a few of them to a common resistance. The 'judges' were only of districts, not of the whole land. Such a state of things could not contribute to the establishment of a central Sanctuary, with exclusive sacrificial worship, one universal priesthood, and the observance of great national festivals in the Sanctuary. It must have tended in quite the opposite direction, and been a mighty factor in preventing the establishment of the Mosaic religious legislation. Even the strict law of inheritance, which confined the tribal lands to members of the tribe, must, in the circumstances, have helped this disintegration of the nation, and, with it, increased the difficulty of central religious institutions. The other civil institutions of the Mosaic code, such as the rule of local authorities—elders, and heads of families and clans—would tend in the same direction. And in this growing religious disintegration, to which so many elements were constantly contributing, we perceive the importance—indeed, the necessity—of the succession of unnamed prophets, to whom reference is made in the historical books, and who were the predecessors of the great prophets of later times, in truth, it seems almost impossible that, without Divine interposition, even the remembrance of Mosaic institutions could have been preserved in Israel.

And it did continue, although these institutions now appeared in forms increasingly tinged by surrounding circumstances, while Israel settled to still lower and lower depths. Even if we were to concede to our opponents that the Canaanitish term for the national Deity, Baal, was at that period applied to Jehovah, that un-Jewish rites mingled in the worship of Israel, and un-Jewish notions appeared in the popular expression of religion, what is this but to own the existence of those influences for which we have accounted on historic grounds? For it will not be denied that these Canaanitish elements did not exist alone, nor even as primary and prevailing, but that by their side there was what we may call Jehovahism as the leading principle—only tinged and tainted, on some occasions even overgrown, by these foreign elements. Indeed, to contend for more than this would be to prove too much, since, according to our opponents, the historical books, which contain all these notices, have undergone a revision which would not have left in them an entirely heathen presentation of the religious state of Israel. And we find a precisely parallel case in the history of the Christian Church, which at one period was similarly tainted and overgrown by heathen elements. Without entering into details, it is sufficiently known that many purely heathen practices were, so to speak, Christianised, and that many notions of pagan origin mingled with the religious belief and observances of the Church in early ages. Their presence would not lead us to infer that the idea of the Christianisation of certain tribes and countries was an after-invention, but rather that in certain circumstances, and at a certain stage of civilisation and religious condition, the retention or introduction of foreign elements by the side of the purer teaching of Christianity was possible, and even natural, however incongruous the two may seem.

But we have to go further. It is evident that tribal separation, tribal jealousies, and local interests would contribute to the decentralisation of the Sanctuary during the period before David—and, similarly, also after the secession of the ten tribes, and the consequent rivalry and hostility of the two kingdoms. We can only repeat that all this would not have happened, if Israel had lived up to its institutions, which, in a sense, were intended to form and mould the people into a political as well as religious unity, for the higher purposes of the Theocracy, in which politics and religion were intended to coincide. But Israel did not rise to the level of its institutions; rather brought them down to its own ever lowering standpoint, although there were individuals, let us hope not a few, who aimed after the higher conformity. Besides these tribal, even communal, separations and jealousies, we have to remember, that intercourse between different parts of the country was more rare and difficult than we can well imagine. As we infer from many notices in the historical books, a journey of a few miles into a neighbouring tribe, still more into a comparatively remote part of the country, was contemplated, and prepared for with the same solemnity, as half a century ago a removal to one of our most distant colonies, or a continental tour.

When in all these circumstances we try to realise the religious condition of the tribesmen before David, the picture may seem strange to modern eyes, but it will be true to the historical notices in the books of Joshua, of the Judges, and of Samuel. We think of the people as arranged in quite separated little communities, between which the intercourse was both rare and difficult, while tribal rivalries and jealousies converted separation into isolation. In each of these little communities, or even districts, a sparse and stationary population tilled the soil. They had been there for generations, and they inherited the traditions, the prejudices, the superstitions, the habits of their forefathers—often without knowing their origin; still more frequently, without perceiving or even suspecting their real meaning, or their possible inconsistency with their ancestral religious principles and ordinances, which in measure were to them a dim sacred tradition. In each district the tone for good or for evil was given by the 'great' people, who were well-to-do farmers or sheepmasters on their own land, without much money, but also with few and simple wants, which their own resources or those of the district could supply. There were good and earnest, and there were corrupt and idolatrous 'great' men and women; simple, primitive, almost idyllic districts, like Bethlehem in the Book of Ruth; and corrupt, debauched places like the Gibeah of Benjamin, of the 19th and 20th chapters of the Book of Judges. The departure of a member of the community, or the chance arrival of a stranger, was a great event. Yet, despite this isolation and separation, they were also conscious of the higher, though too often ideal unity of Israel; and so far under the influence of its legislation, that on great political emergencies all Israel gathered at the Central Sanctuary—or sometimes, to a well-known chieftain; and that the more earnest in Israel, like the parents of Samuel, appeared annually before the Lord, probably at the Feast of Passover. Even these are theocratic institutions which look back upon the Mosaic legislation. But far more than in any single notice or reference does this connection with theocratic institutions, and hence with the Mosaic legislation—the two being inseparably connected, even on the theory of our opponents— impress itself on the mind by the *tout ensemble* presented in the historic books. It is not one or another fact, but everything there, which seems to look back on the theocratic past. We instinctively feel that, whether for good or evil, everything is viewed in connection with it. Every personality, every speech, every action, every event is presented from the standpoint of accord with, or opposition to, the theocratic past. The books as a whole breathe the spirit of the Mosaic history and legislation, and lean upon it; and, surely, it is a sound canon that individual passages, even though seemingly difficult, must be interpreted by the spirit of the whole book.

And as we enter yet more fully into the circumstances of the time and people, the religious condition of these communities, and of the families composing them, stands out more distinctly in our view. We can perceive how the great Central Sanctuary, with the institutions depending upon it, was, to most men, rather an ideal than a practical reality. And yet the two sacraments of circumcision and the Sabbath kept it ever before them, and became a permanent and unsurmountable wall of separation from that heathen world which was in such close proximity. And here we perceive the immense importance of the Mosaic arrangement, by which the Levites were scattered throughout the country, while, at the same time, they had, or might have had, in their Levite- and priest-cities, centres which ought to have kept alive the spirit and traditions of their order. Even this, that the Levites were, according to the ancient arrangement, as a tribe and hereditarily, to be dependent for support on their religion, would tend to keep the old faith alive. In every district or community the Levite was the living impersonation of it in the sight of all men. He connected in the present the past with the future. Thus we find him hired as a kind of domestic chaplain in a wealthy, religious, or superstitious household; while, on occasions, he emerges into view in connection with some event or undertaking. He belongs to all Israel, and all Israel—not his tribesmen— must take care of him, or avenge his wrongs. He does not often appear, nor yet prominently, because in reality no prominence belongs to him. No doubt some of his distinctive functions were occasionally usurped by others, without their thinking of usurpation in what they did. All this is quite natural. A sacrifice might be killed by any one: it was the sprinkling of the blood on the great altar of the Tabernacle, which was the distinctively priestly function. Family or communal feasts would naturally be sacrificial; and even if it were proved that these sacrifices were offered by laymen, there would not necessarily have been an infraction of the old order; or if there was—such a generalising of the old order would not surprise us, in the peculiar circumstances of the people, the land, and the Central Sanctuary, as we have described them; far less would it prove the theocratic order and Mosaic legislation to have never existed.

And if it be still urged that the Mosaic priesthood ought to have occupied a more distinctive place in history, we have only to picture to ourselves the country Aaronite or Levite, as he was; for, in the circumstances, the distinction between the two would naturally be, to a great extent, effaced. He is poor, expropriated, alone without possessions (unless through marriage) in a community of more or less well-to-do peasant-proprietors, mainly dependent for support on hospitality and charity. He is not even like the friar in an Italian or Spanish village, but rather like the Greek 'pope' in a remote district of Roumania or of one of the Turkish provinces; and in the history of those countries the village 'pope' would not form a distinguished or prominent figure. And yet the 'pope' has great advantages.

True, he has not any training or education to speak of, but at least there is a religious literature, not quite inaccessible to him. In any case, he has the service-books and the lectionaries of his Church. But, from the circumstances previously described, we do not wonder at what seems implied in

2 Chronicles 17:9, that, in the great reformatory movement under Jehoshaphat, the priests and Levites, deputed to traverse the country with the princes, had to take with them from Jerusalem the book of the Law. This seems to convey that, even in the more religious southern kingdom of Judah, and in the time of Jehoshaphat, this primal religious document was only rarely found in country districts. In other words, we have a state of general ignorance and absence of religious literature, except in the capital. But why this piece of gratuitous information in the Book of Chronicles, if there was no Mosaic Law in existence, since the compilers of Chronicles are supposed, at least, to have belonged to the same school which produced the Priest-Code? People do not generally go out of their way gratuitously to inform us, that a work, which has been palmed off as the original and fundamental constitution of their religion, was unknown in the country districts so long as five hundred years ago.

And the Priests and Levites were at still further disadvantage in the country-districts, since neither services nor places of worship were provided for them. We can scarcely wonder that the ancient sacred places, 'the heights,' were reconsecrated as centres of communal worship. One has said that these 'heights' took the place of the synagogues of a later period, and that they stood related to the Central Sanctuary as the synagogues to the Temple. This is an exceedingly practical mode of putting it; and we again recall that in ancient times former heathen temples and ceremonies were similarly Christianised. Nor yet can we wonder at the non-observance of the great festivals, far less infer from it that they had not been Mosaically instituted. We have already seen that their observance was dependent on universal resort to a great Central Sanctuary. And when it was established, and the people finally settled, these feasts had already fallen into desuetude. As regards the Feast of Tabernacles, some indication of it may possibly be traced in Judges 21:19. And this also would be significant. But from verse 21 the feast seems to have been chiefly of a local character, and its observances remind us more of the later festivities on the 15th of Ab (Taan. 4:8) than of the Biblical festival. Naturally, it could only have been celebrated after the entrance into Canaan, when, according to an historical notice, it seems to have been observed in the days of Joshua the son of Nun (Neh 8:17). After this, we find it again celebrated by Solomon (2 Chron 7:8-10; comp. 1 Kings 8:65, 66). Subsequently, the times of religious reformation and unification were too brief and troubled, the intrusion of foreign religious elements of too long standing and too general, and the people as a whole in too great measure religiously denationalised, to admit of so radical a change, as would have been implied in a national celebration of that feast. Indeed, we might almost say that the Feast of Tabernacles would, in the then state of the people, have been a moral anachronism.

It was otherwise with the Feast of Passover, with which we may reasonably suppose that of Weeks to have been connected. Manifestly, this would be the first and most natural to be re-introduced. Accordingly we find notices of it, not only in the time of Joshua, although, as we mark, before the possession of the land (Josh 5:11), but in that of King Hezekiah (2 Chron 30:21), and of King Josiah (2 Chron 35:18, 19; 2 Kings 23:21, 22). Several points strike us as peculiar in these last notices—more especially this, that they seem to imply a kind of observance of these feasts in the days of the Judges, specifically in those of Samuel (2 Chron 35:18), as well as in the days of the kings of Judah and of Israel. Another point seems even more noteworthy. In 2 Chronicles 30:21 the Passover under Hezekiah is recorded, although, significantly, only on the part of those children of Israel that were in Jerusalem (2 Chron 30:21; comp. here 7:1-11), consisting (according to verse 25) of worshippers from Judah, Priests and Levites, a number of persons from the northern kingdom, and proselytes ('strangers' both out of Judah and Israel). Yet, a few chapters afterwards, the same Book of Chronicles, in recording the Passover under Josiah, has it, that no Passover like it had been kept since the days of Samuel the Prophet (2 Chron 35:18). Similarly, while in Nehemiah 8:17 the Feast of Tabernacles then celebrated is said to have been unique—at least in its mode of observation—since the days of Joshua, 2 Chronicles 7:8, 10, which, even according to our opponents, is kindred to Nehemiah, records the celebration of this seven-days' feast with extraordinary pomp in the time of Solomon. From every point of view, these seemingly conflicting statements appear at first sight incomprehensible. On the theory of our opponents as to the date and character of these books, it seems inexplicable that such inconsistent statements should have been inserted, or left in the text, and that the writers should have gratuitously gone back a thousand years to the time of Joshua for the Feast of Tabernacles, and to the time of Samuel for that of the Passover, when in the one case they might have mentioned the Solomonic observance, and in the other that of Hezekiah, and when, on the theory under review of the introduction of these observances, it would have been their manifest interest to make the gap as small as possible.

To these difficulties we can, on our view of the case, offer what seems to us a sufficient and a natural solution. The passages in question do not affirm that there had not been any celebration of the Passover between Josiah and Samuel, nor of the Feast of Tabernacles between Nehemiah and Joshua, but that there had not been any of the same kind since those days. We are allowed to infer that there may have been others—less national or less truly Mosaic; we may even speculate, that while, and when, there was a Central Sanctuary, a certain number of the people may have been wont to attend them, even though the observances may have become more local or undergone modification, perhaps owing to the very circumstance that they were no longer kept as general national festivals. With this agrees, not only the notice about the annual attendance at Shiloh of Samuel's parents (1 Sam 1:3), but also the institution by Jeroboam in the northern kingdom of festivals rival to the great annual Mosaic feasts (1 Kings 12:27, 33). This, indeed, is only expressly affirmed in regard to the Feast of Tabernacles, which Jeroboam transferred from the seventh to the eighth month. But this notice is evidently connected with the account of the dedication of the house of high places, which Jeroboam combined with his spurious Feast of Tabernacles, no doubt, in imitation of what Solomon had done on a similar occasion. Manifestly, if there had not been a more or less common observance of that feast in Judah, Jeroboam would not have dreaded the resort of his subjects to the Temple, nor instituted a rival feast. Moreover, the expression used at the setting up of the two calves: 'Behold thy gods, O Israel, which brought thee up out of the land of Egypt,' seems to point to the observance of a kind of Passover feast—an institution which is not likely to have been wholly neglected, when a substitute was sought for the Feast of Tabernacles.

Without entering into particulars, I think I am warranted in saying that the historical notices about the festivals are exactly as might have been expected in the circumstances of the land and people. And our reasoning regarding the scanty mention of the great national festivals seems supported by the frequent references to domestic and communal celebrations, such as the observance of Sabbaths and New Moons, which evidently seems to have been general, because it did not involve the necessity of any central national attendance. And the general conclusion which we derive from a review of the actual state of matters in Israel is to the effect that, so far from the notices in the historical books being inconsistent with a previous Mosaic legislation, they are not only compatible with it, but even presuppose its existence, and that, without such previous religious institutions, the principal events and the leading personages in Jewish history—not only a Boaz, a Samuel, or a David, but even a Gideon, a Saul, or a Joab—would be unintelligible.

On the other hand, the theory of our opponents implies premises which, on consideration, it will be found difficult to accept. Let us still bear in mind that Israel came out of Egypt, a land most advanced in literature, and where religious institutions were settled and established. It seems scarcely credible, on purely historical grounds, that their leaders should not have attempted to introduce something of the same kind in Israel—some religious legislation and order; the more so, as this would constitute a bond of national union, and a distinctive badge of their newly-acquired nationality, which would effectually separate them from that heathen world, active hostility to which was the primary condition of their existence. To this antecedent likelihood of a Mosaic legislation and religious order, we have to add other considerations in the same direction. Can we believe that Israel was settled for centuries in their land; had developed from federal to monarchical institutions, and been brought into contact with so many neighbouring races, and yet that up to their 'golden age' they had possessed only a rudimentary code of religious legislation; that it then suddenly appeared developed at the period of commencing decay, while its greater part was constructed during the banishment of Israel, when the people were so scattered that even the remembrance of the location of the Ten Tribes was lost? Assuredly, that does not seem the fitting moment for a great part of the religious institutions to have been invented, or even formulated, nor for the history of the nation to have been recast, and most of its religious poetry composed. We are asked to believe that so many of the priestly and Temple arrangements, which had not existed while Israel was in their own land, and worshipped in their Temple, originated when Israel was scattered, and had neither centre of religious unity nor of worship; further, that the comparatively small minority which returned to Palestine, and to whose lamentable condition the books of Ezra and Nehemiah bear abundant witness, could impose a fictitious and, in many respects, new, Mosaic law on the great majority of the people—and they the more educated, who, as we know, remained behind in the lands of the dispersion; and, lastly, that this new law, which they introduced, contained, as we shall show, so much that was impossible in the new circumstances of the land and people, while it omitted reference to much that we would have expected in a legislation originating in those times.

At the risk of repetition, I must further urge one part of this argument, leaving the other for the sequel. Let it be kept in view, that it was only a small and comparatively uninfluential minority which returned with Ezra and Nehemiah. The rest remained behind, and rapidly spread over the face of the world. Yet the legislation, supposed to have been then introduced, made no provision for, took not the slightest notice of, the wants of the great majority, not even to the provision of synagogues, which we know to have been among the first requirements of the 'dispersed'—nay, even of those who returned to Palestine. Surely, this seems so strange as to be almost incredible. In times which called for the widest comprehension, they concocted the narrowest conceivable legislation, and that, in the interest of the small number of priests who returned to Palestine; and they not only succeeded in introducing it as the Mosaic Law, but in imposing it upon the educated majority, without eliciting a single contradiction, or raising a single question as to its authenticity—until the ingenuity of critics more than two thousand years later discovered the forgery! Was there not a single individual, among those outside the circle where this fraud was perpetrated, wise enough to discover, or honest enough to expose it—no one, priest or layman, of those who did not return to Palestine? And what had all this time become of JE, or of Deuteronomy, which in some form must have existed, and the provisions of which are supposed to be inconsistent with this new Priest-Code? Were these documents latent, lost, or unknown, except within the small circle of the priestly forgers?

There are other questions connected with what is called the Priest-Code of Ezekiel (Eze 40-48), so important, that we shall have to refer to them separately. Meantime we would challenge evidence of the extraordinary literary activity attributed to the exilian period. We are acquainted with the literary activity of the Prophets at the beginning of that period; but these Prophets had their root in the past, not in the new development. What we know of the undoubted post-exilian literature does not encourage belief in any extraordinary and novel literary activity of the exilian age, and it seems absolutely incompatible with it, that no chronicle or record has been kept of that period. We know actually less of the history of the Jews during that time than of their condition while in Egypt, and before they became a people, insomuch that, as already stated, the very tracks of the Ten Tribes have been lost.

This is the proper place to refer—of necessity quite briefly—to an argument which has been advanced on the other side, although it is not easy to understand that it should be so confidently used. It is to the effect, that the age of the various portions in the Pentateuch may be distinguished by linguistic differences. This pretension, which in any case would necessitate extreme delicacy of literary tact, has been initially discredited by the circumstance that scholars of admittedly equal competence have, on linguistic grounds, declared certain parts to be of latest date, which others have, for the same reason, adjudged to be earliest. It is, indeed, possible to distinguish, at least with approximate reliableness, the style of different authors, and to determine with general accuracy whether a book belongs to one or another period of literature, although a clever forger of what was intended to be passed as an ancient work (as in the case of the 'Priest-Code') might easily mislead critics more than two thousand years later, and who had such scanty *data* by which to judge as the small compass of Biblical literature which we possess. In point of fact, according to Wellhausen's theory, the forgers did so succeed, and that not only in inducing their own contemporaries to accept as archaic what was quite recent, but they similarly eluded the vigilance of succeeding generations, of all the Rabbis, of all the Church, and of all critics—none of whom, till the present century, discovered, or even suspected, the exilian composition of the Priest-Code. And this scantiness of Biblical literature for comparison is admitted, at least by many on the other side, to make it almost impossible to determine whether an expression is old or modern, and whether an ancient usus of expression may not have been continued or taken up anew, or *vice versâ*, or else what may be due to local or educational circumstances. All this has of late been practically illustrated. By a careful examination of the language, a competent scholar, E. Ryssel, set himself to prove the high antiquity of certain portions in that part of the Pentateuch known as the work of the Elohist. Next, and in answer to him, another competent scholar, F. Giesebrecht, endeavoured by a fresh examination to show, that it was of much later date; while, lastly, one of our own scholars, Professor Driver, has, I think, conclusively established, that those linguistic peculiarities, on which Giesebrecht relies, do *not* necessarily prove such a late date as he contends for. From all which the impartial observer will at least conclude, that the arguments on either side cannot be of absolute stringency, and that no certain deduction as to the date of composition can be derived from linguistic considerations. And this inference of common sense is remarkably illustrated by the very interesting comparison which Professor Stanley Leathes has made of the *usus* of certain words by English writers.

Before submitting some considerations which seem to me incompatible with the theory of our opponents, it may be well to take a brief retrospect of the argument, as advanced by them. We have already indicated that we have assigned only a very secondary place to the supposed inconsistencies and contradictions within the Pentateuch-legislation itself: firstly, because they depend on an often arbitrary separation of documents and notices, and the assignment to them of dates *ex hypothesi*, while there is no real inconsistency between them; and, secondly, because it would involve detailed discussions for which this is not the place. Indeed, it seems to me that, without the second branch of the argument—as to the alleged inconsistencies of the Mosaic legislation with the condition of things, as set forth in the historical books—the first, which seeks to prove essential differences within the Pentateuch itself, and on that ground to separate it into documents, widely differing in date—the most important being post-exilian—would lack any historical basis, and degenerate into discussions, in which critical and speculative ingenuity on the one side might be pitted against the same qualities on the other. In fact, however Wellhausen may, in the Introduction to his 'History,' strive to give prominence to the demarcation of the various layers of which he supposes the Pentateuch to be composed, the account which he gives of the *genesis* of his own convictions regarding the character of the Pentateuch shows, that he was mainly led by a review of Israel's history, derived from the historical books, to that disintegration and classification of the Pentateuch, which seemed to him to accord with the *data* he had gathered from the historical books. For, otherwise there would not seem anything in the results of modern criticism inconsistent with the supposition, stated at the outset of this Lecture, of different sources or documents in the Pentateuch, *yet all embodying Mosaic legislation*, adapted to the varying conditions of different periods, or to circumstances arising in the history of Israel— especially, when we take into account later redactions of the book as a whole. It seems to me, therefore, that, in an argumentative defence of the Mosaic origin of the Pentateuch-legislation, main consideration should be given to its relation to the notices derived from the historical books.

This has been the object of our detailed analysis of the condition of Israel in Canaan, with the view of showing that, what might seem inconsistencies, are in reality rationally accounted for by—in fact, the natural outcome of—the then existing state of things. To this it may be added, that in general the *argumentum ex silentio*, even if circumstances could not be otherwise satisfactorily explained, can never be satisfactory or convincing. It may raise doubts, but it cannot establish any facts. The non-observance of a law does not prove its non-existence. Thus, to repeat an oft- quoted instance, in Jeremiah 16:6, the practice is referred to, without special disapprobation, of cutting and making themselves bald for the dead; while it is expressly interdicted in Deuteronomy (14:1), which yet, according to our opponents, existed in the time of that prophet.

On the other branch of the argument I have still some considerations to offer, which shall be presented in popular form. I venture to suggest that, if there is one fact more clearly established than another in the history of civilisation, it is, that the earliest period in the life of all nations is what may be designated as the theological, or else mythological; and that the first on the scene for guidance, rule, and instruction, are the *priests*. These are in due time followed by what may be generally classed as *teachers*, or prophets. Nor is this order infringed, either in the Old Testament, or in the later history of Israel. There also we have first the legislation connected with the Sanctuary, and Priests. And these are afterwards followed by the period of the Prophets. In turn, after the cessation of prophecy, the Prophets give place to teachers and Rabbis. But the theory of our opponents requires us to invert this universal order. It asks us to believe, that in Israel alone it was not first Priests, then Prophets; but first Prophets, then Priests. And the difficulty of such inversion is all the greater since, according to these writers, the period when the Prophets began was one of religious barbarism in Israel, while they were surrounded by nations, such as the Phoenicians, Egyptians, and Assyrians, whose religious rites and institutions were not only fixed, but in a very advanced stage of development. Moreover, the question naturally suggests itself: If the so-called Mosaic legislation was of much later date and very different authorship; and if the history in the historical books has been painted over in the interest of later institutions, does it not seem a strange and unaccountable blunder to have left the picture of religious society in such colouring as to have suggested the objection, that the Mosaic legislation could not then have existed? We can understand that, if there had been a Mosaic legislation, it might have been followed by a period of such decay as is implied in the books of Joshua, the Judges, and Samuel. But what we cannot understand is, how those who introduced a legislation so fundamentally different from, and a religious order and ritual so discordant with, much that characterises society in these books, and who wished to ascribe that legislation and ritual to Moses, could have allowed so incongruous a state of society to appear in histories which owed to them, if not their origin, yet their redaction.

This leads up to another point to which previous reference has been made from a different point of view. It has been argued that the references by the Prophets, and in the Psalms, to sacrifices, ritual observances, feasts, and such like, are antagonistic to those, at least, in the Priest-Code. And it has been answered, that the views expressed by the Prophets presuppose the existence of such institutions, and that their polemics were directed not against these institutions, but against their externalisation, and the separation of their outward observance from their inward meaning, by which their Divine purpose was perverted to opposite results. But the argument admits of further application. Taking the Law simply by itself, and those sayings of the Prophets by themselves, it will be admitted that the latter mark a progress upon the bare text of the former. Their views of the Law, as spiritual and inward; of the priesthood, as one of holiness of circumcision, as of the heart; and of sacrifices, feasts, and fasts, as not merely outward observances, unconnected with a corresponding state of mind, mark an advance on a former state of externalism. We can understand it, if the Mosaic Law had already existed; but not, if the main part of the so-called Mosaic legislation originated afterwards. For, in that case, it would mark a retrogression from the more spiritual standpoint of the Prophets to that Law, which yet was evidently connected with their activity.

This connection will at least not be denied in regard to Ezekiel. What has been called his 'Priest-Code' (chapters 40-48) may be viewed as a symbolical and ideal presentation of the 'New Jerusalem'—the form of the vision being determined, on the principle explained in a former Lecture, by the peculiar modes of thinking and the then circumstances of the Prophet and the people. But even so, and still more—viewing it, from the standpoint of our discussion, as a piece of legislation, it bears reference to the Pentateuch order, and more especially to that portion of it known as the 'Priest-Code.' Historically speaking, it stands, according to our opponents, midway between the Jehovist and the Deuteronomist on the one hand, and the Priest-Code on the other. Indeed, it is said to have formed the model, and in part the kernel, of the 'Priest-Code.' This is a decisive position to take up, but also one which has been proved indefensible. No other part of the controversy has been more exhaustively treated than this of the relation between Ezekiel and the Priest-Code, whether Ezekiel looked back on the Priest-Code, or the Priest-Code on Ezekiel. The contention of Wellhausen is the latter; but it has been shown on conclusive evidence that Ezekiel looks back on the Priest-Code, which, therefore, must have been prior to the Prophet. But, in that case, we shall have to put the Priest-Code a long way back, since, according to our opponents, there is the widest difference between it and the other documents in the Pentateuch, which mark a very different stage and a very different date from the Priest-Code. The detailed proof for the assertion that Ezekiel looks back upon the Priest-Code, and not the reverse, cannot be attempted in this place, and the reader must be referred to where it is specifically discussed. But it would be unfair to the argument, not at least to state the evidence which Hoffmann has adduced in proof that Ezekiel had known the Priest-Code. He quotes not fewer than eighty-one passages from the Priest-Code, which have exact verbal parallels in eighty-three passages in Ezekiel. These prove, even if we were to make some deductions from them, that the one document must have referred to the other. And this is further confirmed by the peculiar use of a particle (Khi כי 'when'), which only in the Priest-Code in the Pentateuch, and, with few isolated exceptions, only in Ezekiel, is placed after the subject which it determines. In evidence, that Ezekiel had derived all this from the Priest-Code, and not the reverse, Hoffmann adduces these two facts: first, that Ezekiel employs a number of other expressions which occur in writings that are undoubtedly older than his prophecies, while the Priest-Code contains no other passages in which such parallelism with other portions of Scripture occurs; and, secondly, that the Priest-Code has merely such parallelisms to Ezekiel as occur only in the latter, but none of those which Ezekiel has in common with other writings such as Jeremiah and Deuteronomy.

We have to submit yet another consideration, which, indeed, is not new, but will, we believe, have its due weight with those who view the subject, not so much from the technical standpoint, as from that of general considerations and common sense. Let it be remembered that the ritual portion in Ezekiel differs in many and important particulars from the laws and arrangements of the so-called Priest-Code. We can understand such modifications by a prophet in his vision of the future, if the arrangements of the Priest-Code had been already in existence; but a later composition by priests of a Code, professedly Mosaic, which contravened the arrangements of an acknowledged Prophet, seems incredible. And this the more, when we remember that, according to our opponents, the arrangements of the Priest-Code were also inconsistent with an earlier legislation, which also professed to be Mosaic—so that the priests who, to speak plainly, foisted the Priest-Code upon Moses, also made Moses contradict himself as well as Ezekiel. And yet it is admitted on all hands that the 'redaction,' which welded into one whole the various parts of which the Pentateuch is composed, displays extraordinary skill. Indeed, the dilemma becomes even more acute. Let it still be borne in mind, that the difference between the earlier legislation and that of the Priest-Code is said, on certain points, to be very great. If so, how are we to account for the introduction of the Priest-Code as the Law of Moses, long after the differing institutions of the earlier legislation had been received as Mosaic? Or, again, if the Priest-Code which modified the earlier legislation was the latest production, and intended to be finally binding, how is it that the Priest-Code was not placed after Deuteronomy in the Pentateuch, when they had the arranging of it? We can understand that Deuteronomy may have been a second and popular version of the earlier Law, when, in view of the immediate entrance into the land, certain of the ordinances, given thirty-eight years before, had to be modified, or, rather, adapted to the new circumstances of the people. But we cannot imagine the publication by the later priesthood of a code professedly Mosaic, by the side of one more ancient, and also professedly Mosaic, which taught differently. Why retain the older code at all, after it had become antiquated for so long a time? why call it Mosaic? why insert it in the Pentateuch? If the priests were able to introduce such an entirely new code, in which the privileges of their order and other arrangements were so much more emphasised than in the old legislation, why retain the latter, and insert it into the Canon? or why should Ezra, for example, have read it in the hearing of all the people—or, did he read it?—and why should he have told them, that the exile had been the punishment of their transgression of the Mosaic ordinances, when, according to our opponents, he was himself bringing in a new code, on many points inconsistent with the old one?

Such questions might easily be multiplied. But I have still to add to the argument some considerations bearing, not exclusively on the date of the Priest-Code, but on my general position, that the Pentateuch as a whole must be considered as embodying the Mosaic legislation. For,—

1. The laws and arrangements of the Pentateuch are only adapted to an agricultural people. Trade and commerce, except of the most primitive kind, are not even contemplated. Not only is there an entire absence of strictly commercial laws, but some of the institutions seem almost incompatible with trade. Among these we only name the prohibition of charging interest on loans or debts, and the arrangement by which all real property, houses as well as lands, reverted to their original owners after a certain number of years, and, indeed, as I infer, could never have passed from the possession of members of one tribe to that of another. It is impossible to conceive that, in a developed state of national life, arrangements should originate which would make the possession of capital absolutely valueless, by depriving the capitalist of all interest and the trader of almost any profit, or by which, within a limited time, at longest fifty years, every house and piece of ground would be restored to the family of the original settlers in the land, so that a family could not have acquired a freehold, although it had been in their actual possession possibly for nearly two generations, unless it could be shown that their ancestry had been the original settlers in the place. Such arrangements could not have been introduced even after the separation of the two Kingdoms of Israel and Judah; they seem incredible as proposed in the time of King Josiah, and impossible as originating, or reproduced, in or after the Exile, considering that only two of the twelve tribes returned to Palestine.

2. The same character of *primitiveness* appears in regard to the administration of justice. In some respects it differed materially, although not in the sense of our opponents, from the arrangements introduced at a later period by the Kings. According to the Pentateuch, the 'elders' of a place would act as judges. Apparently they were the men of greatest repute, dignity, and age, and selected by each community from its own members. They sat in the gate, and heard and decided causes. From this primitive tribunal the parties in a case had not the right of appeal. This lay only with the judges. If any cause were too hard for them, they might refer it to the central authority in the Sanctuary, no doubt to the High Priest and

those around him, who were the religious or national leaders of what was intended to have been a tribal federation. When the nation became consolidated, and monarchy was introduced, we find, indeed, the ancient institution of the eldership continued. But the elders now administered chiefly communal affairs. They were the political or the religious representatives of a district, who would act for the community at large, only in cases of urgency or danger, or punish a criminal, if his delinquency involved the community as a whole. But the general administration of justice seems to have devolved on regular judges appointed by the king, of which new order we have distinct mention, if not in the time of David (1 Chron 23:4), yet in that of Solomon and of Jehoshaphat (2 Chron 1:2; 19:5). But if the Pentateuch legislation was posterior to that period, if it even dated in part from the time of Josiah, it could not have been proposed to discard the more orderly, and go back to the primitive rude mode of administering justice by an eldership sitting at the entering of the gate. In point of fact we find under Ezra judges by the side of the primitive institution of 'elders' (Ezra 10:14).

The argument which has just been urged in regard to the Pentateuch arrangements about judges would equally apply to the very primitive mode of punishments proposed, or allowed, in the Mosaic legislation. Some of these, such as the right of blood-vengeance, or the executing of a rebellious son, could not have been introduced, or renewed, scarcely been allowed to continue, at an advanced period in the life of a nation. To the same class belong those Divine punishments of 'cutting off,' so frequently threatened, which we would not expect to find in a legislative code that had originated otherwise than that of the Pentateuch.

3. But, indeed, it is not in one direction only nor another that we find it impossible to reconcile the theory of a late, in part exilian, origin and date of it with the character of the Pentateuch legislation. The same conclusion is constantly forced upon us. We find it difficult to believe that in any but the most primitive legislation an arrangement would have been introduced, which rendered it imperative on all males three times in the year to quit their occupations, and undertake a pilgrimage to the Central Sanctuary, however remote their habitations from it. In point of fact, these three annual attendances seem never to have been exactly observed. And we remember that the kings of Israel, immediately after the separation of the two kingdoms, made the inconvenience of such an ordinance one of the grounds for setting up a rival worship. A similar remark applies, and even

more strongly, to the laws which enjoined the offering of a sacrifice in the Central Sanctuary, on the many occasions in the life of every family which called for 'purification.' We can understand the introduction of such laws in the infancy of Israel, but not at an advanced period. Least of all can we comprehend how they could have been enacted, or renewed, after Israel was 'dispersed,' and the observance of such laws to the vast majority matter of absolute impossibility.

I might prosecute this argument in reference to the provision for the poor, and some of the ritual and Levitical laws of the Pentateuch; but a striking evidence, that some at least of those arrangements could not have originated during and after the Exile, comes to us from the later Synagogue. We know that the traditional law was intended not only to develop and protect, as by a fence around it, the Law of Moses, but also to apply and supplement it. One of the avowed reasons for this 'second law' was that, in the state of matters which had evolved in the course of time, and especially since the return from the Captivity, new circumstances had emerged, to which the primitive Law of Moses no longer applied, or which it had apparently not contemplated. And there was, as we can see, reason for this contention. It is most curious and instructive to watch the ingenuity with which traditionalism sought to reconcile the old with the new, and to show that there was essential agreement, even identity, between the Law of Moses and the ordinances of the Scribes. For it was the theory of traditionalism that all these cases had been Divinely foreseen, although not expressed, and provided for by oral, although not by written, legislation. One instance—although in regard to the Deuteronomic legislation —may illustrate our meaning. The Mosaic Law had directed the absolute extinction of debt on every Sabbatic or Jubilee year. This, because the Mosaic legislation recognised not the ordinary commercial relations of debtor and creditor, but treated the borrower as one who in his need had received charitable assistance from his richer brother. The Rabbinic Code sought to alleviate the inconvenience of this primitive arrangement by ruling that the remission of debt was to take place, not at the beginning, but only on the last day of the seventh year. And it added this curiously characteristic provision, that while the creditor intimated to the debtor the remission, he might at the same time hold open his hand for the receipt of payment. But even so it was found that 'all needful business transactions were so hindered, that the great Hillel introduced what in Rabbinic Law is called the *Prosbul* (προς βουλη, before the Council), which was a document, duly attested, bearing these words: I, *A B*, hereby declare before you, the Judges of *C*, that I shall have the right to claim at any time payment of whatever debt may be due to me by *D*. This curious provision, dating nearly half a century before our era, may help to show how impossible it would have been to originate at any later period so primitive a legislation as that of the Pentateuch. Indeed, as previously stated, even the Deuteronomic legislation, introduced just before the entry into Canaan, seems already to mark a widening and adaptation of the earlier code. And we may reasonably assume that, if Israel had been faithful to its mission, and developed in accordance with its institutions, the central authority at the Sanctuary, whether the priesthood or the Prophets, would have been able to adapt the primitive legislation to the growing wants of the people.

To these considerations of what we would not have expected to find in the Pentateuch, if its legislation had been other than primitive and Mosaic, we shall, in conclusion, add a few others, indicating what we might reasonably have expected to find, if any considerable part of it had dated from a late, but especially from the exilian or post-exilian, period.

1. In such a legislation the fact of the exile could not have been wholly ignored. We cannot conceive a complete, and minutely detailed, code of religious arrangements, in which no provision whatever had been made for, not even notice taken of, the wants of the great majority, dispersed in all lands. We know that the institution of the Synagogue originated in the necessities of the period of the exile; and we also know how rapidly that institution spread, as meeting the most pressing religious requirements. Is it possible then to imagine a legislation introduced at that very time, which would completely ignore the institution of the Synagogue, and the felt need from which it sprang? Yet the greatest critical ingenuity has failed to discover a reference to it, either in one or another part of the Pentateuch legislation. On the other hand, we ask ourselves what could be the meaning, is those times, of the Urim and Thummim, which no longer existed; of all the fictions about the Ark of the Covenant, which also no longer existed; of the laws about the Levitical cities, about the spoil taken in war, and, as regards the Deuteronomist, of the laws about the Ammonite and the Moabite, which in those days could have no application, and whose relations to Israel seem, indeed, in later times, to have completely changed?

2. A legislation originating in later times must have embodied, if not avowedly, yet really, the results of the past development. The whole

religious history of a people cannot be effaced. Many things will here occur as products of the past, to which we would have expected some reference in the new legislation. It is the primal position in the theory of our opponents, that the Law was after the Prophets. Yet, admittedly, there are in the Law only faint references to what was the constant and great theme of prophetic preaching,—the Messianic hope. There is enough to show that the thought was not absent; nothing, to convey what place it occupied in Jewish thinking. Similarly, we would have expected, if not more distinct, yet different references to royalty; nor can we understand how every indication of a monarchy of such long duration, and of so significant a character as that of the Davidic line, could have been entirely blotted out of the record.

Lastly, even our opponents contend that, during the Babylonish captivity, the theological views of the exiles underwent development. With certain important reservations, we are prepared to admit the correctness of this statement. As might be expected, these new elements came to occupy, in the centuries immediately following, the most prominent place in Jewish teaching. We specially allude here to four points. To the period of the Exile we have to trace: the institution of the Synagogue; the real commencement of traditionalism; the development of certain doctrines, notably those concerning angelic and demoniac influences; and the wider application of the religion of Israel to the nations of the world, consequent on the new relation of the people to the world-monarchies. Such development would, as we can readily see, naturally commence during the banishment of the Jews in the Assyrian Empire. On the other hand, the influence of these new elements proved, in a sense, entirely transforming in the religious history of Israel. And yet no trace of factors, which so powerfully affected the nation, can be discovered in the code of religious legislation, of which a large part is said to have originated at, or after, that period.

We must bring to an abrupt termination a discussion which has, perhaps, been prolonged beyond the bounds proper in this course of Lectures. On a review of the whole, we are the last to deny the ingenuity and brilliancy with which Professor Wellhausen has applied and popularised the theory of Reuss and Graf. He has the merit, not only of developing, but of applying it in all directions. In fact, he has wholly reconstructed, on the basis of it, the history of Israel, and resolved its problems in accordance with it. But in this very thing lies, in our view, the fatal flaw of the theory. We do not profess to be able to explain every difficulty that may be urged; nor, indeed, do we believe that, with the materials at our command, it is possible to do so. But with all deference for the learning and ability of the scholars who have adopted the views of Wellhausen, we must be allowed to express, in plain language, our conviction that their theory lacks the one element which is primary: it lacks a reliable historical basis.

LECTURE 9: THE MESSIANIC IDEA IN THE LATER STAGES OF ISRAEL'S HISTORY: THE APOCRYPHA AND THEIR RELATION TO THE PAST AND THE FUTURE.

For the children of Israel shall abide many days without a king,
and without a prince, and without a sacrifice, and without an image,
and without an ephod, and without teraphim. Afterward shall the
children of Israel return, and seek the Lord their God, and David their
king, and shall fear the Lord and His goodness in the latter days. Hosea
3:4, 5.

From the consideration of Prophecy and of its teaching, and from the vindication of its place in the Old Testament Canon, we proceed to follow the history of the Messianic idea in Israel after the strictly prophetic period. And as regards the condition of Israel during one part, or the great hope set before them in the other part, of this period, a more accurate prophetic description could not have been given than that by Hosea (3:4,5).

We have reached the age of the Exile. The last notes of the old prophetic voices followed the wanderers into their banishment; the last glow of the torch which they had held aloft threw, amidst the encircling gloom, its fitful light on the future. But soon it was extinguished, and silence and darkness fall upon the scene. For a brief time this was once more broken— and yet scarcely broken—at the time of the return of the exiles into Palestine. Broken: for we have such prophetic utterances as those of Haggai, Zechariah, and Malachi, the redaction of certain portions of the Old Testament canon, and the beginning and groundwork of such historical, didactic, and prophetic works, as, with later additions and insertions, may have been edited at a subsequent period. And yet we say that the silence and darkness were scarcely interrupted; for—(1) The whole tone and style of the post-exilian period differs from that of the pre-exilian. A comparison of the prophecies of Malachi, for example, with some of those of the earlier prophets will impress us that we are no longer in the golden age of prophetism. In this I am not referring to their prophetic character, nor to the inspiration of their writings. My remarks apply to the form—the human *media*—through which the Divine Revelation was communicated. And further, while I do not feel called upon here to express an opinion as to the precise date of the groundwork, or of the final redaction, of those historical, didactic, and prophetic writings to which I have referred, it seems to me that they must date either from the end of the exilian or the beginning of the post-exilian period; or else, from a much later time—the close of the Persian, and the beginning of the Macedono-Grecian period, about the end of the fourth century before Christ. For, from the purely literary point of view, and thinking of their writers, we would expect such a renewal of religious literature only in a period of general religious revival and enthusiasm, such as at the return from the Exile; or else in one of rejuvenescence, such as that which marked and followed the accession of Alexander the Great—that Napoleon of the ancient world, whose conquests re-formed and transformed not only the political, but the social and intellectual condition of the world. But there are, to my mind, conclusive grounds against the later date of any integral part of the Old Testament canon. But whether or not the final redaction of such works as Chronicles, Ezra, and Nehemiah—not to speak of others, such as Esther, Proverbs, and Ecclesiastes—belong to the earlier period, or to the Alexandrian, it is at least remarkable, that the first known revival of Jewish religious literature—I mean the earliest of the Apocrypha—dates from the period soon after Alexander the Great.

We may here be allowed a brief digression, if such it be, to note three, to me at least, deeply interesting inferences. The oldest book among the Palestinian Apocrypha is 'The Wisdom of Jesus the Son of Sirach' (Ecclesiasticus). This, whether, according to my view of it, we place its composition—not its translation into Greek, which was later—at the end of the third century before Christ, or, according to that of others, regard it as a century younger. It is, as already stated, Palestinian. But about the same time (somewhere about 280) we place the beginning of the Greek (LXX) version of the Old Testament—that of the Pentateuch. This translation would, in the nature of things, be speedily followed by that of the other portions of the Canon, existing at the time, and which, in the prologue to Ecclesiasticus, are already distinguished as 'the Law, and the Prophets, and the other books of our fathers' (the Hagiographa). Such speedy further version is also otherwise likely. We know that in the second, and, most probably, even in the third century before Christ, there was considerable literary activity among the Jews of Alexandria. Not less than six names of Jewish writers, with notices or extracts of their works, are preserved, all of them, whether historical or poetic, connected with religious subjects. In such circumstances it is not credible that the translation into Greek of the historical, poetic, and prophetic portions of Scripture should have been neglected. And when we turn to the Book of Sirach we find that its language is borrowed in places, not only from that of the Pentateuch version of the LXX, but from their rendering of the Books of Proverbs, of Jeremiah, and of Isaiah. We might go even a step further, and call attention to certain peculiarities in the Greek rendering of Sirach. For the use of any one marked peculiarity, evidently derived from the LXX rendering, on the part of one so capable of writing Greek as the Son of Sirach, not only implies the existence of this LXX version, but leads up to the supposition of its recent introduction. Now, if we suppose the younger Sirach to have arrived in Alexandria some time after 247 B.C., there would remain, roughly speaking, about half a century after the LXX version of the Pentateuch (about 280 B.C.) for the translation of the other parts of the Canon. And, as before stated, the existence of a religious Jewish literature in Alexandria about the end of the third century before Christ seems necessarily to imply a previous translation of the portions of the Canon then existing. We have dwelt at such length on this point, not only from its intrinsic interest, but for its obvious important bearing on questions connected with the Old Testament Canon. We hasten to add that, about a century after the 'Wisdom of Sirach,' the earliest Palestinian Apocryphon, we have (somewhere about 150 B.C.) the earliest preserved Alexandrian Apocryphon, the Book of Wisdom. Alike the original composition of the Book of Sirach (between 310 and 291 B.C.) and the fact of the Alexandrian Pentateuch version (about 280 B.C.)—not to speak of later works—impress us with the conviction that they could not have stood isolated. By this I mean, that they cannot have been the first outburst of a religious literature after a long period of silence. They must have been immediately preceded in Palestine by a revival of religious literary activity. The most cursory reading of Ecclesiasticus will convince that this is not a first religious book. It expresses, so to speak, not a fresh and primitive, but a developed religious state of a certain character. Aphorisms of this kind are, so to speak, the sediment, or else the precipitate, of a religious development. It seems therefore inherently not unlikely, that the redaction, not the composition, of the latest Old Testament literature may date from the revival at the beginning of the Alexandrian period.

I have said only the redaction, and this leads me to my second inference. For if we compare the oldest Palestinian Apocryphon—the Book of Sirach—or the spirit that underlies the LXX version of the Pentateuch, with what are the youngest portions of the Old Testament, say with the prophecies of Daniel,—or, to place side by side works that are kindred, such as The Wisdom of the Son of Sirach and the Book of Proverbs or Ecclesiastes—we instinctively feel, that there is a great gap between them—a difference not only of degree but of kind. From this we again argue, that the youngest Old Testament literature cannot, so far as its groundwork is concerned, date from the period of the revival of Jewish religious literature, although its redaction may. But in that case even this groundwork of the youngest portions of the Old Testament must date from the beginning of the post-exilian period. During the interval between it and the Alexandrian period there was nothing in the political situation to rouse intellectual activity, nothing in the social, to encourage it, nothing in the religious, to be reflected in it—no outstanding event, no outstanding personality, with which to connect it. On that period rest silence and darkness. We may call it the formative age, corresponding to that of infancy and childhood in the life of the individual, when, so to speak, the physical basis was laid for the life of the nation.

Yet a third remark seems here in place. From the period succeeding the return from the Exile—which, so far as regards the form of Old Testament literature, we would designate as its silver, if not iron age—to the Alexandrian period, roughly speaking, about a century intervened. This interval, which can scarcely be said to have a history, in the true sense, nor, so far as we have certain evidence, a literature of its own, was, as just stated, the formative period of the nation in its new circumstances. Its certain outcome, as apparent in the next period, was something quite different from what had preceded it in, what may be called, Old Testament times. In religious literature its outcome was the Apocrypha and the Pseudepigraphic writings; in religion and life, that new direction which, in distinction to that of the Old Testament, is best characterised as *Judaism*, which in its full development we know as Traditionalism and Rabbinism. And yet, in, or near to, a period, the outcome of which is admittedly so different, a certain school of critics would have us place a large portion of the legislation, and of the historical and didactic, if not the prophetic writings of the Old Testament!

But we must turn aside from the many and interesting questions which here occur, and limit our remarks to these three points: (1) What bearing had the period beginning with the Exile on the great Messianic hope? (2) What monuments of it are left to us as its outcome, especially in Apocryphal literature? And (3) What influence did this literature produce on the people in regard to their spiritual training?

1. What bearing had the period beginning with the Exile on the great Messianic hope? It seems a defective, if not a false, view of it to regard the Babylonish exile as simply a Divine punishment for the sins, especially the idolatry, of Israel. I venture to assert that there is nothing merely negative, or exclusively punitive, in the Divine dealings in history, especially in what bears on the Kingdom of God. Every step taken is also a step in advance, even though, in making it, something had to be put down and crushed. It was not otherwise with the Babylonian exile. Assuredly, one aspect of it was punitive of Israel's sin. But that, by which this punishment was effected, also brought Israel a step nearer the goal of its world-mission. In the first great period of its national history Israel had, so to speak, been gathered into a religious unity by the Law. Its watchword had been holiness, or God-separation; its high-point, the priesthood; its character, a symbolism, that ultimately bore reference to the Messiah and His kingdom. In the second period of its history Israel had been under special and constant Divine teaching. Its watchword had been the great hope of the future, or spiritual conquest for God; its high-point, prophetism; its character and object, the formation of spiritual conceptions, with ultimate outlook on the Messiah and His kingdom. And if in the first period Israel was constituted with reference to its great typical object, and, in the second, it was brought within view-point of the nations of the world, as indicating its spiritual mission and goal-point—it was placed in the third and last period in actual contact with them. That period ran to some extent parallel with the previous one, which had begun with the establishment of monarchy in Israel. For, the idea of the kingdom of God could scarcely have been realised without an historical basis in the kingdom of Israel, and the very defects and failures of it, as well as its contests with the kingdoms of this world, would the more clearly point to an ideal reality, set before its view in the grand hope of a universal kingdom of God. But with the deportation to Babylon that stage had not only ended, but was completed. It was now no longer Israel within view of the kingdoms of the world, and in sight of its object and mission; but Israel amidst the kingdoms of the

world, where it could best learn what was the meaning of a universal world-kingdom of God. If Israel had been faithful to its mission, it would have widened to embrace the kingdoms of the world. Israel unfaithful to it, was merged in them, subdued by them. Yet even so, it also fulfilled, in its punishment, its mission—in dying gave up its pearl—bringing mankind a step nearer to the truer realisation of the kingdom of God in its world-wide bearing.

Yet here also Israel had failed. It was the beginning of its last fatal failure. Not only did Israel not understand its mission; but it had not heart for it. In the first of the three periods—that of the Law, holiness, priesthood, and symbolism—Israel had failed through a bare externalism. In the second of the periods—that of teaching, prophetism, and the prospect of conquest of the world for God—Israel had failed, on the one hand, through apostasy to heathenism, and on the other, through national pride, selfishness, and vain-glory. And in the third and final period of completion, Israel utterly and finally failed—misunderstood the teaching of God, and perverted its mission: failed, even in its repentance of past sins, which was not godly sorrow that needeth not to be repented of, but the sorrow of the world which worketh death. Israel's final apostasy in the time of Christ began not at His appearance; this, was only the logical outcome of all that had preceded. And Israel's final rejection also began not with the subjection to Rome, still less with the burning of the City and Temple, but with the return from the Exile.

When Israel went into Babylon, it was once more like the going into Egypt. The return to Palestine was another Exodus. But, oh, how different from the first! That had been marked by the glowing religion of the Old Testament; this, by what we know as Judaism. Israel returned from the Exile not as Israel, but as the Jews; such as history has ever since presented them. They expanded not to the full meaning of their mission in relation to the world; they shrivelled, and became mummified into the narrowest particularism, alike mental, national, and religious. Israel was baptised in the wilderness unto Moses to a new and promising spiritual life; it was ossified in the Exile to a religion of Pharisaism, exclusiveness, and national isolation and pride. No wonder that new forms had to be created for the Divine Spirit, and that no longer Palestinianism but Hellenism became the great factor and connecting link between the Kingdom of God and the kingdoms of the world. Thus the old fig-tree withered at its roots. The Diaspora, rather than the Palestinian minority, became the missionaries of the world; Hellenist thought, culture, and modes of presentation, not Pharisaism or Rabbinism, became the medium through which the kingdoms of the world were to be made the Kingdom of God. And so we can in some measure understand the meaning of the Diaspora, and of that large and ever-widening circle of Hellenist thought, as well as its mission in the world.

2. I have spoken of Israel as emerging on the other side the Babylonian flood, not as Israel, but as the Jews. And of this their later literature bears ample evidence. We have here to reckon with three different tendencies. We notice, first, the working of the old spirit, which in due time would appear as traditionalism and Rabbinism. This means reaction. Next, we have the new spirit, which in due time would appear as Hellenism. This means renewal and re-formation. Lastly, we have the ideal spirit, which, grasping the great hope of the future and of the Messianic Kingdom, would in due time appear either as Jewish Nationalism—in the great Nationalist party (or in close connection with it)—or else, as a pure Apocalypticism. But as yet these three tendencies lay in great measure unseparated in the chaos over which the spirit of the future was brooding—waiting till outward events would differentiate them.

Two centuries had passed since the return from Babylon. At the end of them we find ourselves suddenly in the midst of a new-born activity in religious literature. We have suggested this, as possibly the period of the final redaction—not composition—of some, though perhaps not of all, the youngest portions in the Old Testament Canon. The new literature springs forth in Palestine, but chiefly in Alexandria. It is debased in literary character, chiefly imitative of the Old Testament writings, and, as we would naturally have expected, of the youngest portions among them, so that one might almost infer the comparative lateness of an Old Testament book from its imitation by one or more of the Apocrypha. Briefly to characterise them from this point of view: 1st (III) Esdras is mainly a compilation from 2 Chronicles, Ezra, and Nehemiah; 2nd (IV) Esdras must not come into account, as it really belongs to the Pseudepigraphic writings. Tobit reads almost like a Judaic and apocryphal counterpart of the story of Job, not unmixed with others. Judith contains reminiscences of Deborah, Jael, and even Ruth, but seems modelled on the Book of Esther. The additions to the Book of Esther connect themselves with that work. The Wisdom of Solomon seems to me, in the conception of its ideas, often to present a counterpart to the Book of Job—only that in the one case the philosophy is Eastern and Jehovistic, in the other Western and Grecian. At the same time it also presents, in many of its leading elements, a Grecian development of the two great Solomonic books. The Book of Sirach is connected chiefly with that of Proverbs, but also with Ecclesiastes. Baruch, together with the Epistle of Jeremy, connect themselves with Lamentations, and partially also with Daniel; the Song of the Three Children, and the stories of Susanna, and of Bel and the Dragon, are connected with Daniel; the Prayer of Manasses with Chronicles. The First Book of the Maccabees reminds us more of Nehemiah than of Ezra. The Second Book of the Maccabees is chiefly an epitome of a larger work by one, Jason of Cyrene. It is Alexandrian, as 1st Maccabees is Palestinian and Hebrew. It must be understood that our remarks refer to the cast and tone, not to the contents of these books. In regard to the former, they seem counterparts, or else continuations, of the later portions of the Old Testament Canon. But, in thought and direction, the differences between them and any parts of the Old Testament are so numerous and great, as to afford indirect evidence of the canonicity of the latter. Indeed, one of the earliest Apocrypha expressly laments the absence of Prophets and of Inspiration.

The collection of Apocrypha, as we have it in our English Version, is not only ill translated in many parts, but ill thrown together, being arranged neither according to country, contents, nor age. Their number is really only thirteen, and our collection both contains what should not, and omits what should, have a place in it. Such portions as the Song of the Three Children, the History of Susanna, and that of the Destruction of Bel and of the Dragon, are really only an apocryphal addition to the Greek version of the Book of Daniel. As regards country or—perhaps more accurately— language, the Apocrypha should be arranged into Palestinian and Alexandrian. The former comprise the Hebrew original, of which our present Book of Sirach is a translation, Judith, the First Part of Baruch, the First Book of Maccabees, and, to judge by its contents, perhaps Tobit. I have enumerated them, chiefly, in the probable order of their composition, although considerable doubt attaches to the subject, especially as regards the age of Baruch and of Tobit. But it deserves notice, and it confirms the views previously expressed, that all these books date after the national revival to which we have referred: the Book of Sirach, as I believe, from after the Alexandrian age; the rest probably from the Maccabean period— the 1st of Maccabees from the beginning of the first century before Christ.

As to the others, nothing certain can be predicated. Baruch and Tobit breathe the spirit of later Judaism, although as yet in a more free form than when traditionalism had finally laid its yoke upon the people. With the exception of the books just mentioned, the other Apocrypha were written in Greek. The oldest of them seems the Book of Wisdom, which dates about a century, or probably a century and a half, before Christ. It implies a considerably advanced state of intellectual life preceding it. In truth, it forms an advanced post on the road of that Hellenism which may generally be characterised as the attempt to reconcile the Old Testament with Greek thought. From this there was only a further step—both easy and natural: to seek to combine what had been shown to be harmonious.

To complete this brief review of the Apocryphal writings, it seems appropriate to group them, not only according to country and age, but according to their contents. The task is, however, one of extreme difficulty. Generally speaking, they might, indeed, be distinguished as historical (or pseudo-historical), didactic, and pseudo-prophetic, or rather parenetic, since their object was, under prophetic pretension, to convey admonition or consolation, always with marked reference to the circumstances of the time, the condition of heathenism, and the relation of Israel to it. This anti-heathen element is a very marked characteristic of the Apocrypha, which, variously applied, might serve the purposes of controversy, of apologetics, of confirmation in the faith, of proselytism, and even of Messianic anticipation. More important still is what we gather from the Apocrypha to have been the doctrinal views prevalent at the time.

A brief reference to the differences between them and the Old Testament may here be in place. To begin with: a very marked distinction is made between such writings and the canonical, which are not only designated, in the Prologue to Ecclesiasticus, as 'the Law, the Prophets, and the other books of the fathers,' but for which exclusively inspiration is claimed. Quite in accordance with this is the exceptional manner in which Biblical writers and Biblical works are referred to, or quoted. Thus the Apocrypha themselves mark their line of separation from the canonical books. And this is the more noteworthy, that the Book of Sirach is often quoted in Rabbinic writings in a manner similar to that in which citations are made from canonical books. The distinction in favour of the Old Testament is fully vindicated, the more closely we examine the teaching of the Apocrypha. The presentation of the Divine Being is no longer as in the Old Testament. Sometimes it is Grecian in its form, as chiefly in the Book of

Wisdom, and, in minor degree, in some portions of Ecclesiasticus; in other books, as in Judith and Baruch, it is Judaic, narrow, and nationalistic; while in Tobit we have almost the later Rabbinic view of the propitiation of God by alms. Similar remarks apply to the presentation of the doctrines of Creation and of Providence. As regards the doctrine of Angels, the Apocrypha have much more developed teaching, which in the case of Tobit descends to the low level of superstition.

As might be expected, both Grecianism and Hebrewism appear even more markedly in what such books as Wisdom and Ecclesiasticus have to tell us of man. The pre-existence of the soul, and its fall and degradation through its connection with the body, are taught side by side with a reluctant and almost solitary reference to the fall of man as presented in the Bible. But of the doctrine of original sin, as fully expressed in the New Testament, the Apocrypha, as Rabbinism, have nothing to tell us. In regard to moral duties, the tone of the Book of Proverbs is now absolutely secularised. A respectable religiosity and a sort of common-sense decency take the place of fervour of love and entireness of devotion. Reward in this life, or at most either in the Messianic world or in the life to come, are the leading motives; externalism of work, rather than deep inward spiritual views, characterises the righteousness described. By the side of this we find in the Apocrypha of Grecian cast (Wisdom and partly Ecclesiasticus) a classification of the virtues after the philosophic model; while the Judaic Apocrypha (Judith and Tobit) represent on many points a low standard, not only in the story of Judith, but generally in regard to the relation between man and God. In Ecclesiasticus we find throughout a twofold, somewhat incompatible, direction: the Hellenistic by the side of the Judaic. This strange eclecticism may have been due to the original author of the book, or, as seems more likely, been introduced by the translator.

As regards the 'after death' the characteristics of the Grecian Apocrypha, already noted, once more appear. Ecclesiasticus is not only less pronounced on these subjects than some of the canonical books, but is, to say the least, strangely silent on the "after death." The Book of Wisdom, while acknowledging the immortality of the soul and the judgment, so systematically ignores the resurrection of the body as to lead to the inference of its denial. The same may even more strongly be predicated of 1st Maccabees, which, indeed, has been regarded as representing the views of the Sadducees; while 2nd Maccabees, in this respect, markedly reproduces the views of the Pharisees. In reference to the Messianic hope, we can only say that its personal aspect, as regards the Messiah, if present at all, recedes behind that of Israelitish, national prospects. Of these, alike in the anti-Gentile sense, and in the exaltation of Israel, there is the fullest anticipation.

Thus we have in the Apocrypha—which, as already stated, must be regarded as embodying the outcome of the previous period—a marked divergence, on all main points, from the lines followed in the Canonical Books of the Old Testament. The latter, as has been well remarked (Bissell), led up to the manger of Bethlehem; the Apocrypha may, as regards dogmatic views, be considered only a kind of preface to later Judaism.

The other peculiarities of the Apocrypha can only be lightly touched in this place. They are such as to interest the student, and may open up wider questions. We mark the tone of self-consciousness which Judaism assumes towards a decrepit heathenism, and this, in face of a hostile and unscrupulous political majority. There is something truly noble in this conscious superiority and defiance, when, on the eve of the coming battle, the despised, defeated minority speaks in the haughty language of assured victory. It is the Old Testament spirit, even though it be cramped in narrow, nationalistic forms. We are here thinking of much in the Palestinian Apocrypha. But this element is not wanting in any of the other Apocrypha, although naturally it least appears in those of Grecian tone. Other, and minor, points are also interesting. Thus the story of Susanna, which some writers have regarded as most strongly anti-Sadducean, is in fundamental contradiction with Rabbinic law. According to the Mishnah, false witnesses were to suffer the punishment of death, in obedience to the Law of Moses (Deut 19:19,21), only if an *alibi* could be proved against *them*—that they had been in another place than that where they had sworn to have witnessed the crime. But in the Book of Susanna the perjured elders are put to death simply on being convicted of false witness. Another interesting question is as to the alterations which, whether from misunderstanding, or in a Grecian sense, the younger Sirach may have made when translating into Greek the Hebrew work of his grandfather. Of such even a comparison with the Syriac translation of the book gives evidence; the latter—although containing many needless and jejune paraphrases—having evidently been made with a copy of the Hebrew original before the translator.

3. From these points of chiefly critical interest we turn to the third great question which we had proposed to ourselves: that of the spiritual influence which this apocryphal literature exercised upon the people. They were, indeed, Apocrypha—'Sepharim genuzim'—hidden books, 'books withdrawn'; but we have evidence that they largely circulated among the people. And while they were really the outcome of the development during the preceding period, they must also have truly reflected, though in part they may have helped to form, the spirit of their own time. And it is the general 'spirit of the time' (the *Zeitgeist*), which we encounter and recognise throughout this literature—as appearing in alliance with Judaism: a 'time-spirit' that would fain believe, it could be Jewish. In the new contact with the outer world of Grecianism, it could not be otherwise than that Grecian, philosophical or philosophising, ideas should—perhaps sometimes unconsciously—intrude into Jewish religious thinking. But there they would appear not as metaphysical or speculative, but rather as a rationalistic element. What we call rationalism is never philosophy; it is an attempt to pervade religion with the philosophy of what is misnamed common sense. A jejune, but popularly attractive; treatment this of the great questions of life, which are to be reduced to a kind of arithmetical problems, easily to be solved by well-known rules; an attempt to turn all things in heaven and on earth into ponderable quantities and measurable substances, to which the common Philistine standards can be applied—in utter ignorance that the spirit had long fled from the dead substances which are to be so weighed and measured. This kind of philosophic religion, or religious philosophy, strongly tinged with Eastern elements—alike the sensuous, contemplative, ironical, and *blasé* view of life—had in some measure appeared in the Book of Ecclesiastes—only there as ultimately overcome by the Divine. In the Book of Ecclesiasticus we have mostly the bare prose of all this. Similarly, the rationalistic, or rationalising, tendency in religion, impregnated in Alexandria with Grecian philosophic elements, explains much in the Book of Wisdom, although this is by far the loftiest of these productions, and a long way off from such a work as the so-called Fourth Book of Maccabees. And we have enough, and more than enough, of it in the philosophico-religious platitudes of a Josephus.

It is this same 'time-spirit' in the Apocrypha which, according to circumstances, appears in historical, apologetic, or controversial form. It is an attempt at vindication of the Old; vindication, as regards those that are without; vindication also, as regards existing ideas, with which the Old has to be conciliated, and that, whether these ideas be Grecian or Judaic. Thus, the First Book of Maccabees, which is really historical, is also apologetic, in its long speeches and Jewish reasonings; while the object of 2nd Maccabees seems partly to be eirenical, with the view of preventing a schism between the West and Jerusalem, and partly apologetic of the Old in its Palestinian form, in such legends as about the hiding of the sacred fire, and the mode in which it was rekindled on the altar. Third (I) Esdras is certainly apologetic: the story about the intellectual contest of the three young men, in which Zerubbabel came out victorious, being intended not only to fill up a gap in the history, but to supply a rational motive for the decree of Darius (1 Esdr. 4:42 &c.). Similar remarks apply to the apocryphal additions to the Book of Esther. Of Ecclesiasticus and the Book of Wisdom we have already spoken. Tobit is a haggadic Midrash, conceived in the spirit of the Judaism which was assuming a definite shape. Judith is partly controversial, partly consolatory. Both Baruch and the Epistle of Jeremy are parenetic, apologetic, and strongly controversial; and so are the additions to the Book of Daniel.

We cannot pursue this inquiry farther, nor yet close it without at least stating that there was yet another, and a very powerful, element in the spirit of the time, which found expression in its literature. This element was the all-engrossing anticipation of the prophetic future, set before Israel throughout the Old Testament, but especially in the visions of Daniel. The literature to which it gave birth is represented by such of the Apocalyptic or, as they are called, Pseudepigraphic writings as have been preserved. This must form the next subject for consideration. For the present we only notice, that the spirit of the Apocrypha apparently also influenced the Pseudepigrapha. The Messianic future portrayed in their visions is Judæo-national, not universalistic. And this marks one essential difference between these Apocalyptic visions and the inspired prophecies of the Old Testament. We have observed the same in the Apocrypha, only with wider application. There the Messianic hope had quite lost its definiteness, and been transformed into a Jewish hope. The central figure in the picture of the kingdom is the Jewish nation, not the Person of the Messiah.

All this, in connection with the general religious views which, as the outcome of the past and the preparation for the future development, find their expression in the Apocrypha. The religion of the Old Testament was that of the great prophetic future; the religion and hope of the Apocrypha are of the Israelitish past, which vain- gloriously seeks in the future a realisation, commensurate to its past disappointment. The hope of the Old Testament centred in the Person of the Messiah; that of the Apocrypha, in the nation of the Jews. It is Judaism and the Synagogue with which we have henceforth to do. But not thither had the finger of prophecy pointed. Not to the Jews but to the spiritual Israel; not to the Synagogue but to the Church, belonged the inheritance of the promises and the future of the world.

LECTURE 10: ON THE DIFFERENT MOVEMENTS OF NATIONAL LIFE IN PALESTINE IN THEIR BEARING ON THE MESSIANIC IDEA; ON THE NATIONALIST MOVEMENT IN ITS CONNECTION WITH PSEUDEPIGRAPHIC LITERATURE: THE PSEUDEPIGRAPHA, AND THEIR CHARACTER.

And now I stand here…for the hope of the promise made of God
unto our fathers; unto which promise our twelve tribes,
earnestly seeking God night and day, hope to attain. Acts 26:6.

It were a serious mistake to infer from the post-canonic literature, which we call the Apocrypha—the leading characteristics and contents of which have been briefly sketched in the previous Lecture—that the Messianic idea had died out in Israel after the close of the Old Testament Canon, or even that it had not existed, and indeed, constituted the very life of the nation. It is true that the Apocrypha preserve silence about the Person of the Messiah. But this, not because the Messianic idea was ignored, but because it was apprehended and presented in another form. It was now no longer the Person of the Messiah, but the Messianic times, which engaged the expectancy of the people. This, perhaps, partly from want of real faith in such a Person; partly, to avoid what might issue in politically dangerous movements. In part it may also have been due to the outward condition of Israel, alike in Palestine and in 'the Dispersion.' The hope of the people may, in the pride of self-consciousness, have perhaps rested the more eagerly on the rapt visions of Israel's future, as presented by the Prophets, that it stood in such felt painful contrast to a present, which depended on only brute material force, but could in no way be vindicated from the Divine, or absolute, point of view. But chiefly it also arose from this, that the altered aspect of Messianic expectancy was in accordance with the Hellenist spirit, which some of the Apocrypha represent, and from which scarcely any of them are wholly free. But, for all this change of form, the Messianic hope itself burned none the less brightly that it was concentrated on the Messianic times, when Israel's enemies would be vanquished, and Israel's day of glory arise—and when, so far as this was possible, Israel's blessings would be shared by the nations, although in vassalage to the chosen people. I have called attention to the marked anti-heathen element in the Apocrypha. In measure, it was also necessarily an anti-Gentile element, and it gave its colouring to the Messianic idea. The Messiah was no longer a Prince of peace and the Reconciler of the world. The Messianic times were still those of 'the kingdom'—but of one of conquest, of the reinstatement and triumph of Israel, and of the subjection of the Gentile world. And the more we consider the condition of things, the less shall we wonder that a people which had grown unspiritual should, in the pride of their religious superiority, have no longer dwelt on the Messianic aspect so constantly presented by the Prophets, and, instead of it, accentuated that prophetic future which they now interpreted as belonging to Israel after the flesh, not to the world. The difference between the Messianic hope of the Old Testament and of the later time was that between the utterances of inspired men who spoke the message of God, and uninspired men who spoke of it with the feelings of personal injury burning in their hearts, and the thoughts of the times dominating and moulding the expression of their views. It was still 'the kingdom'—but Judaic, not universalistic: the beginning of that, which was afterwards developed by Rabbinism to all its sequences.

Thus viewed, the Messianic idea underlies all the Apocrypha. Nay, it is found, though in highly elevated, not materialistic, form, even in the extreme representative of Hellenism—Philo—as much as in the utterances of the most bigoted Rabbis. In their realistic mode of viewing, and their Oriental manner of expressing, it, the Rabbis said, that in Messianic days the wheat would grow in Palestine to the height of palm-trees, and that a Jerusalem would rise with walls of gold and precious stones, and in which all manner of jewels would be strewed about for the use of every Israelite; that this new Jerusalem would be wide as all Palestine, and Palestine as all the world, while the Holy City would be the capital of all nations. But, after all, the underlying idea—although in a materialistic form, suited to their standpoint and training—was the same which, not only the Apocrypha (Tob. 13:16-18), but Philo wished, in elevated and philosophic manner, to convey when he described that future, in which all Israel—or perhaps all who owned Israel's Law—would be suddenly converted to virtue. Upon this their masters, ashamed to hold those in bondage who were so much better than themselves, would release them. Then would all the banished be freed in one day, and, as by one impulse, 'the dispersed' throughout the world would assemble, and return to Palestine, led by a Divine, superhuman apparition, invisible to others, but visible to themselves. In Palestine the waste places and the wilderness would be inhabited, and the barren land transformed into fruitfulness. And in another treatise, Philo speaks of that happy time in a manner peculiar to himself. The happier moral condition of man would ultimately affect the wild beasts, which, relinquishing their solitary habits, would first become gregarious; then, imitating the domestic animals, gradually come to respect man as their master, nay, become as affectionate and cheerful as 'Maltese dogs.' This is evidently an anticipation of the literal fulfilment of the Isaiah prophecy about the wolf and the lamb dwelling together. All this would react on the condition of man. There would be universal peace through the subdual of all enemies—of some in supernatural manner, anticipated in a realistic form (by divinely sent swarms of hornets)—and extraordinary wealth, health, and vigour would be the boon of Messianic times. Thus, strictly viewed, there was really not an absolute gulf between the realism of the Rabbis and the most advanced of philosophising Hellenists. And, indeed, it might be argued that the Rabbis had only intended to make use of symbolic language, but meant no more by it than Philo—although it seems difficult to suppose that, in the expectancy of the unlettered masses, the descriptions of the Messianic bliss would be taken otherwise than literally. And such was the spell of the Messianic idea, such the hold it had upon the genius and life of the Jewish nation, that—as we have seen—even so unscrupulously selfish a writer as Josephus could not suppress an reference to it—and this, in works intended for his Roman masters.

And how could it be otherwise? The Jew must cease to be a Jew—in any other than the negative sense of opposition to other creeds—if he gives up the Messianic hope which is the central idea of his religion. In this aspect of it, the Messianic application of Genesis 49:10seems *a priori* established and incontestable. The sceptre could not depart from Judah, nor the staff of command from between his feet before, nor yet could they remain after, the willing obedience of the nations to God. The particular must then give place to the general; the national to the universal. This, and nothing else, is of God. We have followed the history of the great promise through its stages of inception, presentation, and development, till it had reached its largest circumference, when the kingdom of God was shown to be the world-monarchy, with outlook upon the Great Throne, the judgment of the

Ancient of Days, and the coming of the Son of Man. Then the period of promise had run its course, and merged into that of expectancy.

That period really commenced with the Babylonish captivity. It seems difficult fully to realise the changes wrought during its course. In the round numbers of prophetic language, we call it the seventy years' captivity. But it was both of longer and shorter duration than this. From the deportation of the ten tribes, after the destruction of Samaria in 721 B.C., one hundred and eighty-five years elapsed to the decree of Cyrus, about 536 B.C. The first taking of Jerusalem by the Chaldees and the deportation of Joiachim and of a number of the Jews took place in 598 B.C., that is, sixty-two years before the decree of Cyrus; the second taking of Jerusalem, the death of Zedekiah, and the second deportation of Jews, in 588, that is, fifty-two years before the decree of Cyrus; and, lastly, the final deportation of the Jews dates from the year 584 B.C., or forty-eight years before Cyrus. But even as regards the longest of these periods, that of sixty-two years, the change which Israel underwent seems disproportionate to the time—especially as we remember that, with the cessation of the Temple-services, the main institutions of the Mosaic religion had become impossible. We can only conjecture that the exiles from Judah may have found in the land of their captivity new religious institutions, which had been established, or at least commenced, by the earlier exiles under prophetic direction, and that these institutions proved capable of adaptation to the religious wants of the people. At the same time the former temptations to idolatry were not only removed by the Exile, but the new circumstances in which Israel found themselves, the sufferings of banishment, and the longing for their own land and the services of their beautiful Sanctuary, which would be kindled, together with what they witnessed around—all this would crush and wholly remove any leaning towards that great national sin, which had brought on them such Divine judgment. This course of things seems at least much more likely than the theory that the Jews, who were deported in a state of idolatrous apostacy, had derived from Babylon so many entirely new elements of their religion. If a real change, and not a revival of the old, had taken place, we should have expected it in another direction; and post exilian Judaism would have been very different from that rigid Monotheism and purism which we find alike in the Pentateuch and in the practice of those who returned into Palestine.

But, in the nature of them, these can be only conjectures. For silence and darkness rest upon the period of the Exile. The bands of exiles disappear in the vast Assyrian empire, and though we hear echoes of the prophets' voices from the banks of its rivers, and distant dirges of psalmody from harps that had been hung on their willows, we know absolutely nothing of the people itself. When after the dark night morning once more breaks, we perceive, as the mist gradually lifts from valley and hillside, new forms and scenes. Only a small part of the nation—and that chiefly the poorest and least advanced, though religiously the most earnest—has returned, and on those who have remained behind, the mist has again fallen for a time. And they who have returned seem quite other than those who had gone into exile. Not only has every trace of idolatry disappeared, but a fresh, and almost a formative, religious activity has sprung up. The Canon of Scripture is revised and completed; the old institutions are adapted to the new circumstances. Yet so far from any alteration even in the letter of the old, it is developed to the uttermost, and enforced with a rigour that knows no mercy. And a new national life has also commenced—not under the rule of the house of David, to which, despite the intenseness of national feeling, it bore no longer any relationship. This new life fundamentally differed, in one aspect, from that before the Exile, when, speaking generally, religion was dominated by political considerations, whereas political considerations were now dominated by religion. That which then opened was, if I may make the comparison, a kind of Old Testament Puritan period, or rather a Judæan Covenanter period: so truly does history repeat itself in its fundamental tendencies. Those early 'Nationalists,' who resisted the foreigner, and ultimately gathered around the Judæan *Martel*—the 'hammer of God'—Judas the Maccabee, were the *Chasidim*, or 'pious ones.' Intensely religious, intensely Judæan also, they forsook the Maccabees when the religious element receded behind the political, even though the latter was Judæan. And increasingly they went into opposition to their Jewish rulers, till, at last, forsaking or despairing of the national aspect of their cause, they became only a religious party,—the Pharisees. But, after this religious secession, there still remained a strictly 'Nationalist' party. Its adherents obeyed, indeed, the religious direction and ordinances of the Pharisees, but they refused to be confined within the bounds of a purely religious sect, and cherished other and wider aims. It is true that this party afterwards, when driven to bay, ran into wild excesses, and during the last siege of Jerusalem into a kind of fanatical Robespierreism. Josephus, through whose representations, or rather misrepresentations, we chiefly know them, was utterly incapable of sympathising with their loftier ideas, and he denounced them as robbers and *sicarii*. Still, they represented, although in grievously perverted form, much of what was noblest in the national and religious aspirations of Israel. Of this there is evidence even in the circumstance, that in the immediate family circle of our Lord, and among His earliest followers, there were those who had belonged to the nationalist party. Thus to some at least, perhaps to many, in Palestine the nationalist direction was, what Hellenism afterwards became to so many in the West: a schoolmaster unto Christ. We recall here the name of Simon Zelotes, the Cananean, who evidently had been a member of the Nationalist party; and that of Jude, the brother of our Lord, in so far as his general epistle contains one, or more probably two, quotations from that class of writings known as the Pseudepigrapha, which seem to be, in one direction, closely connected with the nationalist movement, or rather with the spirit which underlay it.

To this class of religious literature, and to the tendencies which it represents, viewed in connection with the history of Israel, our attention must now be directed,—in the present Lecture, in only a general manner. The Pseudepigraphic writings represent a peculiar phase in Jewish religious thinking. They express the Messianic hope in its intensest, as well as its most external—I had almost said, realistic—form. They differ in their direction from Pharisaism with its worship of the letter, as issuing in Traditionalism and Rabbinism, as widely, as from the reaction against it in rationalising and supercilious Sadduceeism. Nor have they anything in common with the partly mystical, partly Parsee direction of Essenism, which, in one aspect of it, might almost be designated as a Judæan Stoicism. But the element most closely kindred to the Pseudepigraphic writings is that which is presented by the nationalist movement; perhaps we might rather have said, in the nationalist direction. For its deepest underlying thought was, that Palestine was the land of God, and Israel the people of God; that Jehovah, and Jehovah alone, was King; that His was the sole universal kingdom, against which those outside Israel were in high-handed rebellion. All else—even their excesses—were their inferences from this fundamental position. It will be perceived that this thought lies very close to that idea which formed the foundation of our Lord's teaching and mission—the kingdom of God; or, to put it more specifically, the sole Kingship of our Father in Heaven. Only, the Nationalists of Palestine, like the Roundheads or the Scottish Covenanters of our own history, would have made it an outward reality by means of the sword, and have upheld it by the sword. They would have hewn its way through all opposition, and, if need were, written their own formula of that kingdom in letters of blood on the eternal rocks of history and in the inmost shrine of their sanctuary. But, according to the Word of the Lord, which, in this respect also, is significant in regard to this movement: taking the sword, they perished by the sword. Not so did the God-sent Christ understand, nor yet would He so establish the kingdom of His Father in Heaven. Christ was King—but as meek and lowly, and as, symbolically, making His Royal entry into Jerusalem riding on an ass, the foal of an ass. In view of the opposition of a hostile world, He also must found His kingdom in blood—but in His own Blood, which His enemies shed; not in theirs, which He shed. He also must conquer all enemies, and subdue them to His kingdom; yet not by outward means, but by the moral power of the Truth, and by the constraining influence of His Spirit, working inward and willing submission. His kingdom was not of this world; therefore did His followers not fight for it. The true kingdom of God was within: it was righteousness, and peace, and joy in the Holy Ghost. Such was the Christ, as presented in the Gospels.

We pause to mark the historical contact with—and in this, all the more, the contrast to—the men and parties of His time. In its highest aspirations, the Nationalist movement stood perhaps nearest to the fundamental thought of Christ's mission. Yet, as regards the direction and expression of that thought, it was in absolute contrast to Him. Similarly, His teaching embraced, in its absolute reverence for, and implicit obedience to, the Law, all that was ideally and potentially highest in the direction of Pharisaism. Yet it was in fundamental opposition to the false and unspiritual direction of the Pharisees, in their worship of the letter and bondage of externalism. Or, to pass to the other pole—wide as were the sympathies of Christ, and absolute as was the emancipation from the rule of man, and the liberty of the individual, which He proclaimed, yet His were principles of positive freedom in inward subjection to God, not of mere opposition and negation, such as found expression in the gainsaying, the indifferentism, and the superciliousness of the Sadducees. And, again, in the guardianship of the Sanctuary of the Soul, in its consecration to God, in the avoidance of all that defiled it, or hindered its aspirations and communing with God, in contempt of the world and renunciation of its attractions, Christ touched all that was true and high in Essenism. Yet He was at infinite distance from its foreign and heathen elements, its mysticism, and depreciation of matter, associated as this was with materialistic views of the soul and of all good. His was another way to purity and God-fellowship than theirs; His, other views of the body and of matter: not its contempt, but its God-consecration. And as we thus view the historical Christ—the unlettered carpenter's Son from far-off Nazareth—it is surely impossible not to recognise the transcendent greatness of that contest for the ideal which He sustained, untainted by the thoughts of His time, uninfluenced by its motives and ambitions, undeterred by its threats and torture—pure, holy, and spiritual. And so all ages look up to the absolute light, the infinite loneliness, the unspeakable grandeur of His Divine Majesty.

But to the Nationalist, as we have learned to know him, every embodiment, every outward manifestation of what contravened his deepest idea and highest ideal, was absolutely intolerable. What business had the Roman in Palestine; how dared the idolater profane by his presence the sacred soil that was God's; how could he claim to rule the people, whose sole King was the Jehovah of the mighty Arm and outstretched Hand, that erst had cloven the sea, and Whose breath would subdue nations under Him? Even to admit it as a fact, nay, to tolerate it, was an act of unfaithfulness to God, of deep unbelief, of apostasy. So patriotism and religion—both in abnormal forms—mingled. They whetted their daggers to the sound of psalms, and sharpened their swords to the martial music of prophetic utterances, which to them seemed only denunciations and imprecations on the enemy. And they laid them down to dream in those Apocalyptic visions, which form the subject-matter of so much in the Pseudepigraphic writings.

To be sure, these were the visions of Latter-Day Prophets, not the deeds of the men of action. But the Nationalists sought, in their own rough way, to translate them into history. Yet they contained much besides that which these men heard in them. For, in some respect, the nationalist idea had burned deep into the soul of the Jewish people. In one sense, every true Jew was a Nationalist, and could not help being such, so long as he was a Jew. Nay, it clung to him with all the instincts of centuries of descent, and hereditary disposition; with all the remembrances of his upbringing and surroundings; and with all the latent enthusiasm of his Eastern and Jewish nature—and that, even if he tried to shake off his Judaism. We see it in that knotty problem, which gave every Jew a pang of conscience: whether it was lawful to pay tribute unto Cæsar; we hear it in the proud answer with which they would fain have silenced themselves as well as Christ: 'We be

Abraham's children, and have not been in bondage to any man.' Nay, so mighty was it, that St. Paul, appealing from argument to the irrepressible voice of the heart, could, in a Roman assembly and in presence of the Procurator himself, appeal to that Romanised voluptuary, Agrippa, and his un-Jewish sister Berenice, in such words as these concerning the great common hope: 'King Agrippa, believest thou the Scriptures? I know that thou believest!'

It was this deeper appeal to the Scriptures, or rather to the great Messianic hope contained in them, which in these Apocalyptic Pseudepigrapha presented an element, that found a response in many that were quiet in Israel, and also in some measure kept before their minds the great hope of the future, as so-called Millenarian books do in our generation. Just as many a one must have listened to the stern preaching of the Puritan in his conventicle, or of the Covenanter on the hill-side, who yet would not have sent a Roundhead to battle nor a claymore to the field—even although their hearts might beat faster, and their cheeks flush, at the tale of their deeds; so were there many in Israel—under the shadow of its glorious Temple, in the lonely towns of the Judæan wilderness, and in the far-off places of Galilee—to whom these Apocalyptic visions would bring thoughts, remembrances, hopes of the Messiah and the Messianic Day: of Israel's deliverance, of God's reign, and of the conversion of the world. And all the more dangerous might such thoughts become from their conjunction with Nationalist aims and deeds. Thus we can perceive a new meaning in, and an absolute and pressing need for, the warnings contained in the last Discourses of Jesus about the danger of false Christs. And so the Nationalists, in the frenzy of their despair, plunged with the one hand the dagger in the hearts of supposed 'trimmers,' 'backsliders,' and secret enemies of God—whose very existence and presence among them turned aside the interposition of the Lord—while they lifted the other hand on high, appealing to, and expecting at every moment, the visible help of the God of Israel, Who would rive the heavens, and in some terrible catastrophe annihilate the enemy in the very hour of his triumph and pride. But mark the contrast. In the same hour did the Disciples, who so well knew how steadfastly to believe and calmly to die, warned and directed by Christ, withdraw from the doomed City to the quietness and retirement of Pella. And there and then, in the orderly course of God's trackless Providence, was that effected which, if it had been done immediately after the Death of Christ, would have been a violent and dangerous disruption;

but which was now a peaceful, natural, and necessary separation of the Church of the New Testament from the ancient Synagogue. And this also was of God—and is to us evidential of the Mission of His Christ.

What has been stated will in measure explain the object and the subject-matter of the so-called Pseudepigraphic writings. They take up, and further develop in a peculiar direction, the predictions of the Old Testament; they present them in visions of the future, shaped in that peculiar imagery and language which we call Apocalyptic; and they do so, not as the outcome of the inferences or speculations of their writers, but as bringing direct communications from Heaven, connected with such names as Enoch, Moses, Isaiah, Baruch, or Solomon. This, however, with notable exceptions; since perhaps the most interesting of these books is that which embodies the so-called Sibylline Oracles.

This describes one aspect of these writings. Another, is their intensely Jewish character—not merely as setting forth the advantages and the future bliss of Israel, but in their references to the nations of the world: either hortatory, we might almost call it missionary, or else denunciatory; sometimes scornful, but always triumphant in tone. There are other tendencies, and of a party character, in these writings—mostly, as it seems to me, in opposition to the Pharisaic direction. Some of them are certainly of Hellenist origin—that is, they were the work not only of Western Jews, but are the outcome of Hellenist thought. But even those which may be regarded as springing from the soil of Palestine, have not a Pharisaic cast. On the contrary, they all breathe, more or less, the new spirit. This is very remarkable, and further bears witness to what has already been stated as important in the study of the *origines* of Christianity: that, with all its parade and pomp of Messianic assertion, Traditionalism and Rabbinism had no heart for, and very little sympathy with, the great Messianic hope of Israel. Theirs was another and, in many respects, antagonistic direction, in which the Messiah could only bear the part of a political deliverer. Yet another noteworthy point, of a different character, may here be mentioned. All the canonical books of the Old Testament have come down to us in Hebrew or Chaldee. But, as in the case of the Apocrypha, none of the Pseudepigraphic writings have been preserved in that language, although some of them were no doubt written in the tongue of Palestine. We have them either in the Greek, or else in Ethiopic, in Latin, or other version. This also forms a line of demarcation, not to be quite ignored by those who would dispute the canonicity of some of the Old Testament writings.

The Pseudepigraphic writings cover the period from about 170 before, to about 90 after Christ. Those preserved to us are eight in number: The Book of Enoch, the Sibylline Oracles, the Psalter of Solomon, Little Genesis, 4th Esdras (our 2nd Esdras), the Ascension and Vision of Isaiah, the Assumption of Moses, and the Apocalypse of Baruch. Although, in their present form, some of them contain interpolated portions of a much later date, they are all deeply interesting and instructive. For, first, they give us an insight into the thoughts and expectations of the time—away from Pharisaism, Sadduceeism, and Essenism. Secondly, they present to us the continuance of the great Messianic hope. If certain of the Apocrypha, such as the story of the Maccabees or of Judith, would to the old Jewish world have been what Foxe's 'Book of Martyrs' is to many of us, some of those visions of Israel and of the kingdom may have been eagerly read in Israel as a kind of apocalyptic 'Pilgrim's Progress.' We can imagine a Nationalist poring, with burning cheeks, over these visions and predictions; or some in the far-off lands of the Dispersion dwelling with intense delight on what presented such a blessed contrast to all they saw, and were constrained to experience, in the heathen world around. But our thoughts ever recur to those quiet, deeply pious ones on Palestine's sacred soil, who may have thought with rapt anticipation of the prophetic truths which these works recalled, and the happy possibilities which they suggested. We know that an Apostle quotes from two of these writings—the Book of Enoch (Jude v 14,15) and the Assumption of Moses (Jude v 9). And it awakens a scarcely less deep interest to find, that such of the Pseudepigraphic writings as date after Christ bear evident mark of St. Paul's influence, and this, notwithstanding their own decided anti-Christian tendency.

But what, above all else, appeals to us, is the picture of the messiah and of the Messianic kingdom which these works present. To this our attention must next be directed—as also to the relation which the Pseudepigrapha bear, on the one hand, to the prophecies of the Old Testament, and, on the other, to the reality, as first heralded by the Baptist, and then fully set forth in Christ.

LECTURE 11: ANALYSIS AND CONTENTS OF THE PSEUDEPIGRAPHIC WRITINGS, THEIR TEACHING CONCERNING THE MESSIAH AND MESSIANIC TIMES.

> And this is the record of John, when the Jews sent priests and
> Levites from Jerusalem to ask him, Who art thou?...He said, I am
> the voice of one crying in the wilderness, Make straight the way
> of the Lord, as said the prophet Esaias. John 1:19, 23.

These words and, still more, the thoughts, of him who uttered them, seem to transport us into an atmosphere, different from that of the writings to which attention has been called in the two preceding Lectures. In truth, from the Apocryphal and Pseudepigraphic writings to John the Baptist, there is an immense step backward, as well as forward—a retrogression to the Old Testament: yet not merely to rekindle the old light, but to kindle a new one by its flame.

That this may appear more clearly, we shall have to give a more detailed account than in the last Lecture of the Pseudepigraphic writings—describing their character, titles, and general contents.

1. There cannot, I fear, be any doubt but that many works belonging to this class of literature have perished. It is natural to suppose that writings of this kind would exercise a peculiar fascination on many minds. They were about that future into which we so eagerly peer, and about Israel and its relation to those hateful dominant Gentiles, whose pride was so soon to be laid low. That future belonged to those Jewish readers, who were the 'elect,' and it was painted in such wondrous outline, and with such bright colouring. Even the mystical symbolism of the language and imagery was an additional charm. It implied a peculiar knowledge, which would form an inner select circle among the 'elect,' who would daily make proselytes, as they unfolded the wonders of their discoveries, or produced a new book—a rare acquisition in those days—or discussed the different interpretations offered.

But of all this literature only the following eight books have remained—none of them (as already stated) in Hebrew or Aramæan, and most of them only in first, or even second translation.

a. Probably the oldest of them is the so-called 'Book of Enoch,' numbering 108 chapters. It consists, besides a Prologue and an Epilogue, of five portions, giving an account of the fall of the angels, of Enoch's rapt journeys through heaven and earth, together with certain apocalyptic portions about the Kingdom of Heaven and the Advent of the Messiah. The oldest part of it is supposed to date from about 150 B.C.; the second oldest from the time of Herod the Great; the date of the others cannot be fixed.

b. 'The Sibylline Oracles,' in Greek hexameters, consist in their present form of twelve books. They are full of interpolations—the really ancient portions forming part of the first two books, and the largest part of book 3 (vv 97-807). These sections are deeply imbued with the Messianic spirit. They date from about 140 before our era, while another small portion of the same book is supposed to date from the year 32 B.C.

c. The small collection known as the 'Psalter of Solomon' consists of eighteen Psalms, and probably dates from more than half a century before our era. The work, which I regard as fragmentary, breathes ardent Messianic expectancy.

d. 'Little Genesis,' or 'The Book of Jubilees,' dates probably from about the time of Christ. It is a kind of supplement to the Book of Genesis, and breathes a strong anti-Roman spirit.

e. From about the same time, or a little earlier, dates the so-called 'Assumption of Moses'—unfortunately only a fragment of twelve chapters. It consists of an historical and an apocalyptic portion, and is strongly anti-Pharisaic in spirit, especially as regards purifications. This is very remarkable; nor is it less interesting to find that this is one of the works from which St. Jude quotes (v 9), the other being the Book of Enoch (vv 14, 15); and even more so, that St. Paul seems to have been familiar with it. His account of the corruptness of the men in 'the last times' (2 Tim 3:1-5) so clearly corresponds with that in the 'Assumption of Moses', that it is difficult to believe the language of the Apostle had not in part been borrowed from it.

f. and g. On the other hand, there are two of the Pseudepigrapha which bear evident reference to the writings of St. Paul. Both of them date after the destruction of Jerusalem; but 'The Apocalypse of Baruch' is probably older than 4 Esdras (our apocryphal 2 Esdras). The 'Apocalypse of Baruch' is also unfortunately not quite complete. It consists of eighty-seven chapters. Our interest is stirred by noticing how closely some of its teaching runs alongside that of St. Paul—either controversially, as in regard to the doctrine of justification; or conciliatorily and intermediately, as in regard to the consequences of the fall in original guilt; or imitatively, as in regard to the resurrection of the body. If the author of the 'Apocalypse of Baruch' must have read the Epistles of St. Paul to the Romans and the First to the Corinthians, the influence of Pauline teaching appears even more strongly, almost exaggeratedly, in the statements of 4 Esdras in regard to the fall and original sin.

h. Lastly among these works, we have to mention the so-called 'Ascension and Vision of Isaiah,' describing the martyrdom of the prophet, and containing certain Apocalyptic portions about what he saw in heaven. Although based on an older Jewish document, the book is chiefly of Christian heretical authorship.

2. Such are the monuments left us of the ancient Apocalyptic—or, as from their assumption of spurious authorship it is called, Pseudepigraphic—literature. Its interest is threefold. 1st. Historical. They set before us another direction than either in the Apocrypha or in Hellenism. As previously stated, the Apocrypha are either historical—including the legendary—or else philosophising. They carry us back to the glories of Judaism, or else seek to reconcile it with present thought and philosophy—which, indeed, is the final object of Hellenism. But this Apocalyptic literature represents a quite different tendency. It lays, so to speak, one hand on the Old Testament hope, while with the other it gropes after the fulfilment in that dim future, of which it seeks to pierce the gloom. 2ndly. The Pseudepigrapha are of theological interest, as showing what the Jews before and about the time of Christ—or at least one section of them—were expecting concerning the Messiah and Messianic times. One might indeed long to know something more of the personal views and feelings of yet another class—that represented in New Testament history by such names as Zacharias, Elizabeth, Anna, Simeon, and even Joseph and the Virgin Mother. But beyond the thought that their steadfast gaze was bent on the Eastern sky, where sure prophecy taught them that the Sun of Righteousness would rise, we have not the means of associating with them anything more definite than intense, simple, and receptive expectancy. 3rdly. Yet another, and only in one sense inferior, interest attaches to these writings. We may designate it as exegetical. For, if these books represent the symbolism and the form in which Apocalyptic thoughts presented themselves to a large portion of the Jewish people, it will readily be understood, that knowledge of it must also be of great

importance in the study of the Apocalyptic portions of the New Testament—not, indeed, as regards the substance, but the form and imagery of them.

For our present argument, however, we only require to present a general account of the teaching of these writings concerning the Messiah, and the Messianic kingdom. Here we are not obliged to limit our review to such of them as are strictly pre-Christian, since the views on this subject entertained in the first century of our era could not have been materially different from those in the preceding century.

1. As regards the promise of the Messiah. Here we turn in the first place, and with special interest, to the 'Sibylline Oracles.' In the third book of these, which (in such portions as I shall quote from) dates from about 140 B.C., the Messiah is described as 'the King sent from heaven,' who would 'judge every man in blood and splendour of fire.' And the vision of Messianic times opens with a reference to 'the King whom God will send from the Sun.' We cannot fail here to perceive a reference to Psalm 72, especially as we remember that the Greek (LXX) rendering, which must have been present to the Hellenist Sibyl, fully adopted the Messianic application of the passage to a premundane Messiah. We also think of the picture drawn in the prophecies of Isaiah. According to the Sibylline books, King Messiah was not only to come, but He was to be specifically sent of God. He is supermundane, a King and a Judge of superhuman glory and splendour. And, indeed, that a superhuman kingdom, such as the Sibylline Oracles paint, should have a superhuman King, seems only a natural and necessary inference. One other remark—though somewhat aside from the subject—must be allowed. If, as certain modern critics contend, the Book of Daniel is not authentic, but dates from Maccabean times and refers to the Maccabees, it may well be asked to what king the Sibylline Oracles point, which certainly date from that period; and what is the relationship between the supposed Maccabean prophecies of the Book of Daniel, and the certainly Messianic anticipations of the undoubted literature of that period?

Even more distinct than the utterances of the Sibylline Oracles are those of the so- called 'Book of Enoch,' the oldest portion of which dates, as already stated, from about the year 150 B.C. Our difficulty here is, that a certain class of critics have, although I believe wrongly, assigned a portion of the book, which is full of the most interesting references to the Messiah as 'the Woman's Son,' 'the Son of Man,' 'the Elect,' 'the Just One,' to

Christian authorship and interpolation. In order not to occupy any controverted ground, I propose to omit all references to these portions. But even in the admittedly oldest part the Messiah is designated as 'the Son of God,' not, indeed, in the Christian sense of Eternal Sonship, but as indicating superiority over all creatures; and this is further expressed by a symbolic description of the Messiah as He Whom 'all the beasts of the field and all the fowls of heaven dread, and to Whom they cry at all times.'

A still more emphatic testimony comes to us from the 'Psalter of Solomon,' which dates from more than half a century before Christ. The King who is to reign is described as of the house of David. He is the Son of David, Who comes, at a time known only to God, to reign over Israel. He is a righteous King, taught of God. He is Christ the Lord; He is pure from sin, and thus can rule His people, and banish His enemies by His Word. God renders Him strong in the Holy Ghost, wise in council, with might and righteousness. 'This is the beauty of the King of Israel, Whom God hath chosen to set Him over the house of Israel to rule it.' And yet we remember that no descendant of David was in view in those dark times.

2. I must be even more brief in my account of the teaching of the Pseudepigrapha about the blessedness which Israel would experience in Messianic days. In the Book of Enoch Israel is represented as in the Messianic days coming in carriages, and borne on the wings of the wind from East, and West, and South. Again, the Jewish Sibyl connects these three events: the coming of the Messiah, the rebuilding of the Temple, and the restoration of the Dispersed, when all nations would bring their wealth to the house of God. The Psalter of Solomon bursts into this strain: 'Blessed are they who shall live in those days—in the reunion of the tribes which God brings about.' Then 'the King, the Son of David,' having purged Jerusalem and destroyed the heathen, would by His Word gather together a holy people and rule over it with justice, and judge the tribes, allotting to them tribal possessions, when 'no stranger would any longer dwell among them' (Psa 17). In the 'Book of Jubilees' we are told, that God would gather all Israel 'from the midst of the heathen, build among them His Sanctuary, and dwell with them.' That Sanctuary was 'to be for ever and ever,' and God would appear in view of every one, and every one would acknowledge that He was 'the God of Israel, and the Father of all the children of Jacob, and King upon Mount Zion from everlasting to everlasting.' We pause for a moment at these words of perhaps a contemporary of Christ, to realise what indignation it must have called

forth in the hearts of those who expected all this, when the charge, however false, was spread that He Who professed to be the Messiah, but was really only the carpenter of Nazareth, had actually proposed to destroy the Temple, instead of bestowing upon it eternal glory.

On the utterances of the 4th Book of Esdras it is not necessary to speak at length, as the work forms part of our collection of Apocrypha. This only will we say, that if chapter 13.27-50 is carefully examined, it will be seen how deeply tinged is the prophetic description which it contains with the teaching of the Gospels and the Words of our Lord concerning 'the last things'—although, not as He put it, but in a Judaic form. In fact, it seems impossible to avoid the conclusion, that the writer had been acquainted with the Discourses about the 'Last Things.' The inference to which this leads as to the date of the Gospels of SS. Matthew and Luke need scarcely be indicated.

3. What has been said about the 'Last Things' reminds us of another point connected with the Messianic reign, to which these Pseudepigrapha refer. In common with all Jewish writings, they speak of a period of woe, commonly called the 'Sorrows of the Messiah.' This was to precede the Advent of the Christ. But it would not be difficult to point out the essential differences in regard to this between Jewish thinking and the Discourses of Christ on the subject, much misunderstood as they have been.

We can only notice the account given in the Pseudepigrapha of the 'signs' which were to usher in the Advent of the Messiah. Among these, the Sibylline Books mention a kind of warfare visibly going on in the air, swords in the starlit sky, the falling from it of dust, the extinction of the sun, and the dropping of blood from the rocks. In 4th Esdras we find the expression of distinctly Judaic views, although once more tinged by New Testament influence, especially as regards the moral aspect of these 'signs.' The Book of Jubilees gives a detailed description of the wickedness and physical distress then prevailing upon earth. According to the Sibylline Books, when these signs in air and sky would appear most fully, and the unburied bodies that covered the ground were devoured by birds and wild beasts, or swallowed up by the earth, God would send the King Who would put an end to all unrighteousness. After this would the last war against Jerusalem ensue, when God would fight from heaven against the nations, and they ultimately submit themselves to Him.

Substantially the same views appear in the Book of Enoch expressed in symbolic language. We are told that, in the land, now restored to Israel, the

Messiah-King would reign in a new Jerusalem, purified from all heathen elements, and transformed. That Jerusalem had been shown to Adam before his fall, but after that withdrawn, as well as Paradise. It had been again shown to Abraham, to Moses, and to Ezra. Its splendour baffled description. As regards the relation of the heathen nations to that kingdom, views differed according to the more or less Judaic standpoint of the writers. In the Book of Jubilees, Israel is promised possession of the whole earth, and 'rule over all nations according to their pleasure.' In the 'Assumption of Moses' this ascendancy of Israel is conjoined with vengeance upon Rome. On the other hand, in the Sibylline Oracles the nations are represented as, in view of the blessings upon Israel, turning to acknowledge God, when perfect mental enlightenment, absolute righteousness, as well as physical well-being, would prevail under the rule (literal or moral) of the Prophets. This, as we know, was the Hellenist Messianic ideal. Lastly—and this marks another point of divergence from the New Testament—the Pseudepigrapha uniformly represent the Messianic reign as eternal, and not broken by any apostasy. Then would the earth be renewed, and the Resurrection follow. The latter would, at least according to the Apocalypse of Baruch, be under the same conditions in which men had died, so as to prove that it was really a resurrection of the old. Only after that would the transformation of the risen take place— the just appearing in angelic splendour, while the wicked would fade away.

After this brief review, it will, I hope, be admitted that the evidence is complete of the existence of a Messianic hope during the interval between the close of the Canon and the coming of Christ—and this, alike in the Grecian and the Palestinian Jewish world. To say that it had grown out of Old Testament prophecy, and was intertwined with the life of the Jewish people, seems now only a truism. On the other hand, it must also be clear, that the Old Testament Messianic idea had undergone great, I had almost said terrible, modifications. As regards its form of presentation, it had become external and almost ossified. The figurative language of the Prophets had been perverted into a gross literalism, which gave its coloring to the picture of the Messiah and of His kingdom and reign. As regards the substance of the prophetic hope, we remark that there was not any enlargement, nor spiritual development, of the Old and preliminary dispensation, nor yet any reference to the new law to be written in the heart, and to the new spiritual blessings in forgiveness and righteousness. In short, we perceive not any outlook on a new state and condition of things: only an apotheosis of the old. The grand universalism, when all mankind would become children of the Heavenly Father, is lost behind a mere triumph of Judaism, thus giving place to an exclusive and narrow nationalism. Lastly, the moral elements regarding sin, repentance, spiritual preparation, and universal mercy—in short, the distinctively Christian and, we may add, eternal elements, are wanting. Not so did the Old Testament present the Messianic hope; not so could it have presented it as good tidings to all men.

Before proceeding to point to the period of fulfilment in Christ, we may here pause to mark the contrast between the Messianic idea, as presented in almost contemporary literature, and the preaching of the Baptist, and still more, that of the Christ Whom he announced. We think of that herald-voice in the wilderness calling to repentance and spiritual preparation; still more, of the Christ Himself, with the words, 'Our Father' ever on His lips; with the deeds of eternal compassion and eternal mercy ever in His life; with the love of absolute self-surrender and self-sacrifice in His death; and we realise this as the meaning and outcome of His Mission—that He has opened the Kingdom of Heaven to all believers. We think of His world-Mission and of the regeneration of man, and of His teaching to all mankind, whether Jews or Gentiles. We remember that, of the many hopes which He kindled, of the many expectations of which He brought the realisation, He, a Jew and the Jewish Messiah, was only silent on one, but this the only one which occupied His contemporaries—the glorification of Israel, and its exaltation. His kingdom was to be within the soul: of righteousness, and peace, and joy in the Holy Ghost. Surely, this Christ, Whom the Gospels present to us—so Jewish, and yet so utterly un-Jewish—this King of Israel and Desire of all nations, was in very truth the fulfilment and the completion of the Old Testament promise—the Sent-of-God—not merely Jeshua, the Carpenter's Son of Nazareth in Galilee, nor yet the outcome of the Messianic thoughts and expectancy of His time and of its conceptions. And as we realise the essential difference between this Christ of all humanity, Who meets the inmost wishes and the deepest craving of our hearts—and that of the Jewish ideal, we feel that both He and His teaching must have been of God.

LECTURE 12: THE LAST STAGE IN MESSIANIC PROPHECY; JOHN THE BAPTIST; HIS CHARACTER AND PREACHING. THE FULFILMENT IN CHRIST.

And thou, child, shall be called the prophet of the Highest: for thou shall go before the face of the Lord to prepare His ways. Luke 1:76.

The more we succeed in transporting ourselves into those times, the less shall we wonder that multitudes flocked to the preaching of the Baptist, from 'Jerusalem and all Judea, and all the region round about Jordan.' It was, indeed, in more than the barely literal sense, 'A Voice crying in the wilderness.' Never before in the history of Israel had there been such absence of every prospect of a new life. If, on the eve of the rising of the Maccabees, heathen opposition had been more systematic and cruel, imperilling the very existence of Judaism, there was at least a reaction in Israel, a conflict, and the possibility, if not the prospect, of national deliverance. But only wild fanatics could, unless maddened by despair, have hoped to shake off the rule of Rome, represented by the insolence and tyranny of a Pilate. With such a governor in place of the Son of David, with the High Priesthood almost hereditary in the proverbially corrupt and avaricious family of Annas, the condition of things seemed hopeless; while within Israel itself the life-blood of the Old Testament could scarcely pulsate any longer through the ossified arteries of Traditionalism and Rabbinism. The self-righteousness and externalism of the Pharisees, the indifference and pride of the Sadducees, the semi-heathen mysticism of the Essenes, the wild extravagance into which Nationalism was running,—all this was, indeed, making the once pleasant land a moral wilderness.

And now, of a sudden, 'the Voice' was heard in the wilderness! It was not that of Pharisee, Sadducee, Essene, or Nationalist—and yet the Baptist combined the best elements of all these directions. He insisted on righteousness, though not in the sense of the Pharisees; nay, his teaching was a protest against their externalism, since it set aside the ordinances of Traditionalism, though not after the manner of the Sadducees. John also practised asceticism and withdrew from the world, though not in the spirit of the Essenes; and as regarded Nationalism, none so zealous as the Baptist

183

for the Kingship of Jehovah and the rule of heaven, though not as the Nationalists understood it. The Baptist was an altogether unique personality in that corrupt age. Even a Herod Antipas heard him; even a Josephus recorded his life and work; even the Pharisees and priests from Jerusalem sent a deputation to inquire—nay, to ask him (so truthful was he, and so little suspected of mere fanaticism)—whether he was 'the coming One,' or Elijah, or one of the prophets. Let us see what light his history and preaching reflect on the great Messianic hope of old, and on its fulfilment in the New Testament.

1. The character and life of the Baptist prove him to have been sent of God. It is not easy to speak of him in moderate language. Assuredly, among those born of women there was none greater than he. We can picture to ourselves his child-life: how, specially God-given, he was trained in the home of those parents whom Holy Scripture describes as 'righteous before God, walking in all the commandments and ordinances of the Lord, blameless.' When he had attained the legal age, he would (or might) take part in the services of the Temple as a priest; and he must have witnessed them, long before that period. In Jerusalem he must have been brought into contact with the world of Jewish thought and religious life. But neither of these could hold, nor yet turn him aside from that calling for which at his Annunciation the Angelic message had designated him.

What the years of solitude and meditation in the wilderness, that followed, were to him, we can only infer from his after-life and preaching. That they were years of self-discipline, we learn from his self-abnegation, which rises to the sublimity of entire self-forgetfulness. That they did not issue in mental and moral hardening, to which such ascetic life might naturally lead, we infer even from his openness to doubt, and from the intense sensitiveness of his conscience, which appears in that sublimely heroic and most deeply touching incident of his closing life—the embassy of inquiry which he sent to Christ from his dungeon. And that he was most true and most truthful, who can doubt that considers what it must have cost such a man at the close, nay, near the martyrdom, of such a life, openly to have stated his difficulties, and to have publicly sent such a message. That he was simple, absolutely self-surrendering, and trustful, almost as a child, every act of his life testifies. That he feared not the face of man, nor yet courted his favour, but implicitly acted under a constraining sense of duty as in the sight of God, his bearing alike towards the Pharisees and before Herod amply proves. But above all, it is his generosity, and his unselfishness, and absolute self-abnegation, which impress us. In a generation pre-eminently self-righteous, vain-glorious, and self-seeking, when even on the last journey to Jerusalem the two disciples nearest to Christ could only think of pre-eminence of place in the kingdom, and when, in the near prospect of suffering to the Master, a Peter could ask: What shall we have? when, even at the last meal, the disciples marred the solemn music of this farewell by the discord of their wrangle about the order of rank in which they were to be seated at the Supper—the Baptist stands alone in his life and in his death: absolutely self-forgetful.

Here we would specially remind ourselves of the two high-points in the personal history of John. The first of these is marked by the events recorded in St. John 3:25-30. Nay, the ascent to it had begun even before that. It was on the very first Sabbath of John's emphatic testimony to Jesus as the Lamb of God that taketh away the sin of the world, that the two who stood beside him, his most intimate and close disciples—shall we not also call them his friends—John and Andrew, following the heavenly impulse that drew their souls, forsook their master for the yet silent Christ. It was only the beginning of a far wider defection. Not long afterwards his remaining disciples—and we almost love them for this generosity of their wrongful zeal of affectionate attachment—came to him with these, to them, so distressing tidings: 'Master, He who was with Thee beyond Jordan to Whom thou bearest witness, behold, the same baptiseth, and all men come to Him.' So then it seemed as if every tangible token of success in a life of such self-denial and labour were to be utterly taken away! The multitude had turned from him to another, to Whom he had borne witness; and even the one solitary badge of" his distinctive mission—baptism—was no longer solely his. But immediately we have the sublime answer which the Baptist made to his disciples: 'Ye yourselves bear me witness, that I said, I am not the Christ, but that I am sent before Him. He that hath the bride is the bridegroom; but the friend of the bridegroom, which standeth and heareth him, rejoiceth greatly because of the bridegroom's voice: this my joy therefore is fulfilled. He must increase, but I must decrease.' Not to murmur, but even to rejoice in his seeming failure of success, so that his preparatory work merged in the greater Mission of the Christ; and—not in the hour of exaltation, when most of us feel as if we could find room for nobler sentiments, but in the hour of failure, when we, mostly all, become intensely self-conscious in our disappointments—to express it, not in the resignation of humility, but with the calm of joyous conviction of its rightness and meetness: that he was not worthy to loose the latchet of His sandal—this implies a purity, simplicity and grandeur of purpose, and a strength of conviction, unsurpassed among men. And, to me at least, the moral sublimity of this testimony of John seems among the strongest evidences in confirmation of the Divine claims and the Mission of Christ.

There was yet another high-point in the life of the Baptist—though in a very different direction. Here evidence comes to us from the opposite pole in his inner life: not from the strength, but from the trial of his faith. Months had passed since his dreary imprisonment at Macchærus and yet not one step would, or perhaps could, the Christ take on behalf, or for the vindication, of him who had announced Him as the coming King. And the tidings which reached the Baptist in his lonely dungeon about the new Christ, as One Who ate and drank with publicans and sinners, were seemingly the opposite of what he had announced, when he had proclaimed Him as the Judge Whose axe would cut down the barren tree, and Whose fan would throughly sift His floor. Or—oh, thought too terrible for utterance!—might it all have been on a dream, an illusion? In that dreadful inward conflict the Baptist overcame, when he sent his disciples with the question straight to Christ Himself. For such a question, as addressed to a possibly false Messiah, could have had no meaning. John must have still believed in Him when he sent to Christ with the inquiry— reported both by St. Matthew (11:2-6), and St. Luke (7:18-23): 'Art Thou He that should come, or do we look for another?' But at what cost of suffering must it have been that the Baptist did overcome, and what evidence of truthfulness, earnestness, and nobility of heart and purpose does it reveal! And there is yet another aspect of it. Assuredly, a man so entirely disillusioned as the Baptist must have been in that hour, could not have been an impostor, nor yet his testimony to Christ a falsehood. Nor yet could the record which shows to us such seeming weakness in the strong man, and such doubts in the great testimony-bearer, be a cunningly devised fable. I repeat, that here also the evidential force of the narrative seems irresistible, and the light most bright which the character and history of the Baptist shed on the Mission of Christ.

2. In what has been said we have already in part anticipated the next point in our argument. And yet something remains here to be added. For the character and life of the Baptist cannot be viewed as isolated from his preaching. On the contrary, they reflect the strongest light on it, even as, conversely, his preaching reflects light on his character and life. One who

was, and lived, as the Baptist must also have been true in his preaching; one who believed, and therefore preached, as the Baptist must have been true in his life. And both his preaching and his life shed light on the great Old Testament hope, and on its realisation in Christ.

When we ask ourselves what had determined the Baptist, after so many years of solitude in the wilderness, to come forth into such blazing light of publicity, to which his eyes had been so unaccustomed, and to face those multitudes, to whom he had so long been a stranger, with a message so novel and startling, his own account of it leaves us not in doubt of the motive for a change so complete, and, as we view it, so uncongenial to him. Unhesitatingly, to every kind of audience and inquiry, and with unwavering assurance, he tells it—yet not in fanatical language—that a direct call had come to him from God; a direct mission and definite message had been entrusted to him from heaven. It was to announce the Christ, and to prepare for Him. His public appearance, his call to repentance, his proclamation, his warnings, his baptism, his instruction to his converts—all imply, that in his inmost soul he felt, and that he acted, as sent directly from God. And not only so, but he also expressly tells us that he had a sign Divinely given him, by which actually to recognise Him, Whose near Advent was to be the burden of his preaching. 'And I knew Him not; but He that sent me to baptise with water, the same said unto me, Upon whom thou shalt see the Spirit descending, and remaining on Him, the same is He which baptiseth with the Holy Ghost.' From this it at least follows, that the Baptist himself entertained no doubt of his Divine commission to his special work.

One theory in explanation of his assertion we shall, I think, all dismiss almost instinctively. Certainly the Baptist did not speak conscious falsehood; certainly, he was not an impostor. Of the other alternative remaining we may, with almost equal confidence, put aside the supposition that his had been the dream of a fanatic. This is contradicted by all the facts of his life. There is not anything connected with it which we could designate as fanatical. And there is much to be urged in the opposite direction. To begin with: it were difficult to understand how fanaticism could at once attach itself to One Whom, as he tells us, he had not even known before He came to him for baptism, and Whose life had hitherto been one of the utmost privacy, and under so unpromising circumstances as a carpenter's home in the far-off Nazareth of that Galilee, which the Judæans held in such supreme contempt.

Other considerations also are opposed to the theory of fanaticism. A fanatic would, in the circumstances, have at once identified himself with, and attached himself to Him, Whom he proclaimed as the Messiah; and he would have appeared prominent in His following. John remained alone, content to do his humble work, and willing to retire from the scene when he had done it. Again, a fanatic would have been alienated by the loss of his own adherents, and disappointed when he had to retire into obscurity and forsakenness. John accepted it, and rejoiced in it, as the goal of his mission. A fanatic would, in the peculiar circumstances, have been thoroughly, and also irretrievably, disillusioned by imprisonment and the prospect of martyrdom. And the Baptist *was* disillusioned of many of the expectations which he had apparently connected with the kingdom, when he had announced that the axe was already laid to the root of the tree. He was disillusioned of these, and therefore he sent his final inquiry to Christ; but he *was not* disillusioned of the Christ, and therefore he sent his disciples to Him. But why should we hesitate to believe what so naturally suggests itself in view of the character and life of the Baptist: that this good, true, unselfish, strong man, spoke what was real, and therefore acted what was true, when he declared himself to have been Divinely commissioned to announce, and to prepare for, the coming Saviour?

And, as we further look at it, is it not quite opposed to the theory of fanaticism, and quite accordant with belief in his true Divine commission, that what the Baptist enjoined as preparation for the kingdom was so simple and unfanatical. He preached not asceticism, nor long days of fasting and devotion; not enforced poverty, nor prescribed sacrifices, but repentance, and then a return into ordinary life,—only with a new moral purpose, and a new resolve to sanctify every occupation, however lowly or full of temptation, by a simple and earnest walk with God. It is not thus that a Jewish fanatic of those days would have spoken to the soldiers of Herod, nor to the publicans of Rome, nor to sinners, nor even to the self-righteous who gathered to his baptism, and asked his direction. Nor is it in such manner that a Jewish fanatic of those days would have spoken—nor yet even the most advanced in what represents the extreme opposite, or Hellenist, direction—when he addressed the Jewish people as a 'generation of vipers,' or referred to them as a tree to the root of which the axe was laid. We cannot find anything elsewhere, in any sense, parallel or even analogous to it. For such language we must go back to an Isaiah or a Jeremiah. Nor yet would a Jewish fanatic of those days have said to the

Jewish people: 'Begin not to say within yourselves, We have Abraham to our father: for I say unto you, That God is able of these stones to raise up children unto Abraham.' From all that we have learned of the history of Israel; from all that we have gathered of its literature, whether in the Apocrypha or the Pseudepigrapha, we can at least draw this one unassailable conclusion—that anything more un-Jewish than what John preached, or more unlike his times, could not be imagined. Assuredly, it must have come to him as a new fact, and a new message, directly from heaven.

And, lastly, as we compare the descriptions in the Pseudepigrapha, the utterances of the Rabbis, and the well-known expectations entertained by the people, with what John the Baptist announced concerning the coming kingdom, as one not of outward domination and material bliss, but of inward righteousness and acknowledgment of God—even the most prejudiced must admit, that if he were a Jewish fanatic, it was at least not in the language of Jewish fanaticism that he spoke by the banks of Jordan.

A similar conclusion is reached when we approach the subject from the opposite direction, and ask ourselves what light the preaching of the Baptist reflects on his character and life. Here the one clear outstanding fact is, that the burden of John's preaching was the announcement of the Advent of the kingdom and of its King. And this, not as something new, nor yet, on the other hand, as answering to the expectations of his contemporaries, but solely as the fulfilment of the Old Testament promise. All else in his work and preaching was either preparation for, or the sequence from, this announcement. At the very outset of his mission this is placed in the forefront: 'As it is written in the book of the words of Esaias the prophet, saying, The voice of one crying in the wilderness, Prepare ye the way of the Lord, make His paths straight.' And this key-note of his preaching is heard in almost every recorded utterance of his. It would be difficult, without a detailed examination, to convey how constantly the Baptist recurs to Old Testament prophecy, and how full his language and its imagery are of it. His mind seems saturated with the Old Testament Messianic hope, especially as presented in the prophecies of Isaiah, and we cannot but conclude that, during those many years of his solitary life in the wilderness, this had been the very food and drink of his soul. If—with reverence be it said—the Mission of Jesus Christ might be summed up in the words: 'Our Father which art in heaven,' that of His forerunner is contained in these: Lo, the kingdom of God, promised of old to our fathers!

To make this statement more clear, let us think of the Old Testament sources of the few recorded sentences in the Baptist's preaching. For such expressions of his as: 'generation of vipers,' we refer to Isaiah 59:5; for the 'planting of the Lord,' of which he speaks, to Isaiah 5:7; the reference to these 'trees' recalls Isaiah 6:13; 10:15, 18, 33; 40:24; that to the 'fire' reminds us of Isaiah 1:31; 5:24; 9:18; 10:17; 47:14; the 'floor' and the 'fan' are those ofIsaiah 21:10; 28:27, &c.; 30:24; 40:24; 41:15, &c.; the duty of the penitent to give 'bread and raiment to the poor' is that enjoined in Isaiah 58:7; while 'the garner' of which John speaks is that of Isaiah 21:10. Besides these we mark the Isaiah reference in his baptism (1:16; 52:15), and especially that to 'the Lamb of God' (Isaiah 53); while, lastly, in reply to his final inquiry through his disciples, Christ points to a solution of his doubts, in accordance with the prophecies of Isaiah, 8:14, 15; 35:5, 6; 61:1.

And—to sum up in one sentence this part of our argument—if what has been stated in detail is incompatible with the theory that John spoke and acted as a Jewish fanatic, it is, on the other hand, the fact, that his character, life, and history, as set before us in the Gospels, are absolutely consistent with the declaration which he so solemnly made, and upon which he died,—that he had been directly sent of God to announce the near fulfilment in Christ Jesus of that great Messianic hope of the Old Testament which had set his own soul on fire.

One step in the argument still remains—although I almost shrink from taking it. I have in the preceding course of Lectures endeavoured to show how the great hope of the Old Testament gradually unfolded; I have followed its progression through the long ages to the period when the last prophet came, who summed up all Old Testament prophecy, concentrated and reflected its light, and pointed to Him in Whom was the fulfilment. If I were to attempt describing how completely the Reality answers to the portraiture by the Prophets, I would have to pass in review the entire history of 'the Man of Sorrows,' the Sacrifice of the Great High Priest, the teaching of the Prophet of the New Covenant, the spiritual glory of the King in His beauty, and the provision which He has made, to which not they of that generation, but all the faithful and true-hearted, from East and West, and North and South, are bidden welcome, together with Abraham, Isaac, and Jacob.

Here we must pause—since any attempt at comparison between our Lord and even those who stood closest to Him, and were most transformed into

His likeness, seems almost irreverence. This only I say, that if we think of the Baptist, or of his utterances, by the side of those of Christ, we feel that, however pure and elevated, they still occupy merely Old Testament ground. Christ stands alone in His Kingdom. John is within the porch; Christ has stepped forth into the free air, into the new light and the heavenly life. And He has brought it to us and to all men.

In conclusion, I desire simply to indicate three great points which seem to mark the fulfilment of all in Christ. They are:—First, the *finality* of the New Testament. We are no longer in presence of preparatory institutions, nor do we expect any further religious development in the future. All is now completed and perfected. Secondly, we mark the *universality* of the New Testament dispensation and Church, as no longer hemmed in by national boundaries, or narrowed by national privileges, nor yet hindered by any limitation, intellectual or spiritual. It is a universal Church: for all men, for all times, for all circumstances. Thirdly, we are in view of this great characteristic—*spirituality*. To every one of us the Kingdom of God, with its blessings, comes directly from God; everyone is to be taught from above, and taught by the Holy Spirit; and to each the teaching is in its principle, perfect; in its character, heavenly; and in its nature, a spiritual life planted within the heart, unfolding and developing even to the completeness of the better state, and the 'many mansions' of the Father's house. If Christ had taught mankind no more than this, 'Our Father, which art in heaven,'—if He had opened no other vision, given no other hope than that of the 'many mansions,'—He would have reflected the light of heaven upon earth, removed its woes, lightened its burdens, sweetened its sorrows, and smoothed its cares. Even so would He have been to mankind the fulfilment of the great Messianic hope of a universal brotherhood of peace and of holiness. But He has been more than this. He hath done what He hath said; He hath given what He hath promised. In Him is the Reality of all, and to all ages. In the fullest meaning of it, He is 'the Light to lighten the Gentiles, and the Glory of His people Israel.'

A NOTE TO THE READER

WE HOPED YOU LOVED THIS BOOK. IF YOU DID, PLEASE LEAVE A REVIEW ON AMAZON TO LET EVERYONE ELSE KNOW WHAT YOU THOUGHT.

WE WOULD ALSO LIKE TO THANK OUR SPONSORS **WWW.DIGITALHISTORYBOOKS.COM** WHO MADE THE PUBLICATION OF THIS BOOK POSSIBLE.

WWW.DIGITALHISTORYBOOKS.COM PROVIDES A WEEKLY NEWSLETTER OF THE BEST DEALS IN HISTORY AND HISTORICAL FICTION.

SIGN UP TO THEIR NEWLSETTER TO FIND OUT MORE ABOUT THEIR LATEST DEALS.

Made in the USA
Columbia, SC
10 August 2020